SECRETS OF
SPIDER-MAN
REVEALED

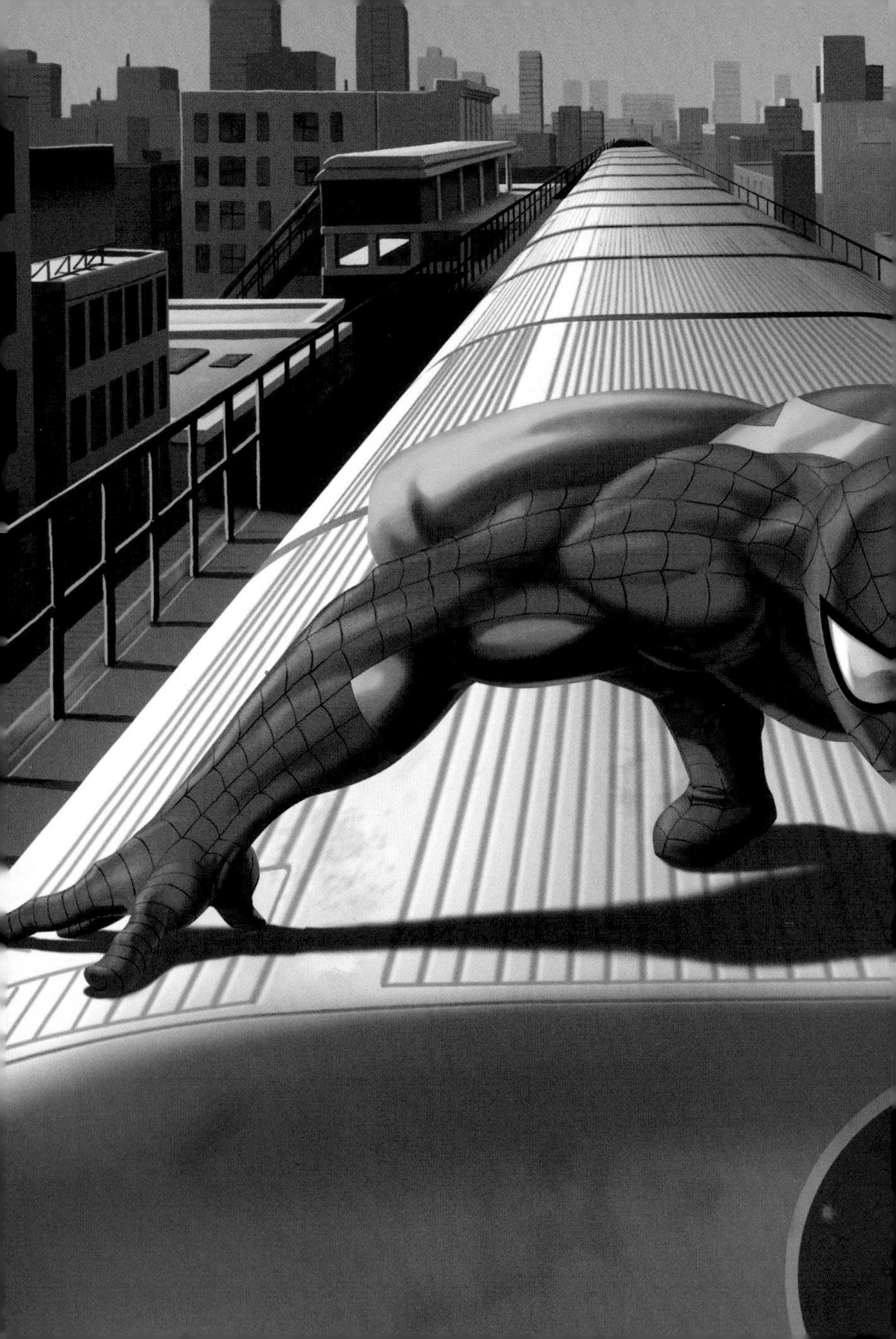

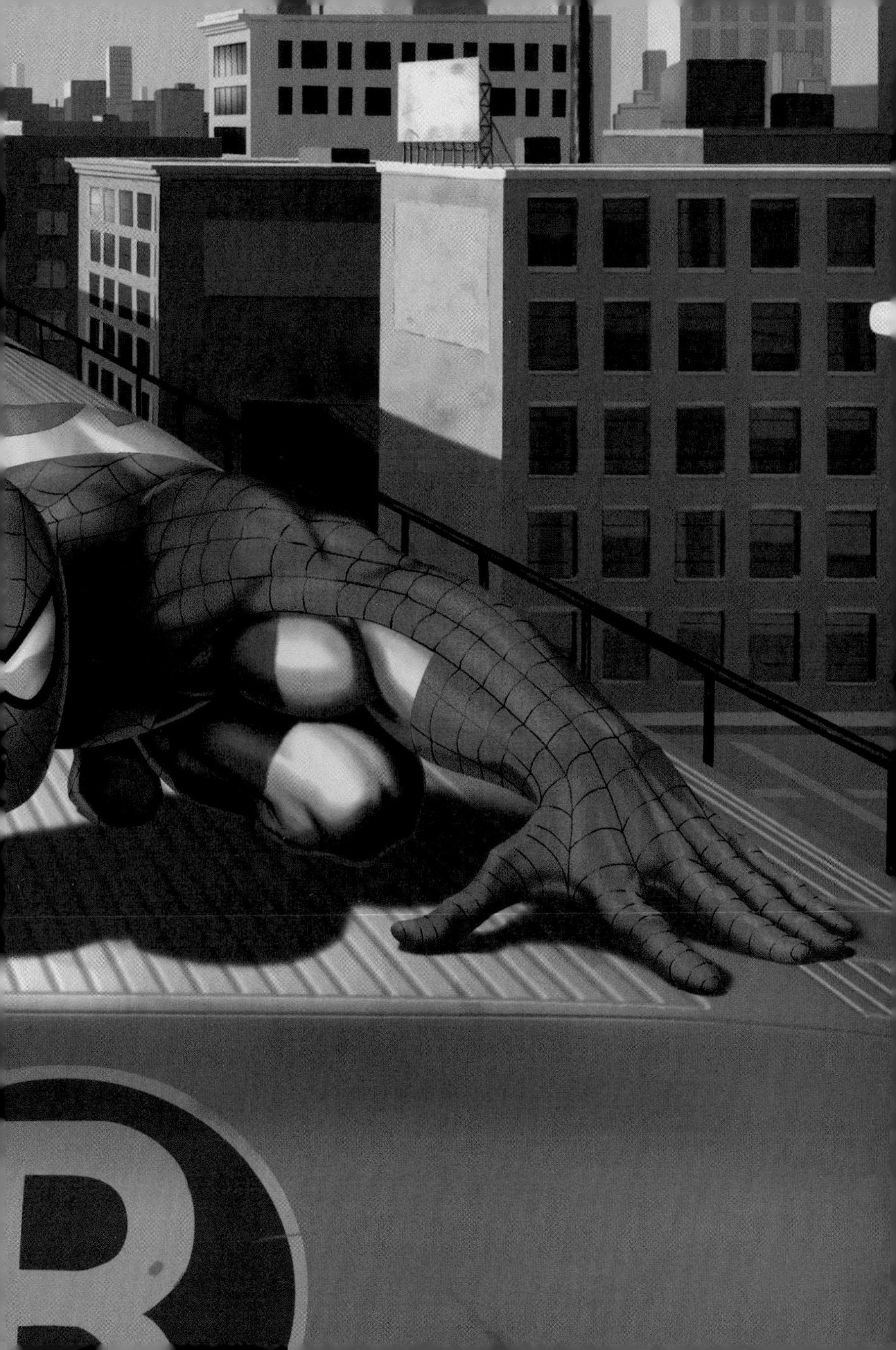

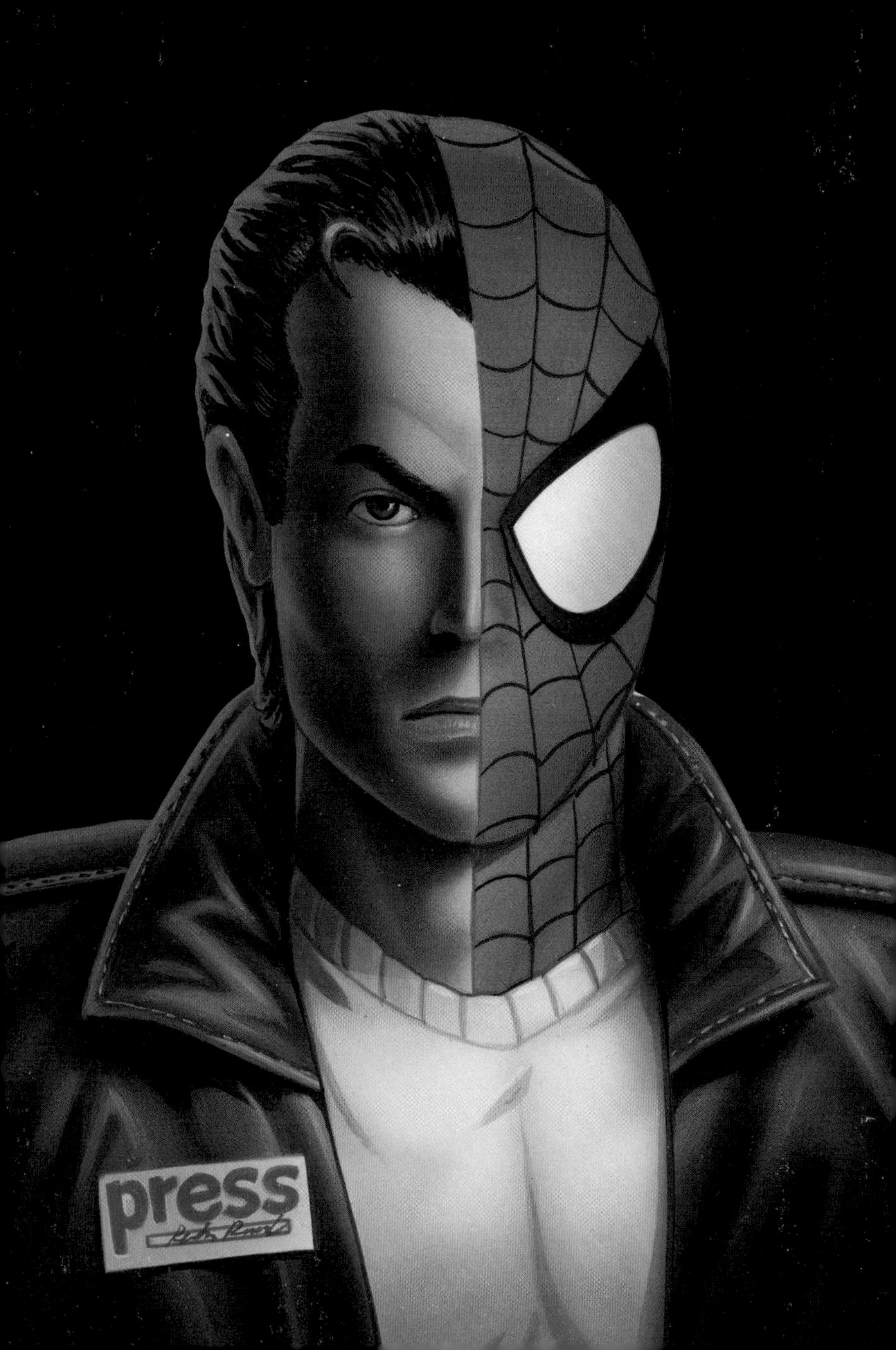
press

SECRETS OF
SPIDER-MAN
REVEALED

ROBERT WEINBERG

STERLING PUBLISHING Co., Inc.
New York

Published by Sterling Publishing Co., Inc.
387 Park Avenue South, New York, NY 10016

For information regarding advertising in Marvel Comics or on Marvel.com, please contact Joe Maimone, Advertising Director, at jmaimone@marvel.com or 212-576-8534

Distributed in Canada by Sterling Publishing
c/o Canadian Manda Group, 165 Dufferin Street,
Toronto, Ontario, Canada M6K 3H6

Distributed in the United Kingdom by
GMC Distribution Services,
Castle Place, 166 High Street, Lewes,
East Sussex, England BN7 1XU

Distributed in Australia by Capricorn Link
(Australia) Pty. Ltd. P.O. Box 704,
Windsor, NSW 2756, Australia

ISBN-13: 978-1-4027-4655-0
ISBN-10: 1-4027-4655-5

Thanks to Tom Murphy, Michael Willows, Robert Shatzkin, Yuri Veynblat, and Ruwan Jayatilleke for their help.

Text by Robert Weinberg

Cover and text design by Kevin McGuinness

Printed in the United States of America

10 9 8 7 6 5 4 3 2 1

For information about custom editions, special sales, premium and corporate purchases, please contact Sterling Special Sales Department at 800-805-5489 or specialsales@sterlingpub.com.

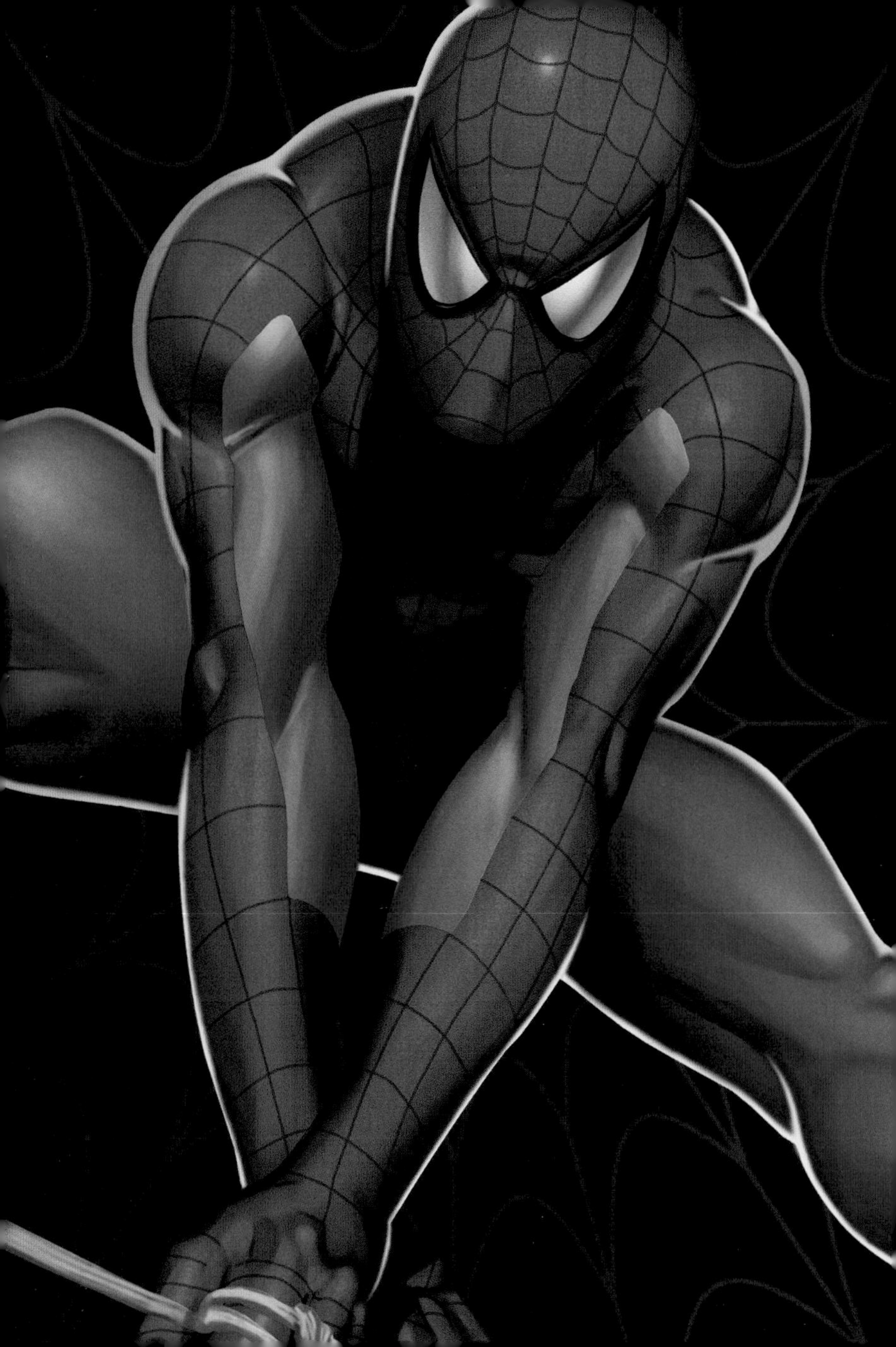

PART I
SPIDER-MAN

THE AMAZING SPIDER-MAN

PART II
COLLEAGUES AND ASSOCIATES

88
DOCTOR OCTOPUS

92
SANDMAN

96
MYSTERIO

100
LIZARD

104
ELECTRO

108
GREEN GOBLIN

PART III
ENEMIES

114
HOBGOBLIN

118
KRAVEN THE HUNTER

122
JACKAL

126
KINGPIN

130
SCORPION

134
VENOM

140
CARNAGE

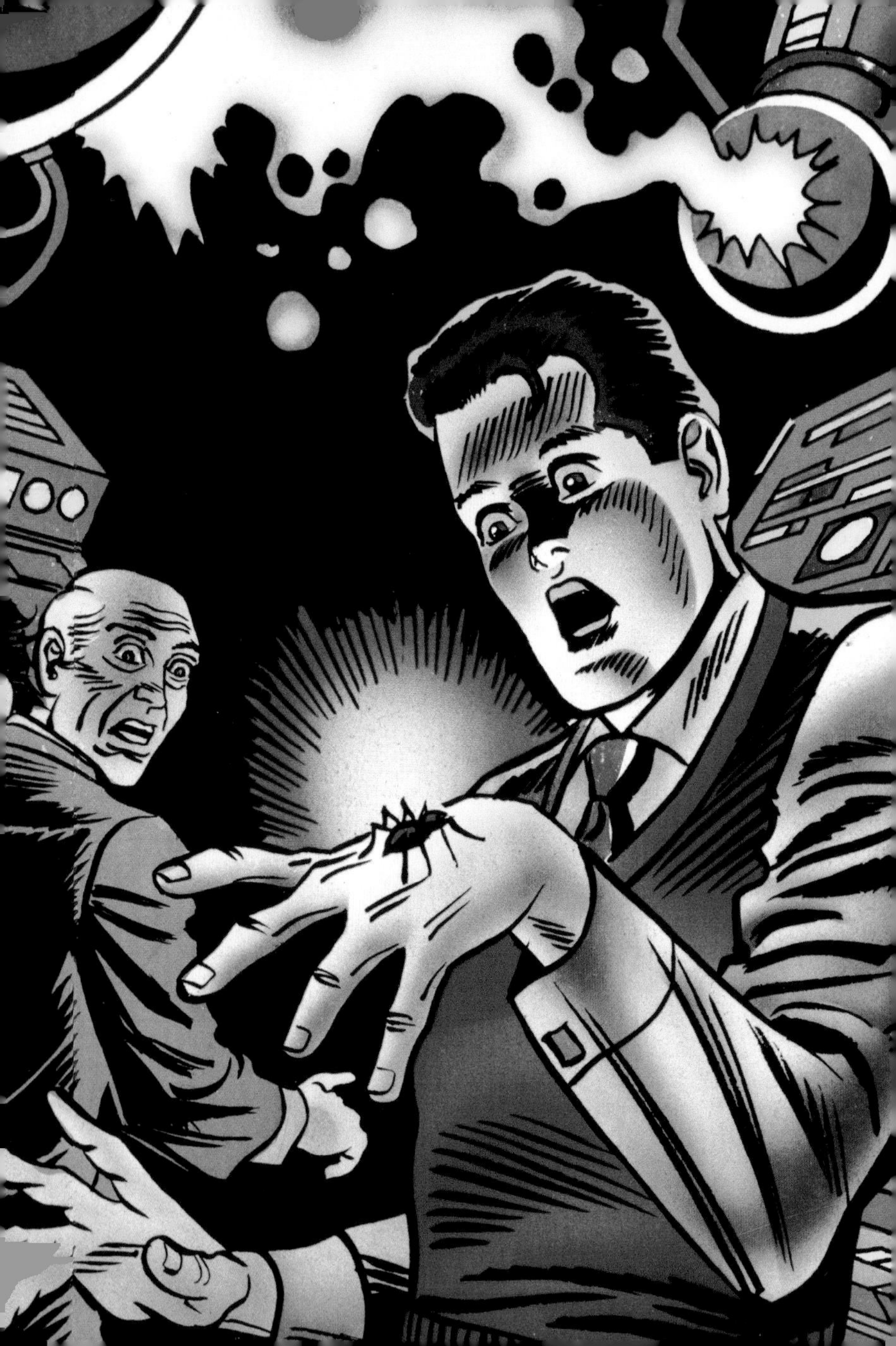

PART I

SPIDER-MAN

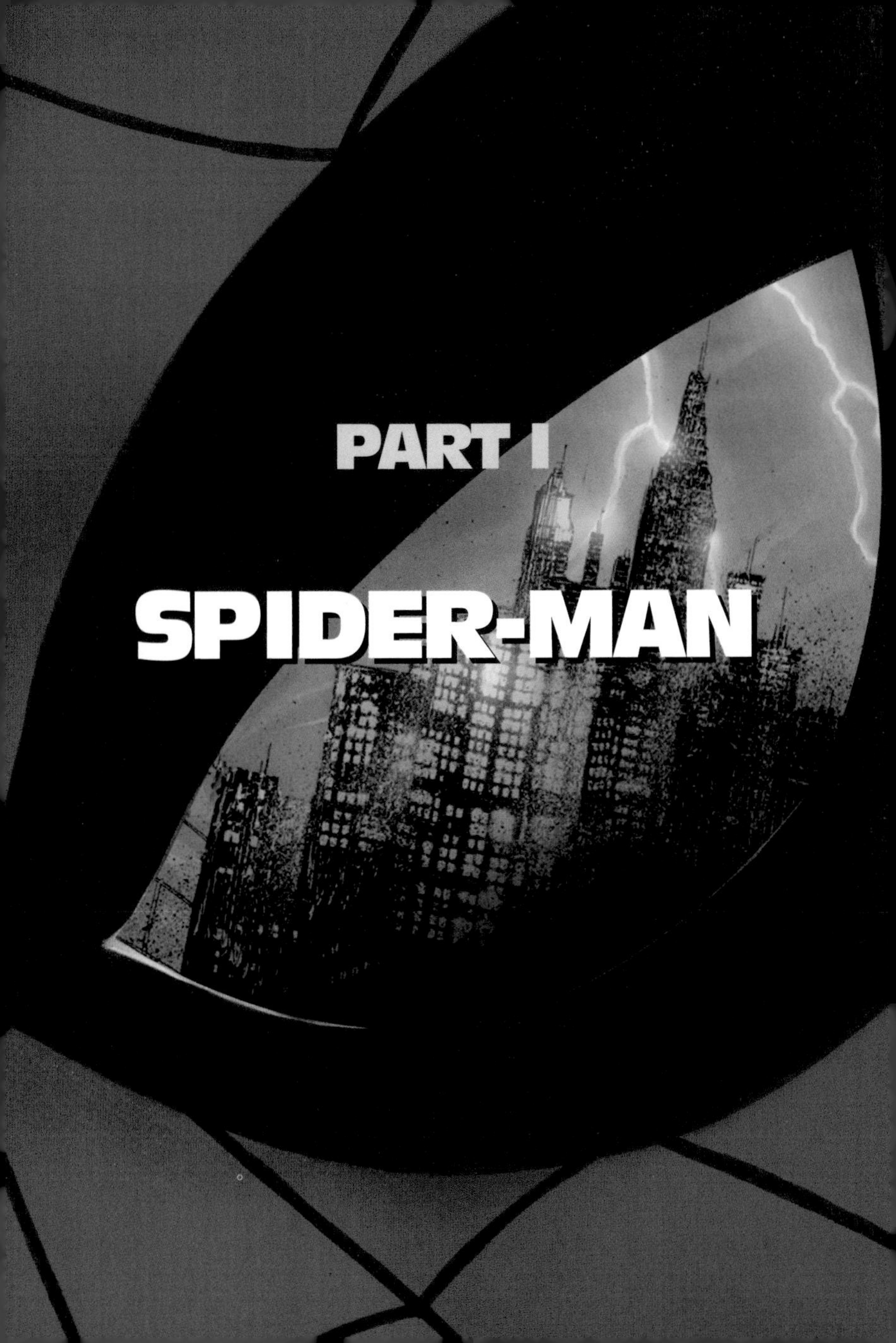

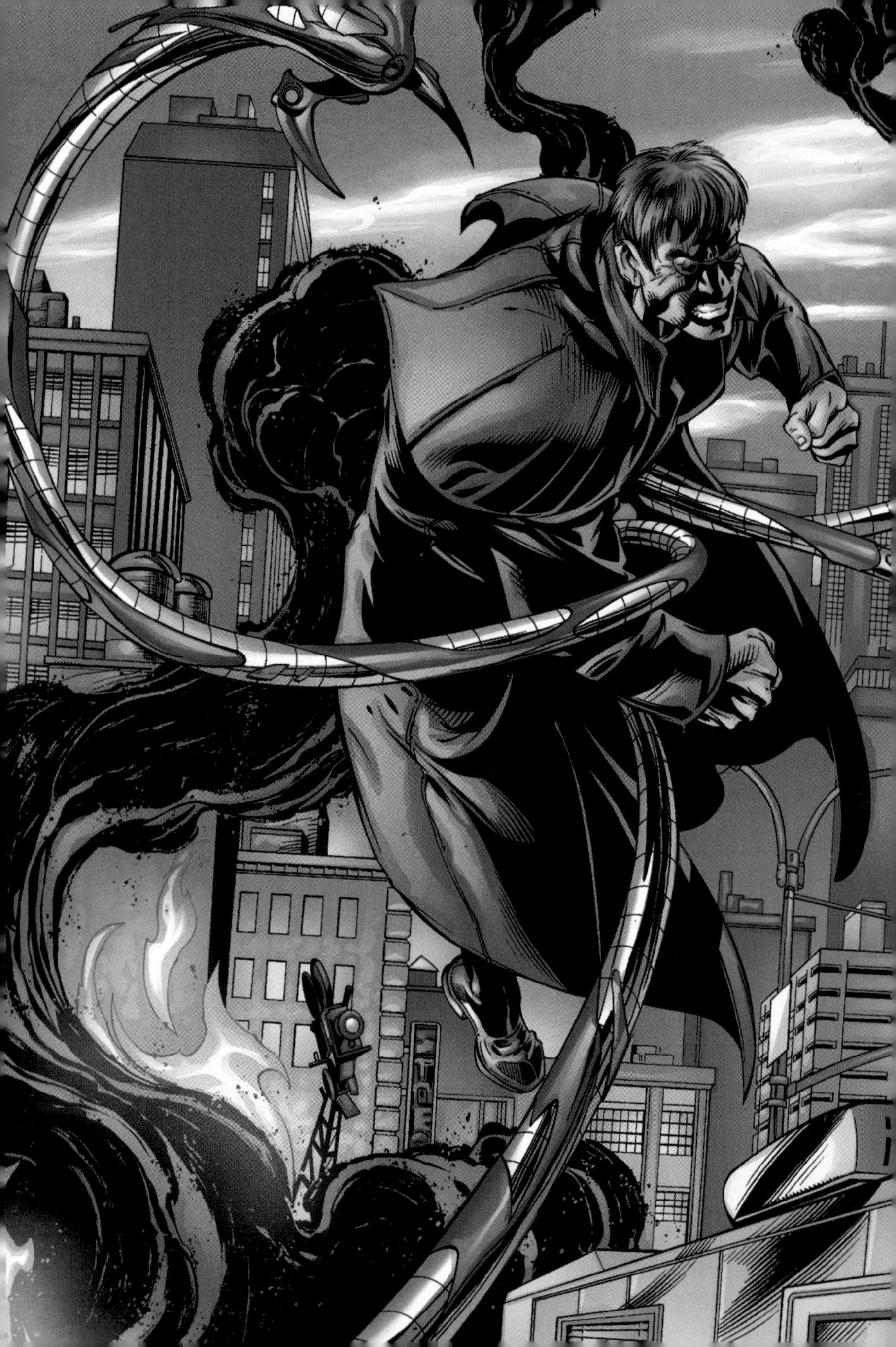

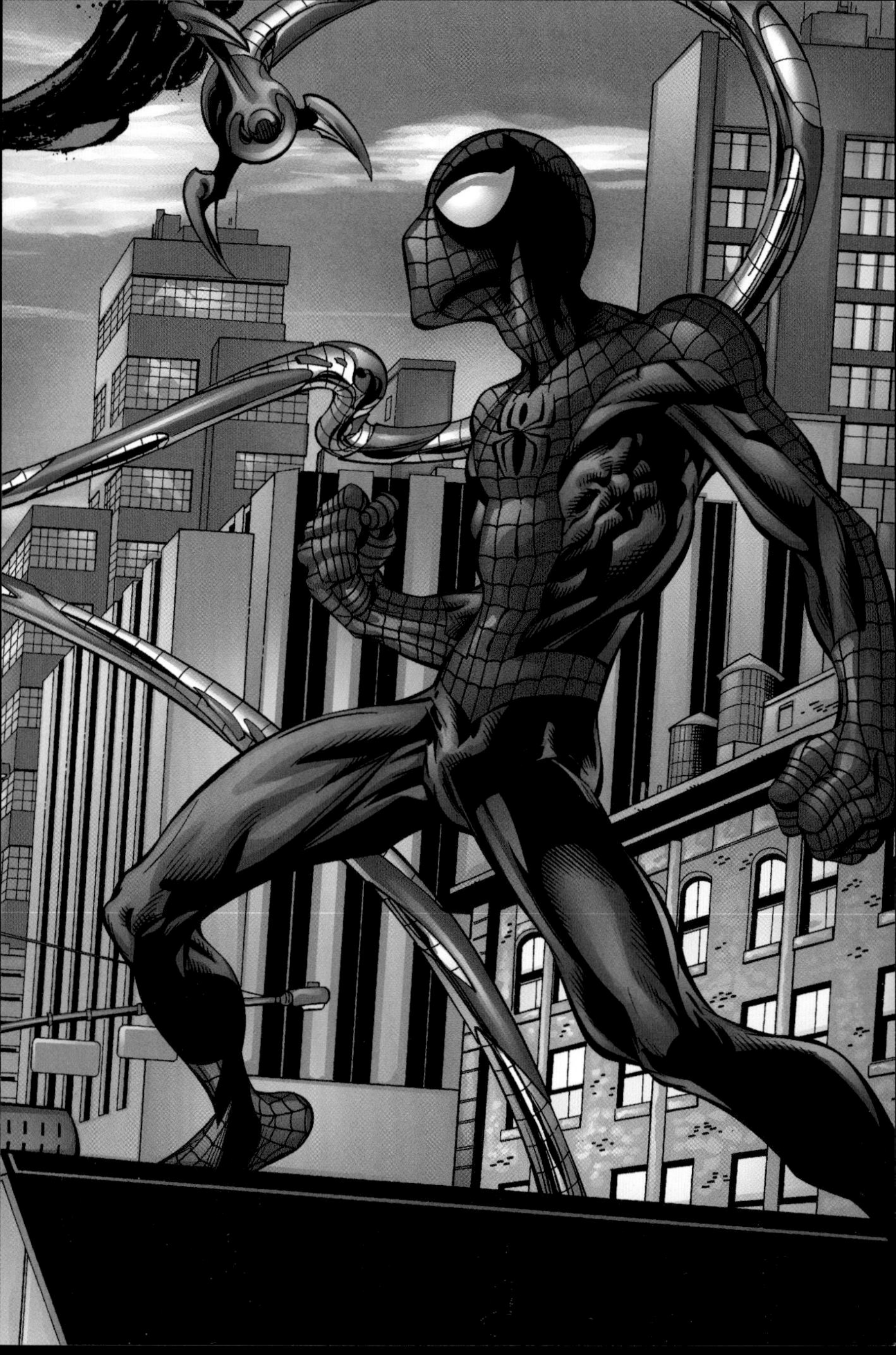

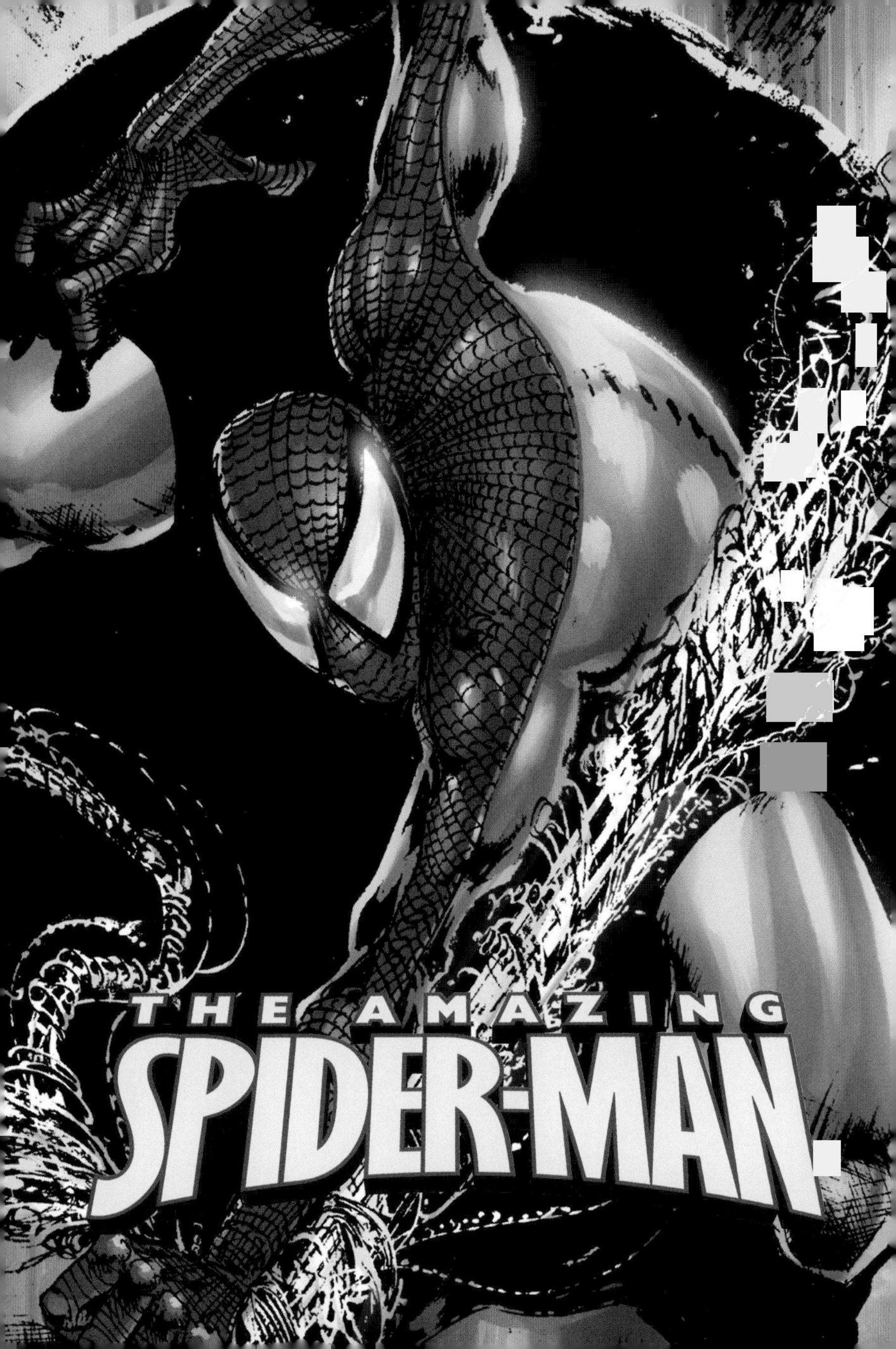
THE AMAZING
SPIDER-MAN

SPIDER-MAN

Before he became Spider-Man, Peter Parker was an ordinary boy. Orphaned when his parents, Mary and Richard Parker, died in a plane crash, Peter was taken in by his father's older brother, Ben Parker, and Ben's wife, May, who raised him as though he was their son. It wasn't until years later that Peter learned his parents were spies for the government and that they had died while on a secret mission.

Uncle Ben and Aunt May were not wealthy, and Peter grew up in humble surroundings. As a teenager, he attended Midtown High School in New York City. He was a shy and bookish student who was fascinated by science, and he regularly attracted the attention of bullies who resented him for being a know-it-all.

When he was fifteen, Peter was bitten on the hand by a spider while attending a science exhibition with his classmates. No one knew at the time that the spider had been exposed accidentally to a "particle beam" and had become highly radioactive. Peter soon began to feel nauseous and dizzy.

On the way back home, Peter was nearly sideswiped by a car, but he escaped injury by leaping out of the way—and onto the side of a building. To his astonishment, he found he was able to cling to walls just like a spider. He also was suddenly possessed of super strength, incredible agility, the ability to adhere to nearly any surface, and a power he would dub "spider-sense," a seeming sixth-sense that warned him of approaching danger.

At first, Peter thought of his newly developed powers only in terms of the wealth and fame they could bring. Donning a makeshift mask, he fought professional wrestler Crusher

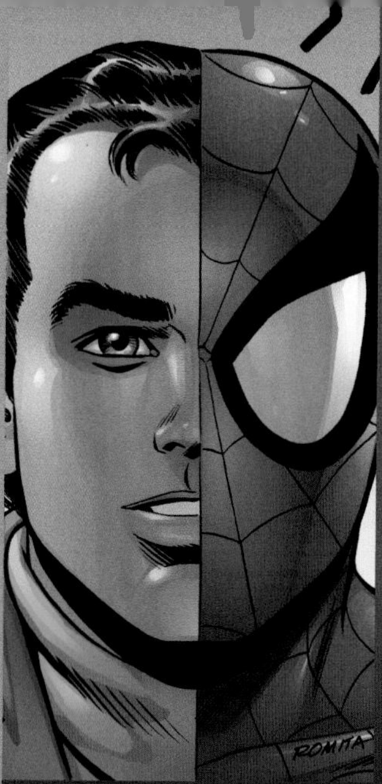
ROMITA

Name Peter Parker

AKA Spider-Man, Webhead, Friendly Neighborhood Spider-Man, Amazing Spider-Man, Spidey, Web-slinger, Captain Universe, Masked Marvel

Groups The Avengers

Height 5' 10"

Weight 167 lbs

Eyes Hazel

Hair Brown

Hogan in a challenge match for cash and easily defeated him. A producer who saw the match offered Peter a spot on television, and Peter accepted, going so far as to hire an agent and to design a costume for his appearance. Mindful of his spider powers, and of the web-spinning skills that distinguished spiders, Peter invented a pair of web-shooting devices to attach to his wrists. The web-shooters ejected a thin stream of liquid that, in seconds, turned solid and formed nearly unbreakable strands. With his new outfit and its accessories, Peter Parker became Spider-Man.

Spider-Man was a huge hit on television and Peter became increasingly self-absorbed with dreams of fame and stardom. One evening, as he was leaving the studio, a burglar ran past with the police in pursuit. Reasoning that it was the police force's responsibility to catch the crook, Peter did nothing to stop the criminal. Several days later, however, Peter returned home to learn that Uncle Ben had been shot and killed at the factory where he worked as night-watchman. As Spider-Man, Peter tracked down the murderer, and was shocked to discover that he was the same criminal he had let escape at the TV studio. Overwhelmed with guilt, Peter realized that with great power comes great responsibility. At that moment Peter dedicated his life to fighting crime as Spider-Man.

Peter soon discovered that being a super hero did not pay the bills. To help Aunt May manage day-to-day living expenses, he took work as a freelance photographer for the *Daily Bugle*. Most of the pictures he sold were close-ups of Spider-Man catching criminals—pictures that only he could take. The publisher of the newspaper, J. Jonah Jameson, hated Spider-Man and used his paper to portray Spider-Man as a criminal vigilante and a menace to society.

At Midtown High School, Peter was still picked on by bullies, including football star Eugene "Flash" Thompson. Complicating the situation, Flash soon became one of Spider-Man's biggest fans.

Over the next few years Spider-Man fought a number of dangerous criminal masterminds, including Doctor Octopus, the Chameleon, the Vulture, the Sandman, and Doctor Doom. Mean-while, working at the Bugle, Peter Parker met and fell in love with Jameson's secretary, Betty Brant. But Betty's brother Bennett was killed during a fight between Spider-Man and Doctor Octopus, and Betty initially blamed Spider-Man for the death. Although she realized later that it wasn't his fault, her lingering distrust of Spider-Man doomed any meaningful relationship with Peter.

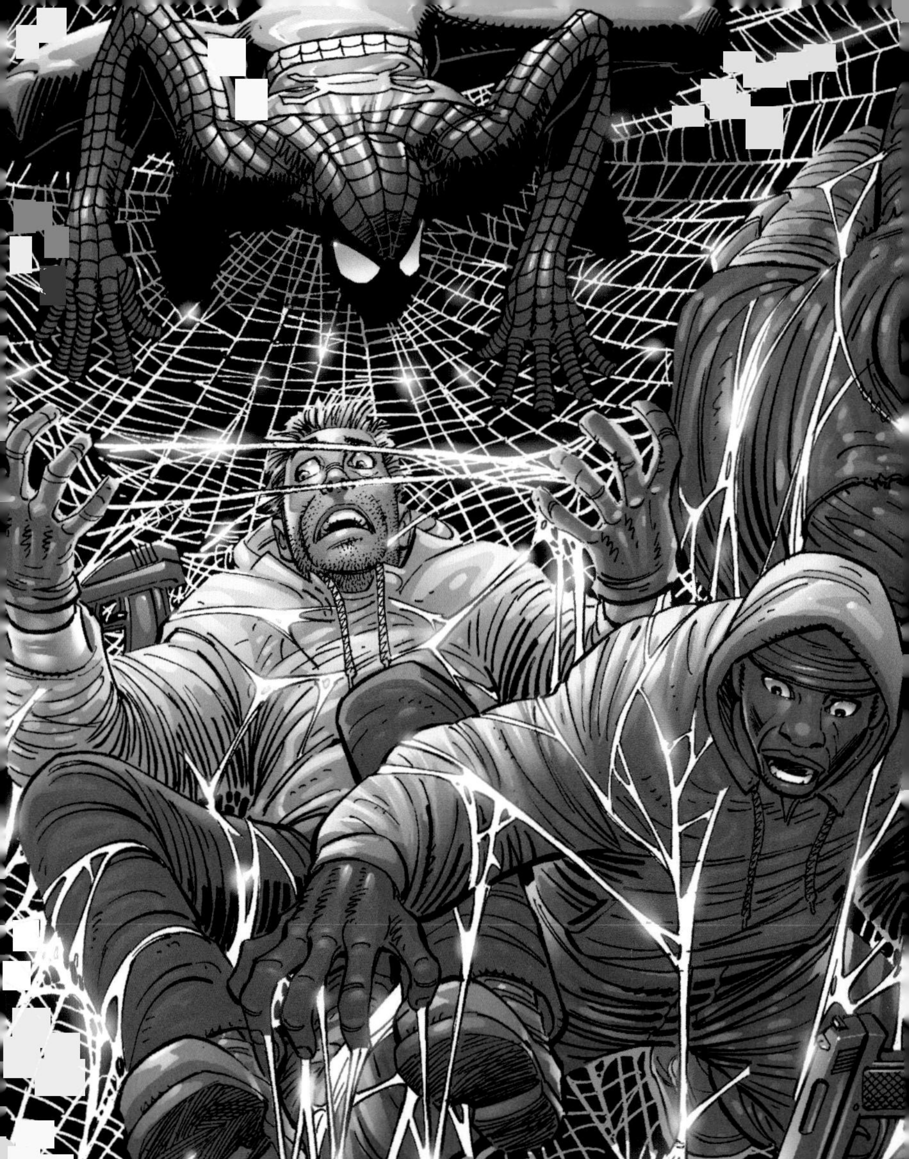

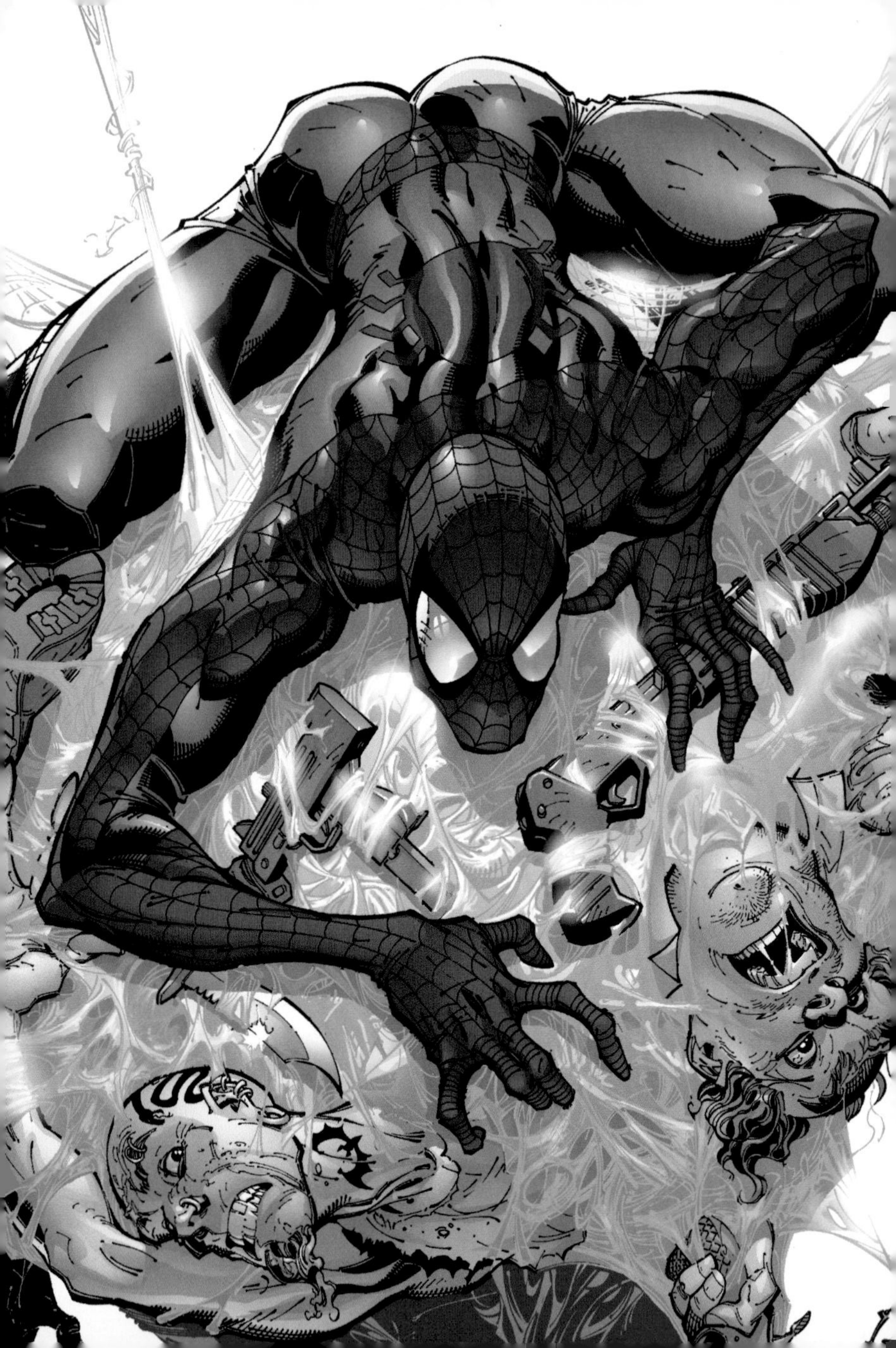

Peter graduated from Midtown High with the finest academic record in the school's history and enrolled at Empire State University on a full science scholarship. Flash Thompson attended ESU as well on an athletic scholarship. It was at ESU that Peter met two fellow students, wealthy Harry Osborn and beauty queen Gwen Stacy. Peter and Harry became close friends and rented an apartment together. Both young men were attracted to Gwen. Peter's life grew increasingly complicated when he discovered that one of Spider-Man's worst enemies, the Green Goblin, was actually Harry's father, Norman Osborn.

Around the same time Peter gave into Aunt May's repeated efforts to get him to go on a blind date with her neighbor's daughter, Mary Jane Watson. To his surprise, he found Mary Jane vivacious and fun-loving, and she soon became a close friend and confidante.

Peter's relationship with Gwen Stacy gradually deepened into love, and Gwen's father, retired police captain George Stacy, approved of it. When Captain Stacy was killed rescuing a child during a battle between Spider-Man and Doctor Octopus, he told Spider-Man with his dying words, "take care of Gwen, Peter," revealing that he knew Peter's secret identity. However, the diabolical Green Goblin kidnapped Gwen and dropped her

off the top of the Brooklyn Bridge. Spider-Man tried to save Gwen but despite his best efforts she died. In a ferocious battle afterwards, Norman Osborn was impaled on the point of his Goblin Glider. Harry Osborn saw his father die and swore vengeance against Spider-Man.

Professor Miles Warren, who had taught both Peter and Gwen biology in college—and who secretly loved Gwen—blamed Spider-Man for Gwen's death. In the guise of the villainous Jackal, Warren created a Spider-Man clone to kill the web-slinger. Warren's plan failed, however, and everyone believed that he and the Spider-Man clone died in an explosion.

It took Peter months to recover from Gwen's death, but with the help of

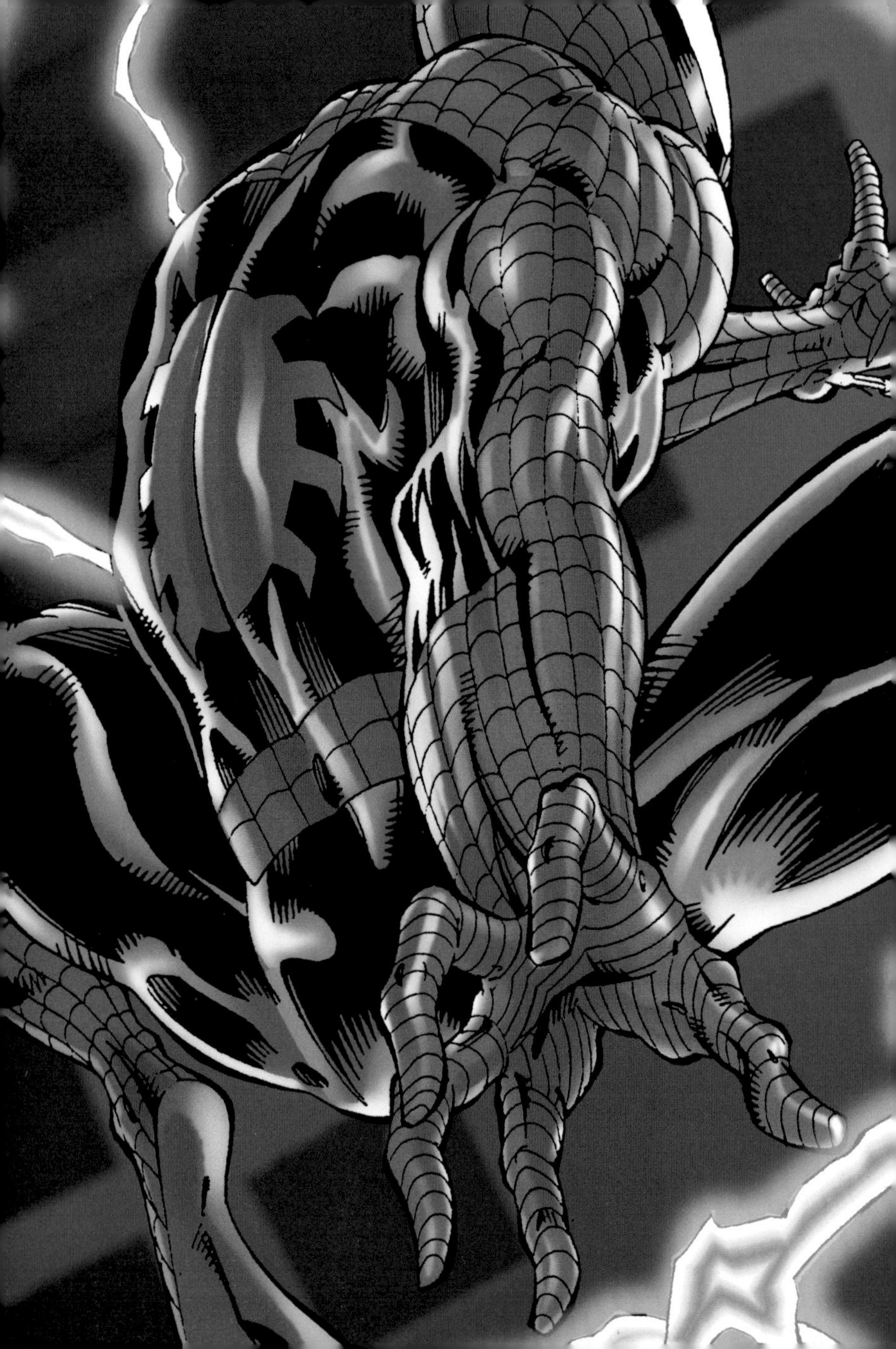

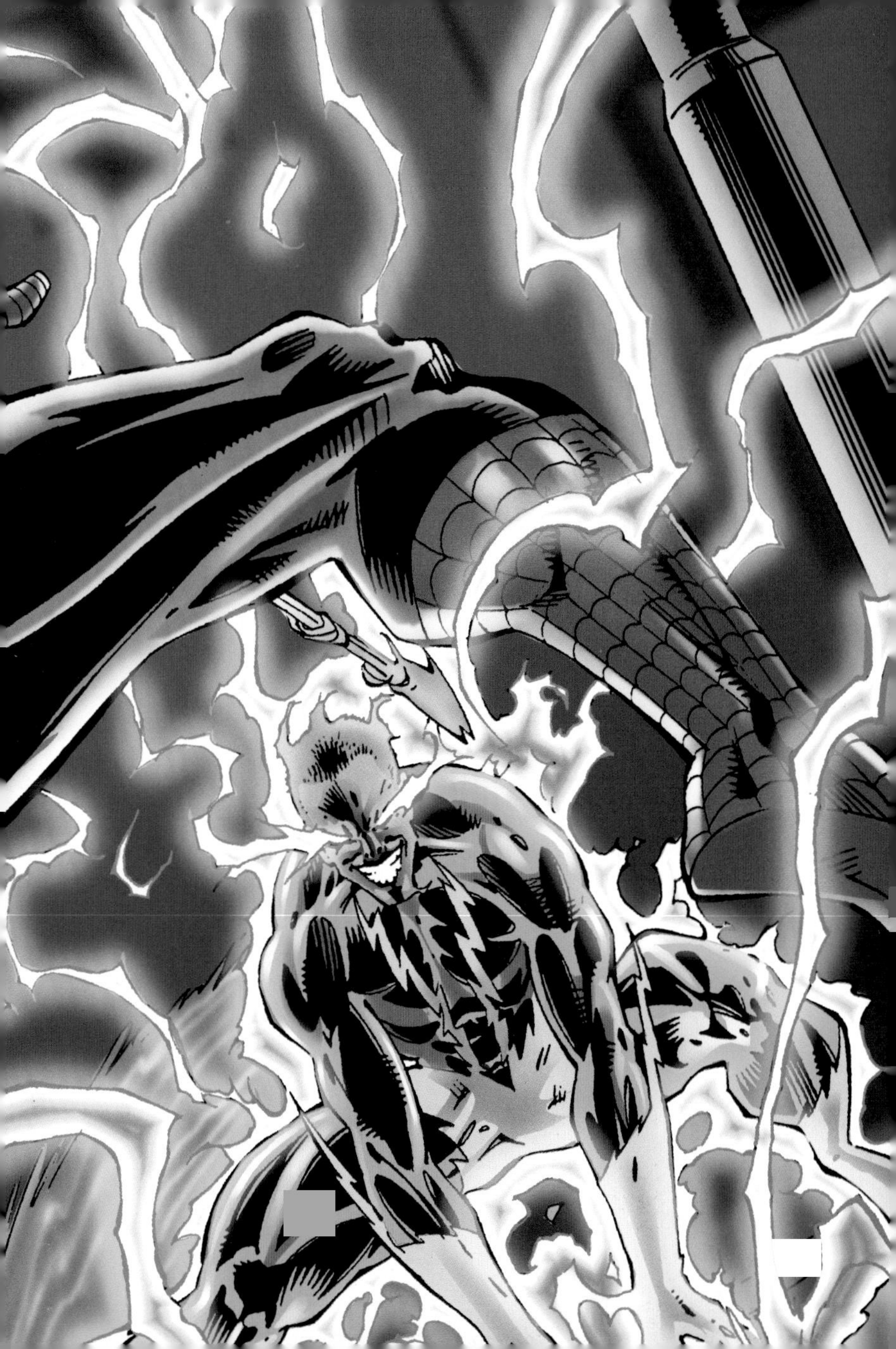

Mary Jane he gradually returned to normal. By then, he had come to realize how much Mary Jane meant to him and understood that love shouldn't be postponed or hidden. Peter proposed to Mary Jane, but she turned him down and moved to Florida. Peter finished college and began graduate school.

Peter dated several women afterward, including Felicia Hardy, a beautiful thrill-seeker obsessed with Spider-Man. Felicia was a burglar who masqueraded as the Black Cat. She and Peter dated briefly, but Peter quickly realized that Felicia was more interested in the thrill of fighting super criminals than in him. Since she had no super powers of her own, she was in constant danger of being killed. Peter would not let another person die because of him, so he broke off his relationship with Black Cat, just as Mary Jane re-entered his life.

Finally understanding how much Peter meant to her, Mary Jane revealed that she had known for years that he was Spider-Man. With no secrets between them any longer, Mary Jane finally accepted Peter's proposal of marriage. Marriage made Peter's life even more complicated, and in the months that followed, he fought numerous old villains as well as many new ones.

He was caught totally off-guard when a couple claiming to be his natural par-

ents returned to the United States, saying that they hadn't really been killed, only captured during a spy mission, after which they had lost their memories. Aunt May didn't trust the pair's story but Peter did, and he revealed his secret identity to them. Soon afterward, the two were discovered to be robots deployed by Harry Osborn, who had stepped into his father's shoes as the Green Goblin.

Peter was then visited by a young man named Ben Reilly, who was actually the Spider-Man clone thought to have died years before. Not only was the clone still alive—so was the villain who created him: the Jackal. Ben arrived in New York just as Aunt May died from a heart attack. Peter and Ben became friends and that was when Jackal

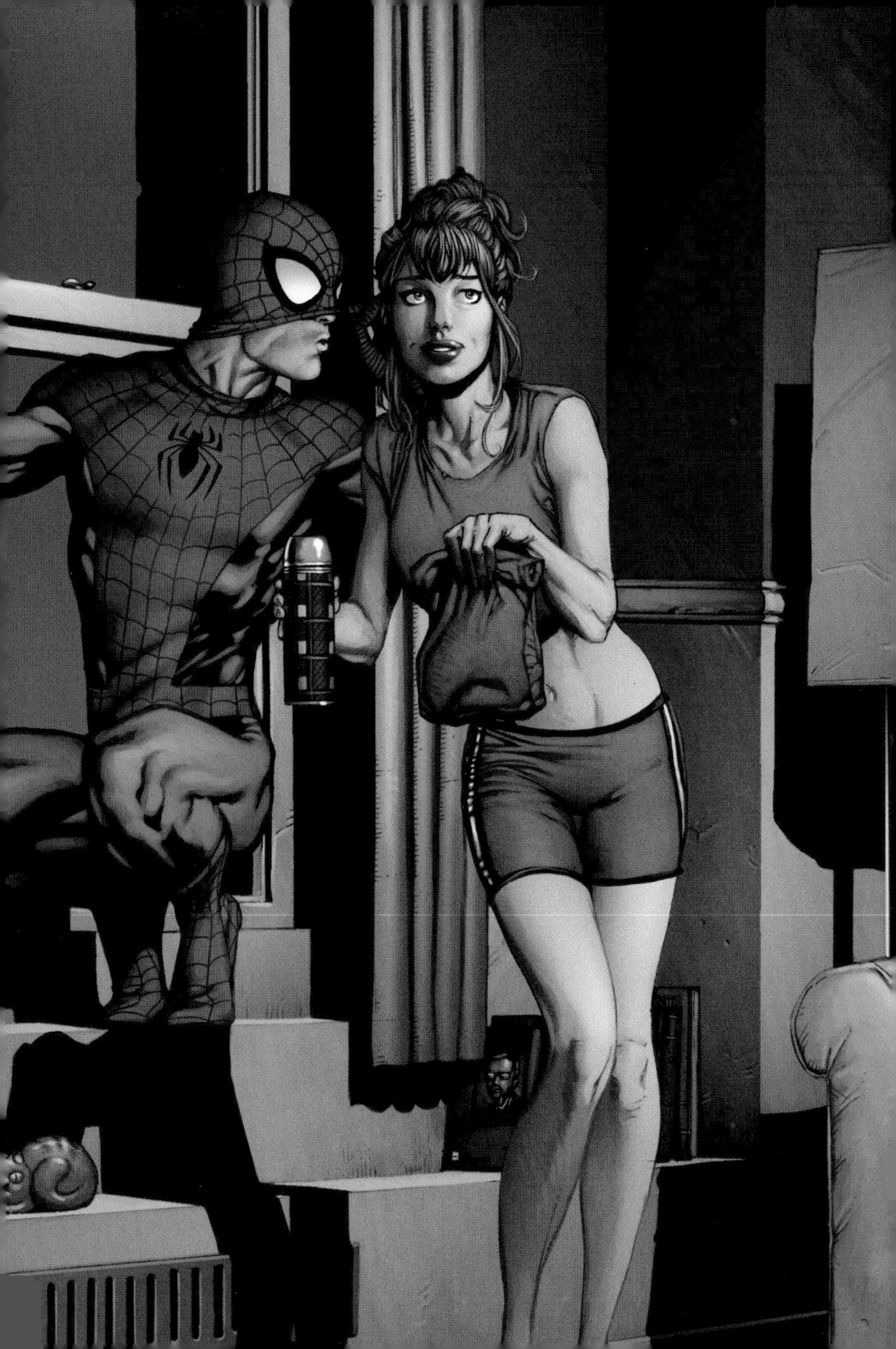

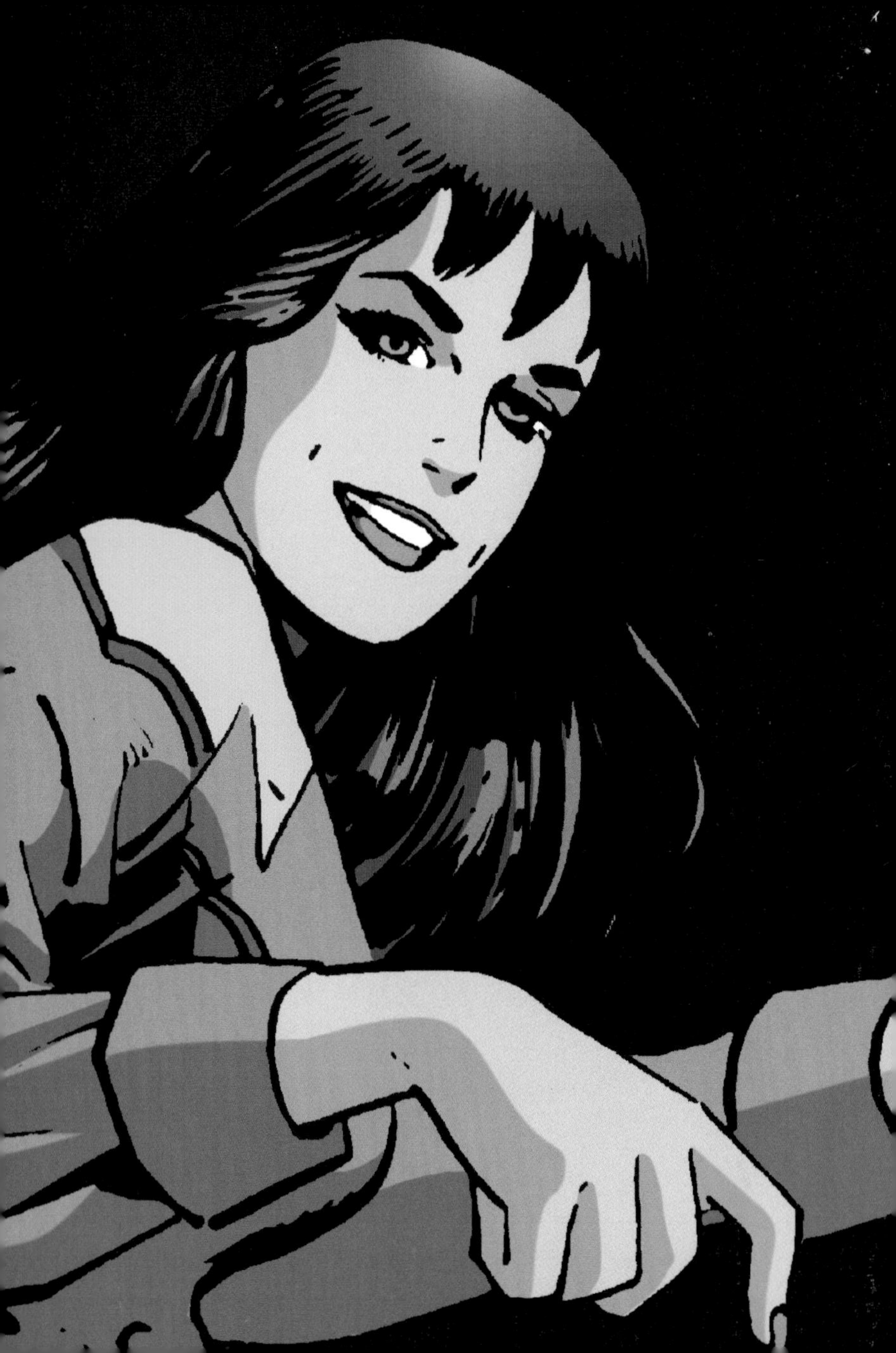

returned to Manhattan and declared that Ben was the real Spider-Man and Peter the clone. Ben took over as Spider-Man, letting Peter and Mary Jane live a normal life. Mary Jane became pregnant and she and Peter prepared to start a family.

It was then revealed that Norman Osborn, the original Green Goblin, had never died. The goblin formula in his blood had kept him alive after his impalement. Escaping from the morgue, he had fled to Europe where he became the leader of a clandestine organization named the Scriers. Norman had worked in secret for years as the mastermind behind numerous plots against Spider-Man. It was during one of Spider-Man's battles with Osborn, once again in his Green Goblin guise, that Mary Jane went into labor. Her baby was stillborn.

After several titanic battles, Spider-Man defeated Norman Osborn once again. In one of those fights, Ben Reilly was impaled on the Goblin's Glider while saving Peter. Ben's body turned to dust, proving that he was the clone. Spider-Man also learned that Aunt May's "death" was a hoax perpetrated by the Green Goblin, and he rescued her from the Osborn estate where she was being held captive.

After numerous other complications in their lives, Peter Parker, Mary Jane, and Aunt May have reunited and they live together at the headquarters of scientific genius Tony (Iron Man) Stark. After a stint as an inner-city schoolteacher, Peter took a job as Stark's assistant.

Recently, the United States government passed the Superhuman Registration Act, which requires all members of the super hero community to register as living weapons of mass destruction, as well as reveal their secret identities. Believing the Act to be a good idea, Spider-Man agreed to do so and revealed to the world at large that he is Peter Parker. His decision put him at odds with his partner, Tony Stark.

Peter has since come to regret his action, but some choices are not easily reversed.

SECRETS

- When Mary Jane Watson-Parker went into labor and gave birth to a child fathered by Peter, the infant was kidnapped by an agent of Norman Osborn. Mary Jane and Peter were told that the baby had died.

- Mary Jane and Peter are the godparents of Norman Harold Osborn, the son of Harry Osborn (the 2nd Green Goblin).

- Aunt May discovered that Peter was Spider-Man when he collapsed in bed still wearing his costume after an exhausting battle against the villain Morlun.

COSTUME

When Peter Parker first decided to become Spider-Man he realized that he needed a costume to hide his features from the public and to keep Aunt May safe from any criminals seeking revenge. Peter sewed together the first Spider-Man costume himself, making it out of ordinary department store materials.

The original uniform was constructed from form-fitting fabric that covered Peter from head to toe. From the waist down, it was dark blue. His boots were mid-calf height and featured a black web pattern on a red background. From his waist up, the material showed a red and black web pattern. The back and insides of his upper arms were dark blue. On his chest he wore a black spider emblem, and on his back a large red spider emblem. His mask had large white eyes, rimmed with black. He was able to see through the mask while it hid his face and eyes from view.

Years later, Spider-Man was one of the many super heroes and super villains that a mysterious being known as the Beyonder transported to the Secret Wars, a battle fought on a distant planet. During the fighting, Spider-Man's costume was ripped nearly to pieces. Using what he thought to be a costume-making machine, he requested a new outfit. The costume produced was a form-fitting black bodysuit with a large white spider emblem on the chest and the back. The new uniform boosted his spider-powers and even came equipped with built-in web-shooters for the back of his hands and a seemingly unlimited supply of webbing.

When Spider-Man returned to Earth, he decided to stick with the new outfit. This almost proved his undoing, as the costume was actually a symbiotic lifeform, which tried to merge with Peter Parker. With the help of the Fantastic Four, Spider-Man was able to rid himself of the symbiotic suit. However, he continued to wear a similar black costume until Mary Jane voiced her objection to it and he reverted back to his original costume.

Recently, Spider-Man changed costumes for a third time. The new outfit, designed by Tony Stark, is made from a liquid metal nanofiber that makes it possible for Spider-Man to change it quickly, through simple mental command, into any outfit, ranging from Peter's street clothes to any of his other costumes. It even can act as a camouflage suit that blends in with the colors of the surrounding scenery.

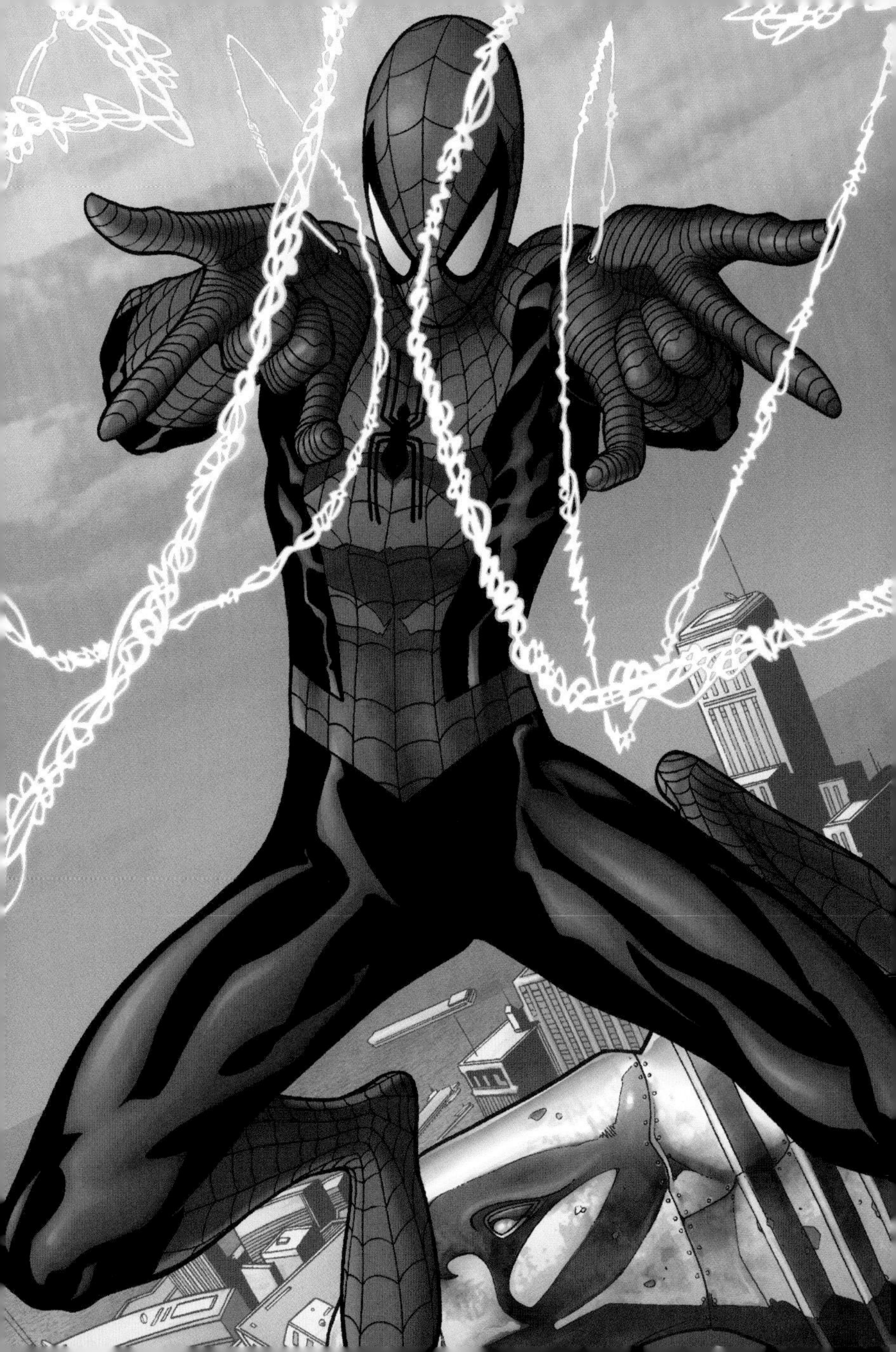

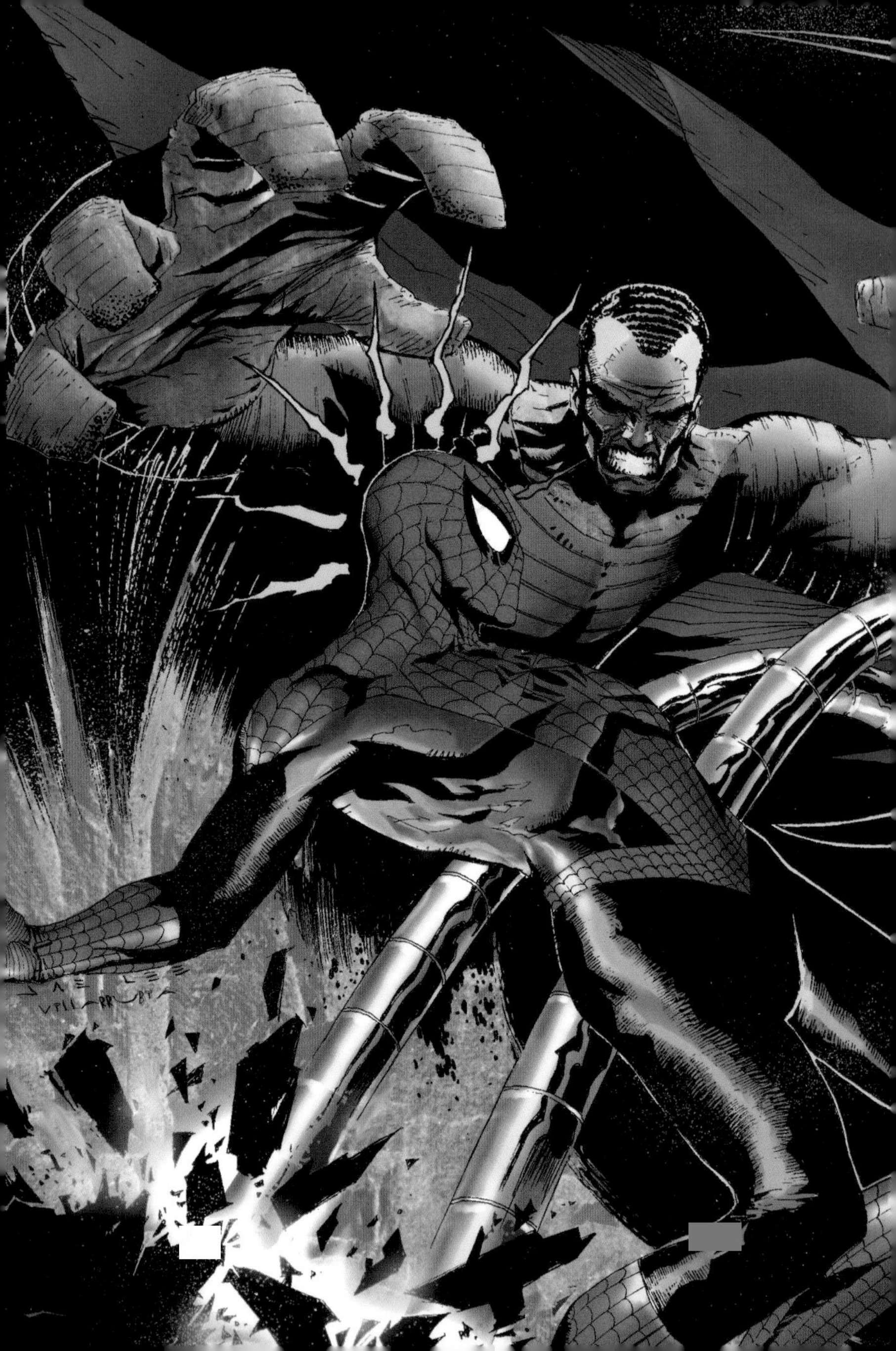

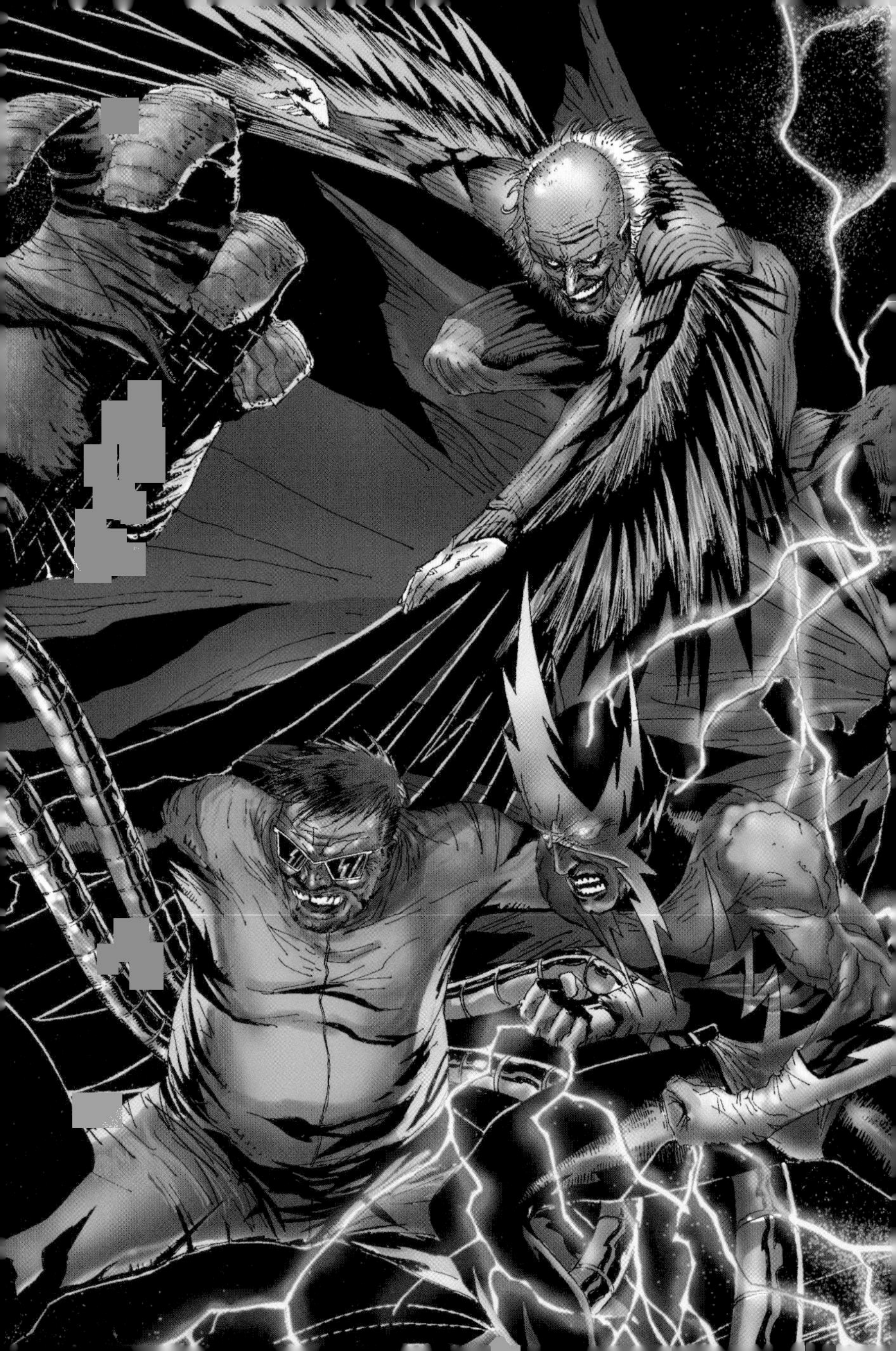

The new costume has three "spider legs" on the back. These mechanical limbs have cameras embedded in the tips that make it possible to see around corners. They also can be used to manipulate small objects. In this regard, they're very similar to waldos, the mechanical arms used by scientists to handle radioactive materials. The suit is bulletproof, equipped with carbon filters to keep out airborne poisons, and contains an underwater breathing system. It has retractable webbing beneath the arms that makes gliding for short distances possible. The outfit has a police and emergency scanner built in, provides audio and visual amplification (both infrared and ultraviolet), and features a short-range GPS communication system.

SECRETS

- Spider-Man's symbiotic black costume was forced off his body by the extremely loud sound of a church-bell ringing.

- Spider-Man uses his three new "spider legs" in combat, even though Tony Stark has warned him that they are extremely fragile.

GADGETS

When Peter Parker was bitten by a radioactive spider, his body was transformed in numerous ways. He gained super-strength, the ability to walk on walls, ceilings, and virtually any surface, superhuman agility, and a sixth-sense that warned him of danger.

Parker's genius enabled him to construct a number of machines and devices that helped him immeasurably in his war against crime. Without these gadgets, Spider-Man would never have made his mark on the underworld. Parker's special powers enabled him to capture evildoers, but it was his scientific creations that delivered the villains to the police.

Once he discovered that he had gained some of the powers of a spider, Peter Parker realized that to be effective as Spider-Man he needed to develop the spider powers he was missing. Chief among those talents

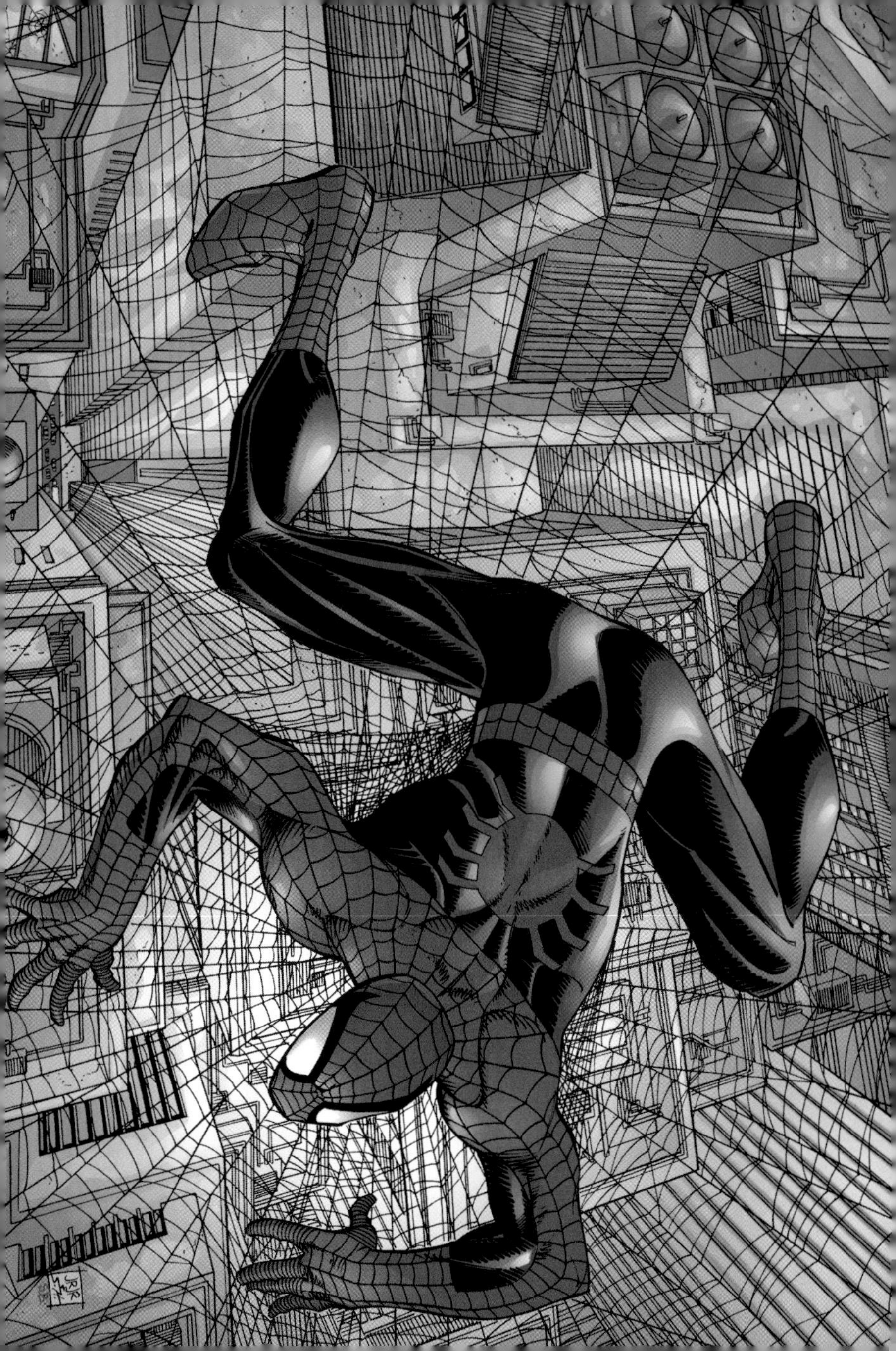

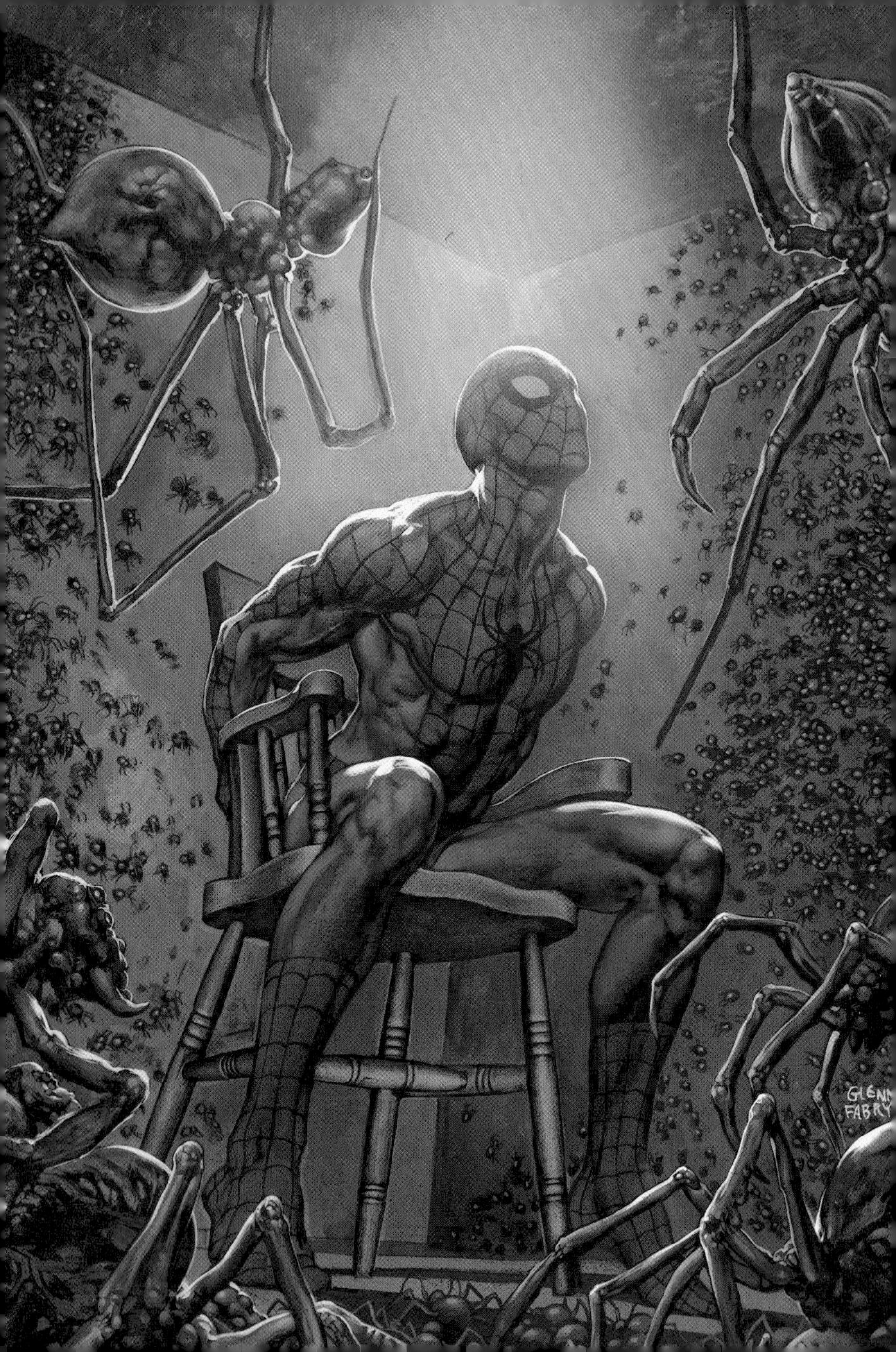

was the ability to spin webs, so Parker set out to create artificial web-spinners that he could use for a multitude of purposes in his battle against crime.

Although he had little money or equipment, Parker developed a unique synthetic liquid that had both adhesive and web-like properties. To use this liquid, he built special devices to be worn on the insides of his wrists that would shoot out small streams of the webbing solution toward any direction in which he pointed his hands. The trigger for these web-shooters rested at the top of his palms and required a double tap from the middle and ring fingers to activate. Once released into the air, the web solution dried almost instantly into long fiber-like strings. A single strand of the webbing is as strong as piano wire.

Spider-Man's webbing enabled him to use his super-powers in the most effective way possible. He quickly developed a technique of shooting a thin web at nearby tall buildings and swinging through the air on a strand, much like Tarzan does with jungle vines. By repeating this action again and again, Spider-Man is easily able to swing his way through Manhattan.

Spider-Man uses thicker strands of webbing to tie up criminals and the super-villains he leaves for the police to find. He's proficient at throwing small globs of webbing at crooks to cover their eyes, making it impossible for them to see. A small amount of web liquid thrown across the muzzle of a firearm jams it. A large amount can be tossed across a street to stop a moving car or a fleeing suspect.

At times, Spider-Man has even built small items out of webbing, such as parachutes, gliders, gloves, bandages, slings, bulletproof shields, and a hammock. The webbing dissolves into a gas approximately one hour after it is spun. During his early days as a crime fighter, Spider-Man regularly had to refill his web-shooters with cartridges of web fluid. He carried extra amounts of the liquid in a utility belt he wore around his waist. Later, realizing that a loaded web-shooter could mean the difference between life or death, he equipped the devices with bracelets of web fluid that would rotate a new cartridge into the shooter when needed. Recently, after his death and resurrection, Peter Parker developed organic web-shooters in both of his wrists.

Another testament to Spider-Man's genius IQ is the miniature tracking devices he invented known as spider-tracers. Shaped like spiders, these tiny electronic bugs emit a signal that he can detect for miles with his spider-sense. Using the tracers, Spider-Man has been able to track more than one criminal back to his hide-away or secret lair. The only short-coming of the spider-tracers is that, if they are discovered by one of Spider-Man's enemies, they can be used to lure him into a trap.

Spider-Man keeps his spider-tracers, extra webbing solution, and camera in a utility belt he wears around his waist. The belt buckle contains a powerful light that can project a picture of Spider-Man's mask. This spider-signal has been used in the past to frighten criminals.

Peter earns his living working as a freelance photographer, selling his pictures to the *Daily Bugle*. His first camera, which originally belonged to his father, had an extended rear plate that allowed him to anchor it with his webbing across from where he would be fighting. It also had a motion sensor, so when Spider-Man and his enemy came into sight, it would immediately snap pictures of their battle.

Working as a freelancer, Peter sells all rights to his photos to the *Daily Bugle*. The newspaper has published a book of his photos entitled *Webs*.

SECRETS

- Spider-Man's webbing has a tensile strength of 120 lbs per square millimeter.

- With the help of the Human Torch, Spider-Man once designed a car called the Spider-Mobile. Since Spider-Man had never learned to drive, he crashed it into the Hudson River soon after it was finished.

- Mary Jane Watson wears an amplified spider-tracer in a necklace pendant so that Spider-Man can find her if she is kidnapped.

- After Spider-Man's death and rebirth, physical changes to his body made his old web-shooters obsolete, so he turned them into bracelets and gave them to Mary Jane as a Valentine's Day present.

POWERS

From the day he was bitten by the radioactive spider, Spider-Man has possessed four powers. He can cling to almost any surface, in any position, up, down, and even sideways. He has incredible strength: he is able to lift more than 25,000 pounds at one time and he has to pull his punches when fighting an ordinary person to avoid killing them with his fists. He possesses superhuman agility: he can balance on narrow surfaces, and his powerful leg muscles enable him to leap from building to building with superhuman precision. And he possesses a sixth-sense, or "spider-sense," which warns him of approaching danger.

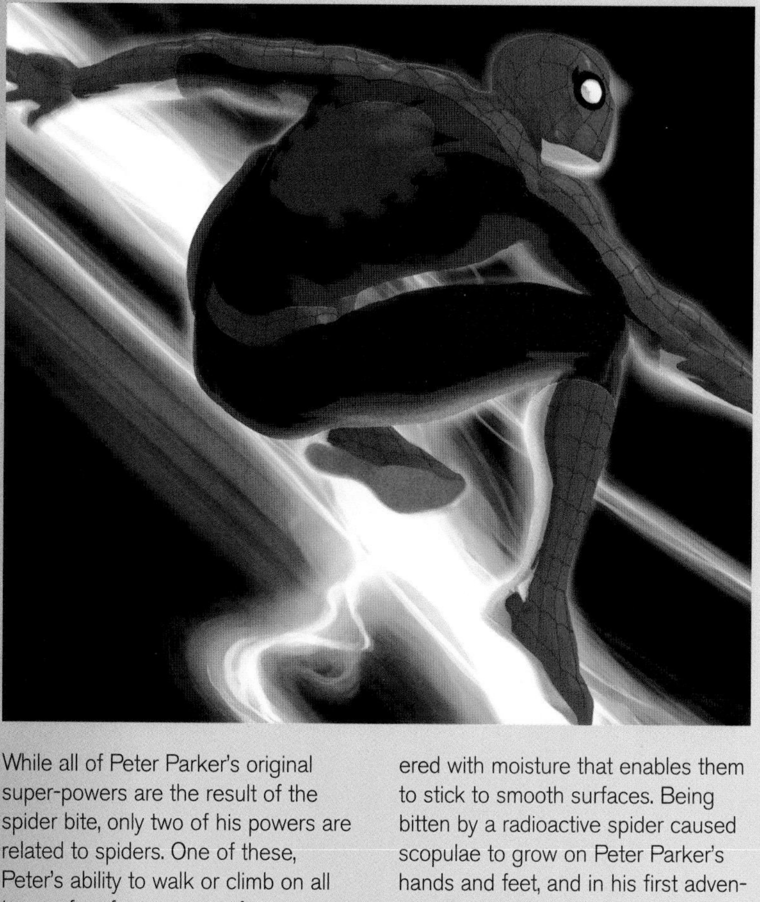

While all of Peter Parker's original super-powers are the result of the spider bite, only two of his powers are related to spiders. One of these, Peter's ability to walk or climb on all types of surfaces, comes from a species of hunting spider. Spiders possess a thick group of hairs known as scopulae on the inside of their limbs. Each hair is made up of thousands of microscopic filaments covered with moisture that enables them to stick to smooth surfaces. Being bitten by a radioactive spider caused scopulae to grow on Peter Parker's hands and feet, and in his first adventure, Peter climbed the side of a building using his bare hands. Later, when Spider-Man donned gloves, he undoubtedly made them porous enough so that these microscopic hairs could extend out from the mate-

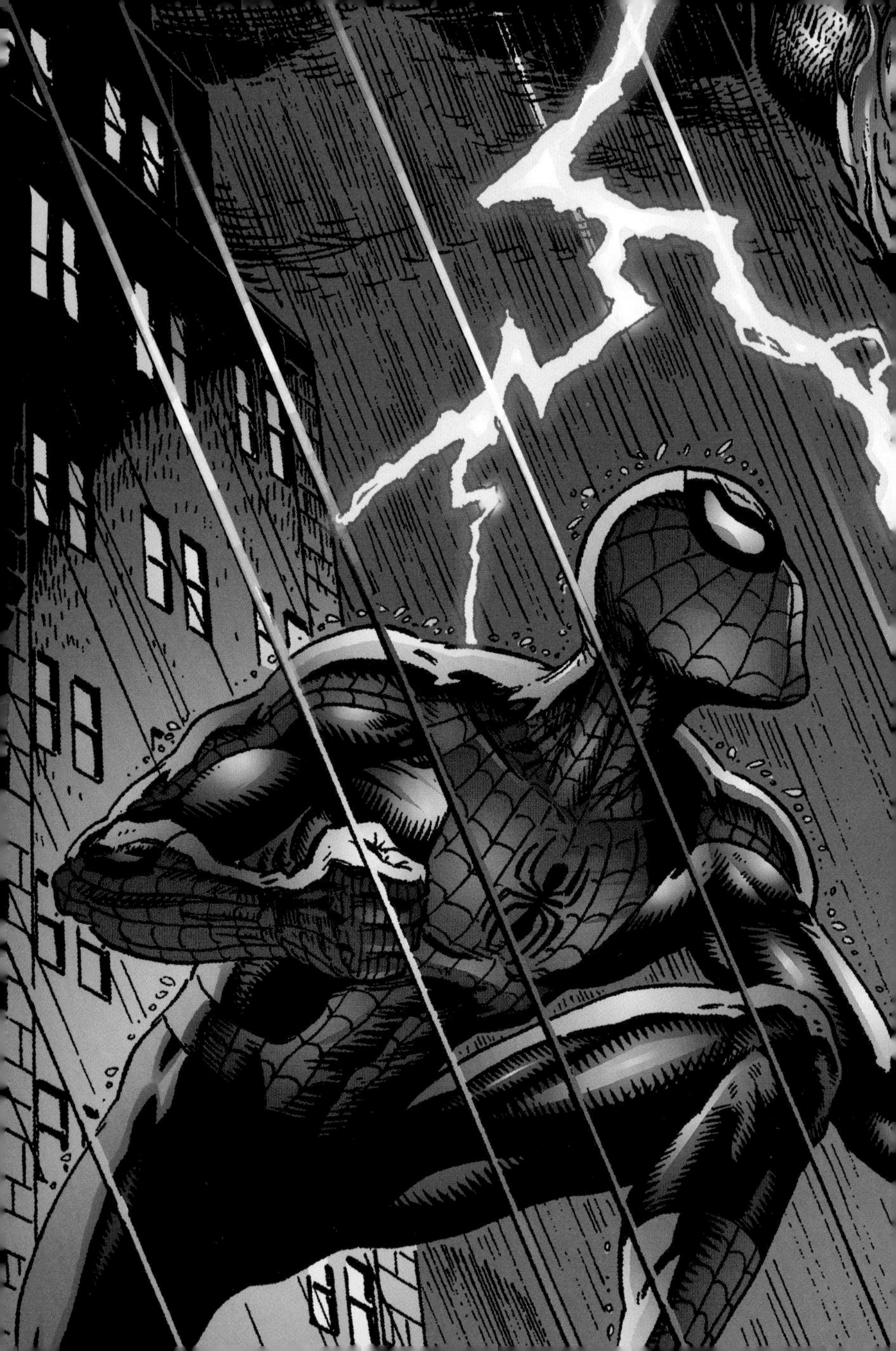

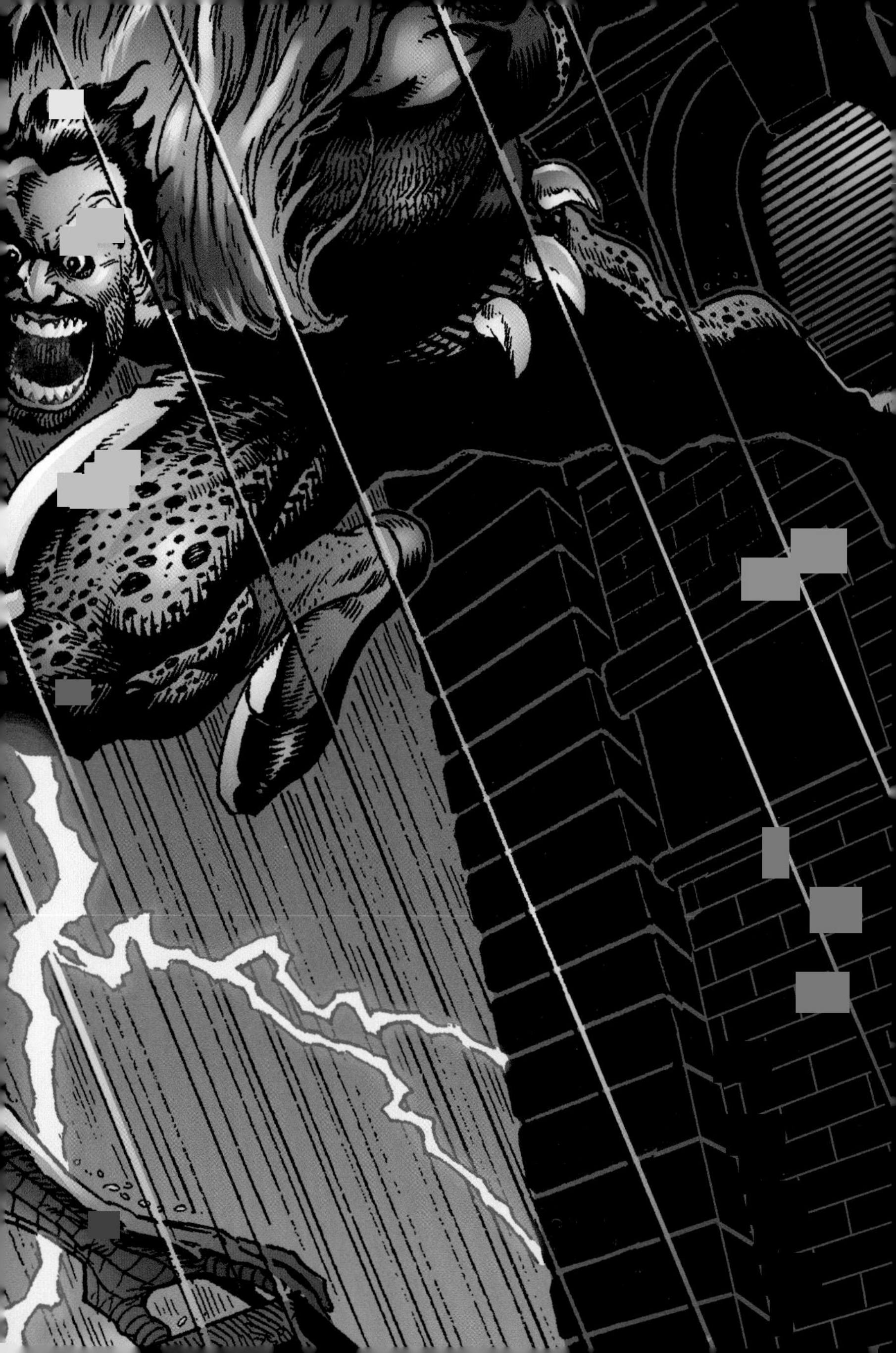

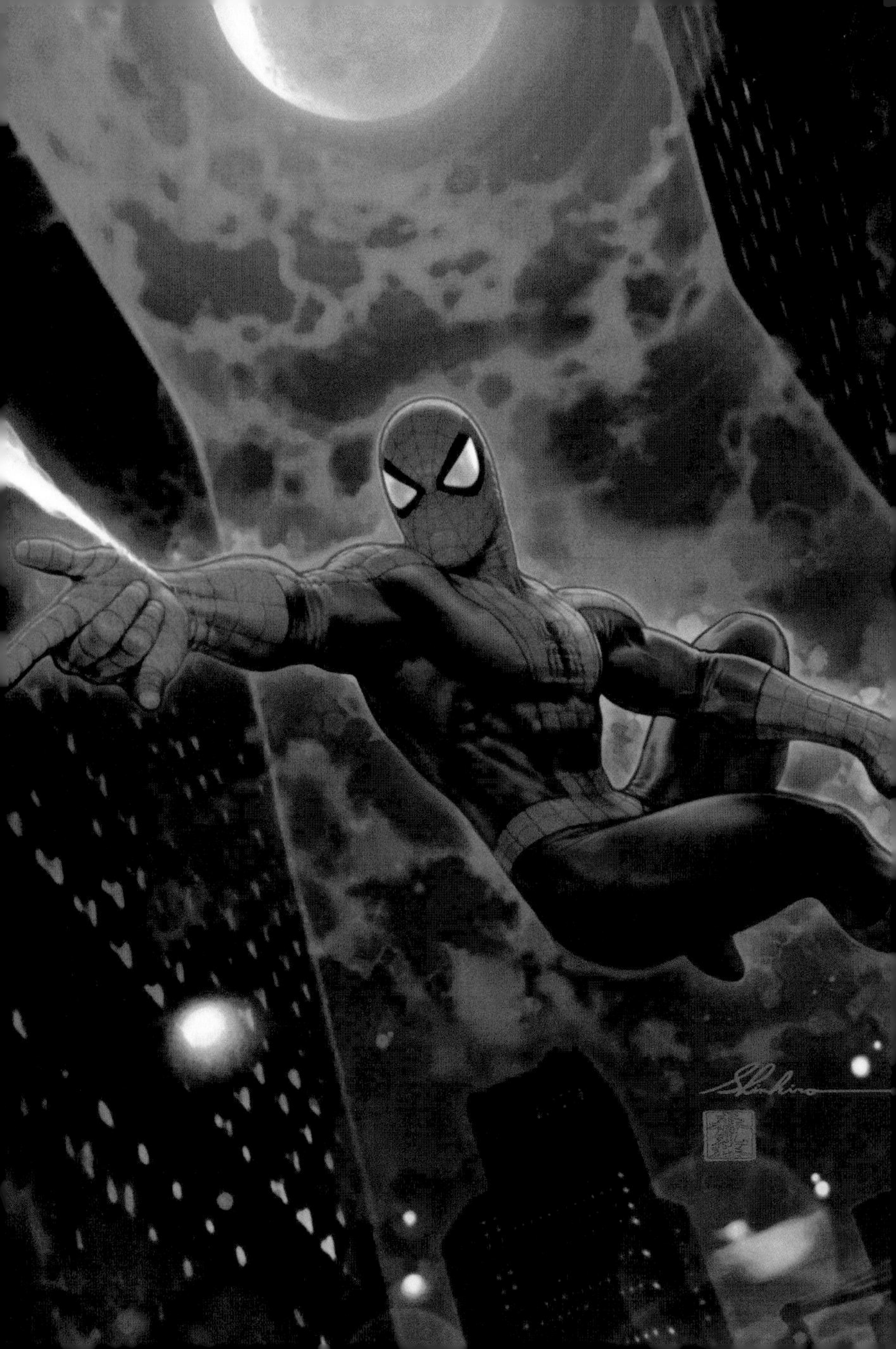

rial. In instances where he wanted to walk up buildings using his feet, he first removed his shoes.

Peter's spider-sense comes from tiny hair bristles known as setae. These minute spines are extraordinarily sensitive to chemical compounds, as well as to the slightest disturbances in the air. Their hypersensitivity gives Peter a heightened awareness of his surroundings and any changes taking place in them. Setae are common to all spiders, and they make Peter immune to surprise attacks. Spiders are not known for great strength or incredible agility. These two abilities are most likely human traits mutated and magnified by the radioactivity in Peter Parker's bloodstream.

After the death of Captain Stacy, Peter Parker felt guilty about his powers and experimented with a chemical compound that would transform him back into an ordinary human being. Instead, the concoction changed Spider-Man into a six-armed human, more spider-like than ever before. With the assistance of Dr. Curt Connors, Spider-Man brewed a potion made in part from blood taken from Morbius, the Living Vampire, which helped him return to human form.

For a short time after his marriage to Mary Jane, Peter gained the cosmic super-powers of Captain Universe. These heightened powers came from the Uni-Power, an extra-dimensional force that possesses super heroes during periods of crisis. The Uni-Power is a manifestation of the Enigma Force, about which little is known. Tapping into the Uni-Power, Spider-Man became indestructible; he was able to fly and fire blasts of cosmic energy. His super strength was multiplied by a power of fifty. The Uni-Power left Spider-Man as mysteriously as it arrived, and he reverted to his original powers.

During an adventure with the super villain known as the Queen, a toxic kiss released an enzyme into Spider-Man's body that transformed him into a grotesque humanoid spider hybrid with extra arms, extra eyes, and deadly fangs. A further mutation changed Spider-Man into a giant spider. However, the huge creature died before the Queen's plans for it could be put into action. The Queen abandoned the dead body and thus didn't witness Peter Parker's rebirth from the creature's corpse as Spider-Man with enhanced spider powers. These enhancements included a strong psychic bond with nature, particularly with arachnids and insects, as well as the ability to create organic spider-webs.

After a titanic battle with the near-immortal Morlun, a villain who lived

off the life-force of super heroes, Spider-Man "died" again, only to shed his old skin and return to life. The newly resurrected hero soon discovered that he had developed new spider powers, including night vision and enhanced sensory perceptions. Peter also learned that he could now fasten any part of his body, not just his hands and feet, to smooth surfaces. Equally important, his mask adhered to his face like a second skin and could not be removed unless he allowed it to. Perhaps the most potent change to his powers was the addition of deadly stingers that emerge from his wrists during extreme emergencies. These stingers are coated with a neurotoxin that causes temporary paralysis in those stung.

SECRETS

- Spider-Man possesses incredible healing powers. His immune system fights off the effects of deadly drugs and gases fairly easily—yet, he still suffers from colds.

- Spider-Man has a normal man's tolerance to alcoholic drinks. Drinking affects his balance, reflexes, and coordination.

- Spider-Man's reflexes are fifteen times faster than those of an ordinary human's.

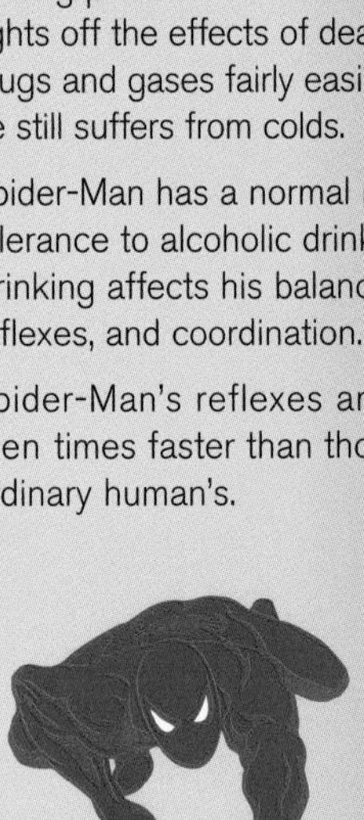

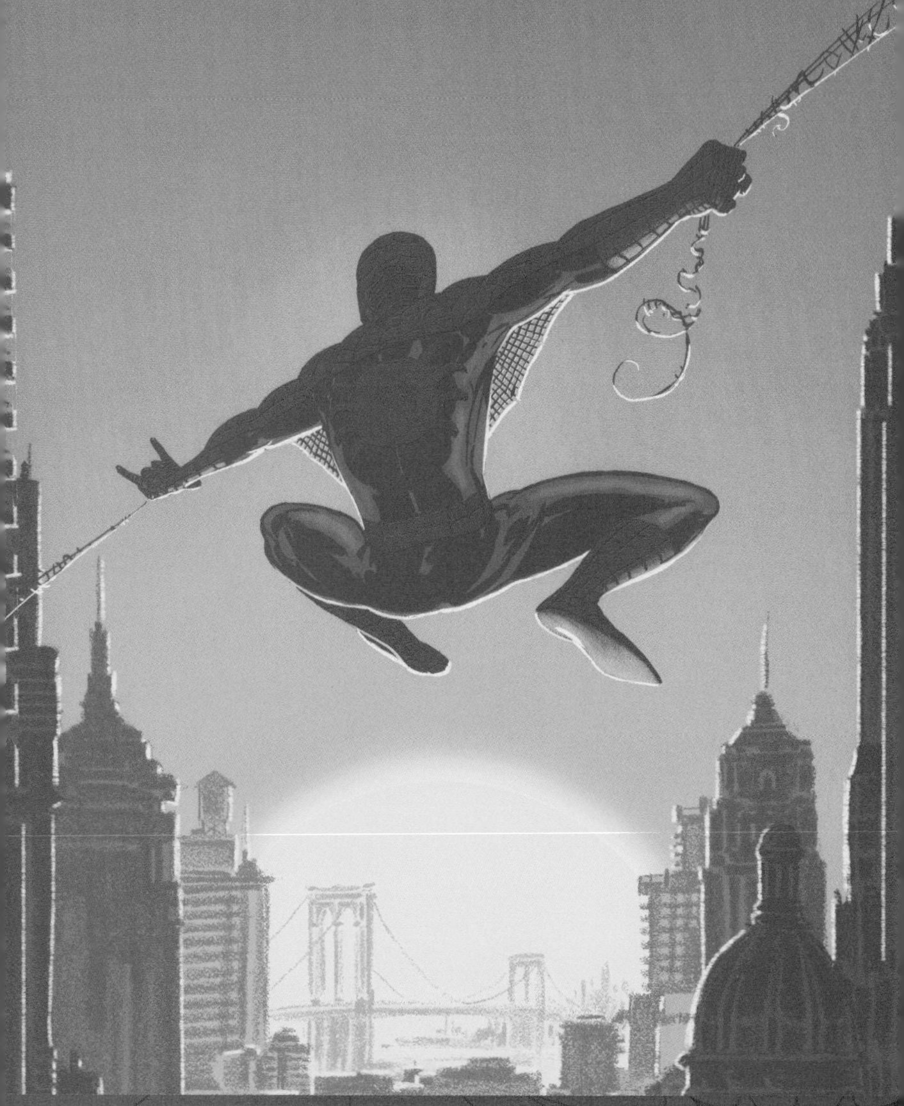

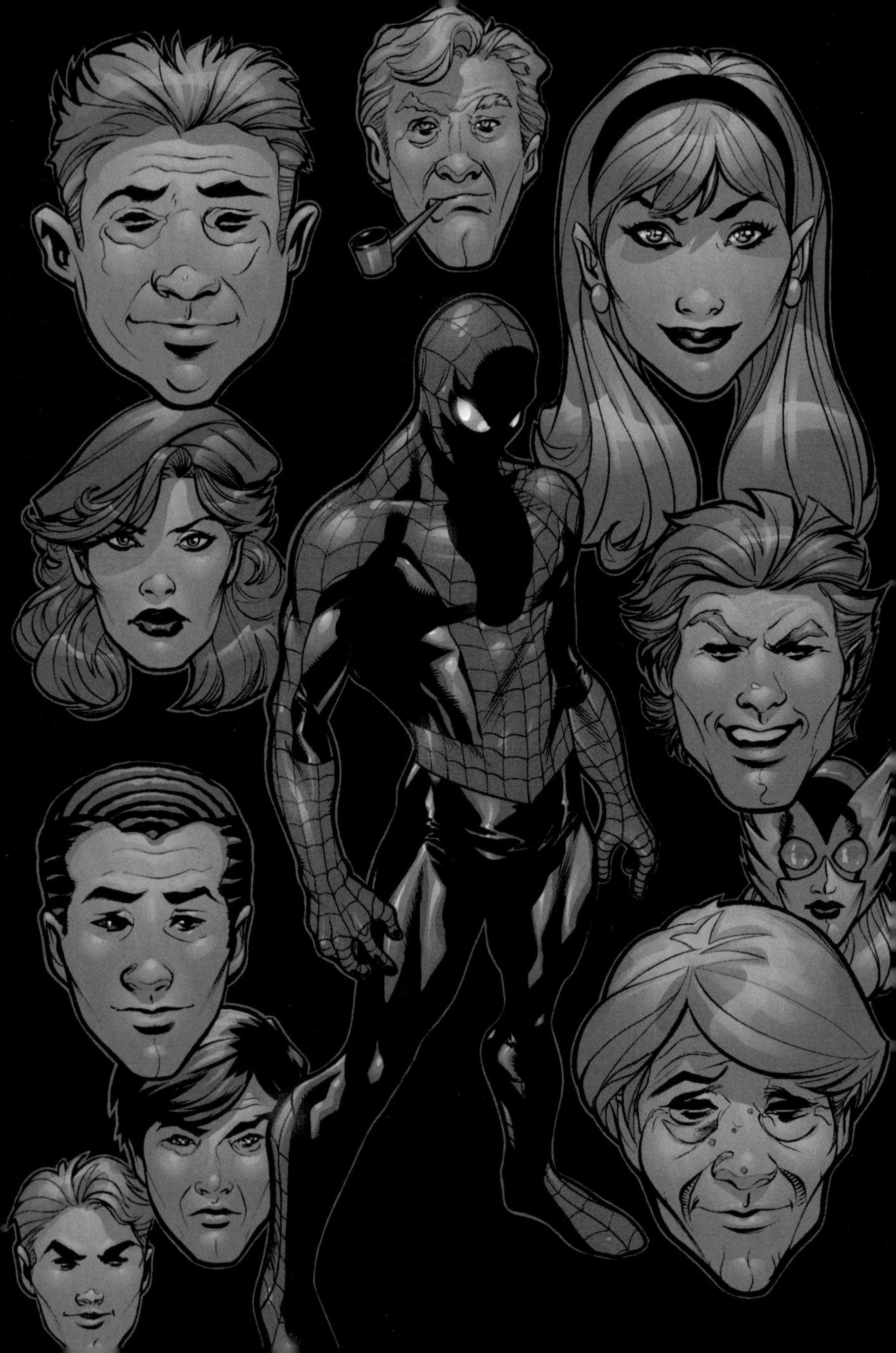

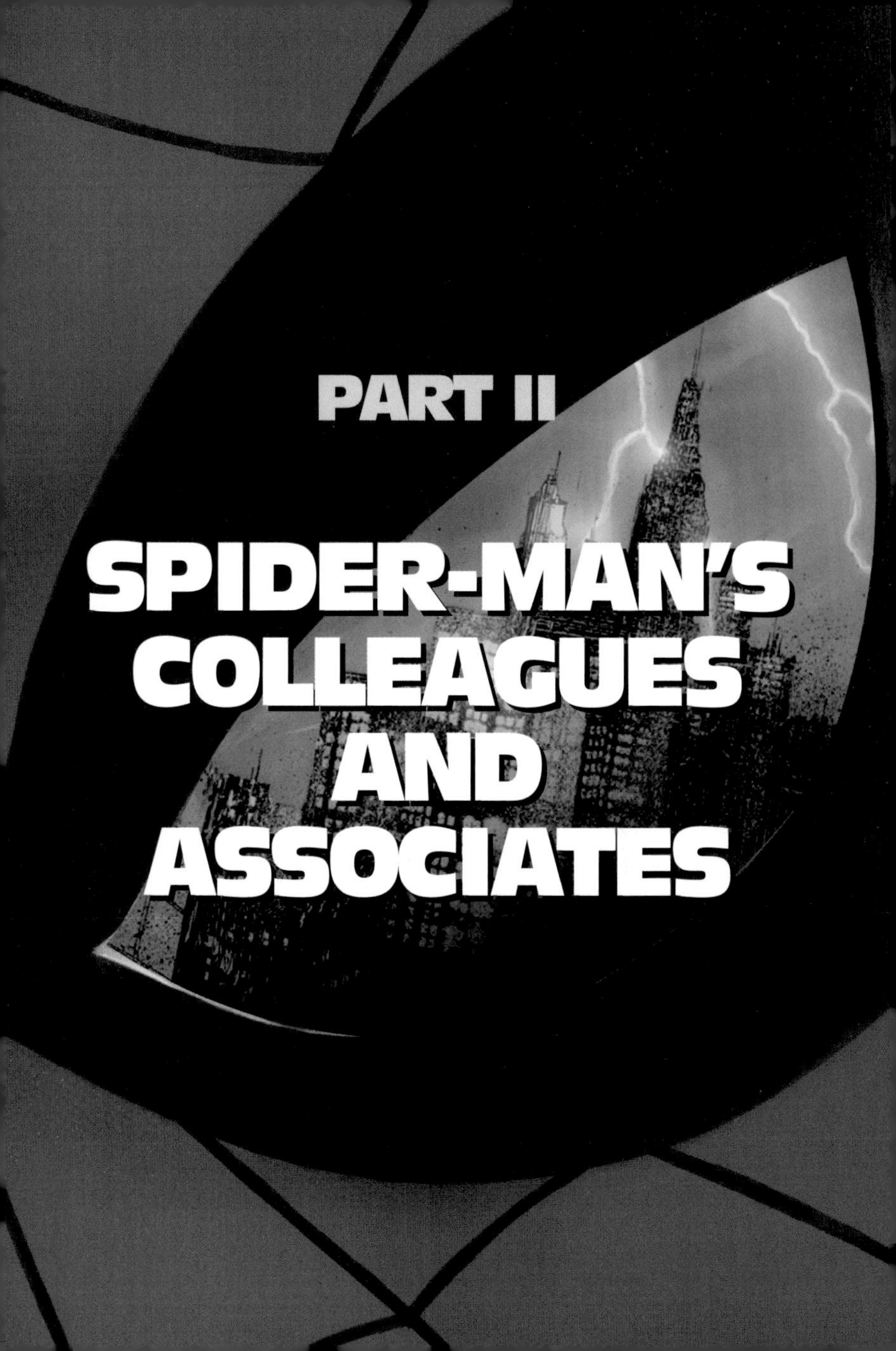

PART II

SPIDER-MAN'S COLLEAGUES AND ASSOCIATES

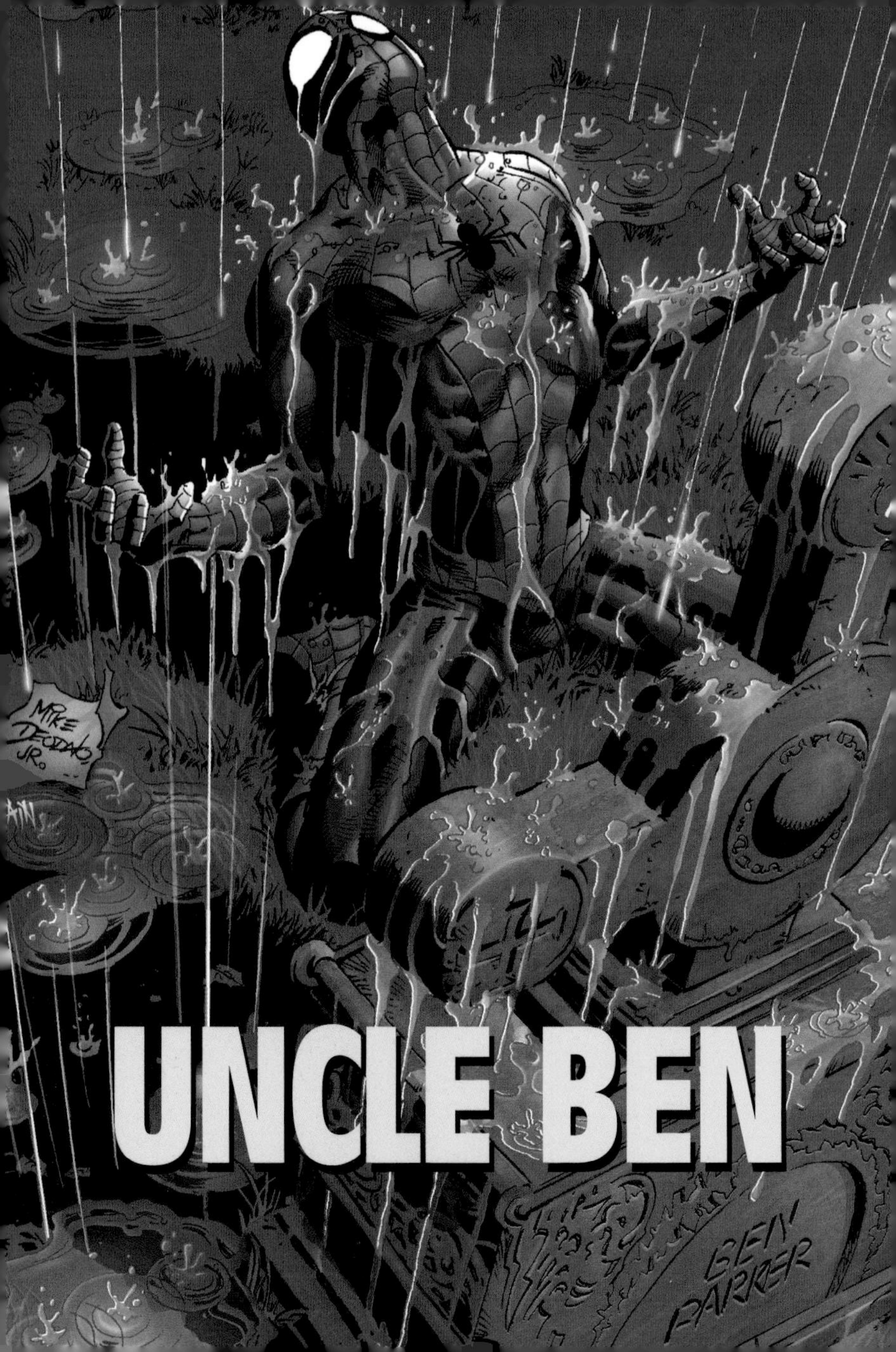
MIKE DEODATO JR.
BEN PARKER

UNCLE BEN

UNCLE BEN

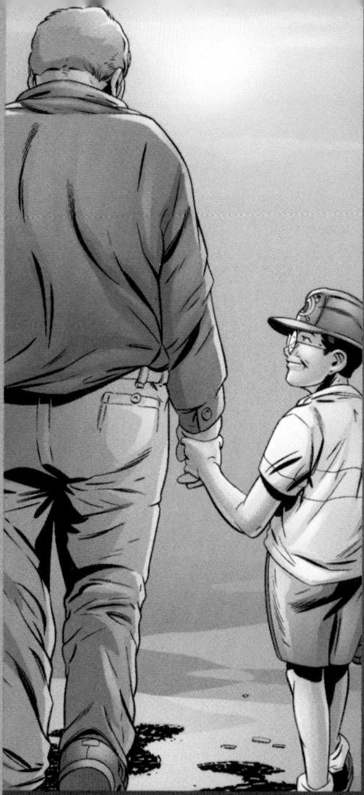

When Richard and Mary Parker were killed on a trip to Europe, Richard's older brother, Ben, and Ben's wife, May, took in their orphaned nephew, Peter, and raised him just like he was their own son. Ben and May didn't have much money, but they provided Peter with everything he needed.

Ultimately, Ben played an important role in Spider-Man's decision to become a crime-fighter. When Ben was murdered on his job as night-watchman Peter, as Spider-Man, tracked the killer down and discovered he was a criminal whom Peter had seen the police pursuing days before. Although Peter had been in his Spider-Man outfit at the time, he chose not to help the police. By ignoring the crime, Peter was indirectly responsible for the death of his uncle. It was a harsh lesson but one that he never forgot for, as Ben had instructed him: "With great power there comes great responsibility."

SECRETS

- When Ben first met May Reilly, she was dating a crook named Johnny Jerome. Ben convinced May to leave Johnny and marry him.
- Uncle Ben once returned for five minutes from the hereafter as part of a birthday present from Doctor Strange for Peter Parker.
- Uncle Ben shared his collection of Golden Age super hero comics and science fiction magazines with Peter; these helped to build up his nephew's confidence and spark Peter's interest in science.

Name
Benjamin Parker

Height 5' 9"

Weight 175 lbs

Eyes Blue

Hair White

Powers None

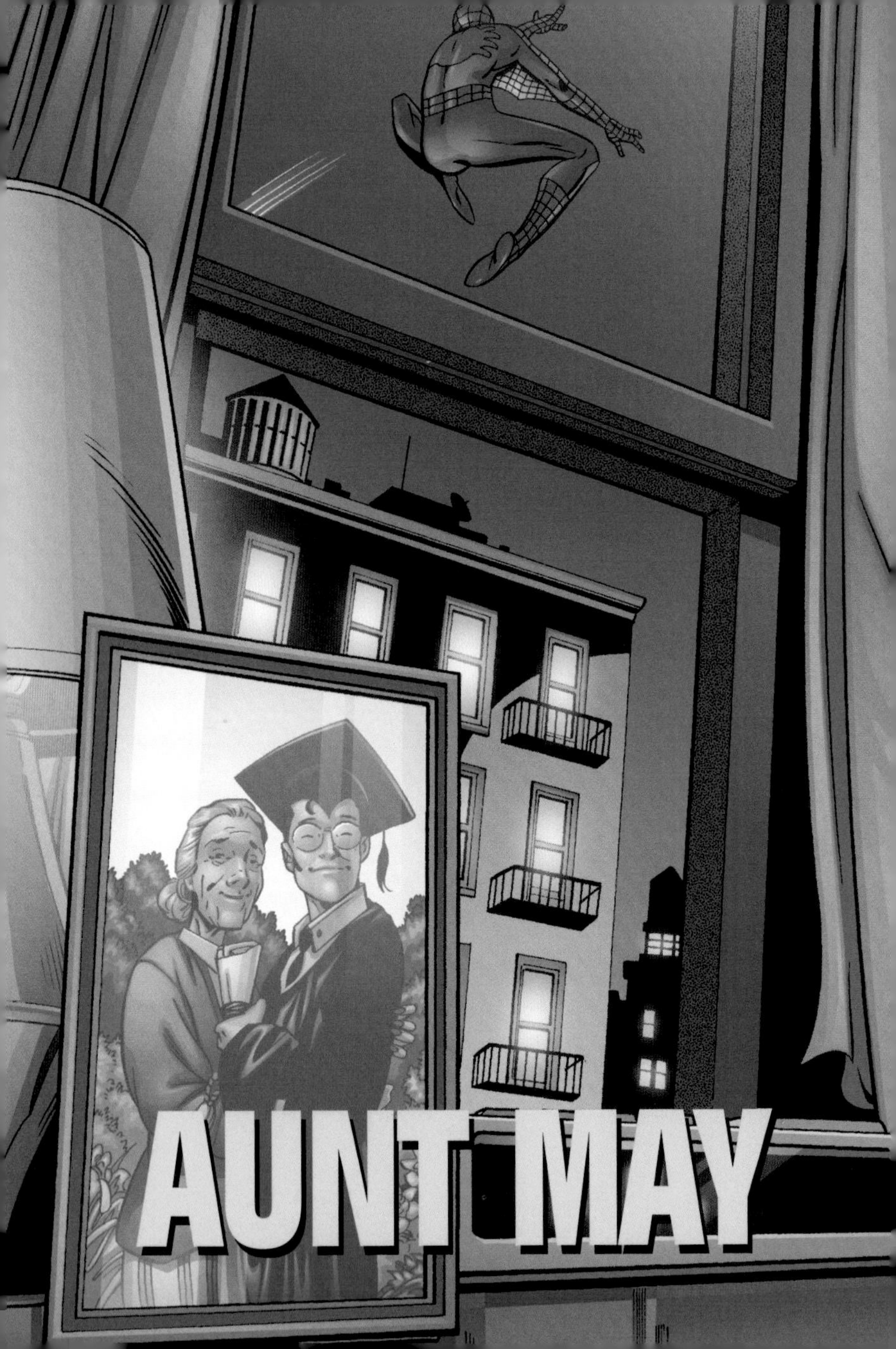
AUNT MAY

After the death of Peter Parker's parents, his Aunt May and Uncle Ben took him in and raised Peter like their own child. Although Ben was glad to do this, May was hesitant at first. Her own parents had blamed her birth for the end of their marriage, and she was afraid that Peter's presence might cause her relationship with Ben to deteriorate. After a while, she came to love Peter and his presence seemed to strengthen her marriage.

Home life became a struggle with money problems when Uncle Ben died. Peter did his best to help pay the bills. May worried about her nephew, whom she considered too frail to be working as a freelance photographer for a newspaper. Peter, on the other hand, was always concerned that Aunt May might find out someday that he was Spider-Man. Aunt May was a regular reader of the *Daily Bugle* and she believed everything negative that J. Jonah Jameson wrote about Spider-Man.

When Peter moved out and into his own apartment, Aunt May turned her home into a boarding house for retired persons. Romance entered her life when she met wheelchair bound Nathan Lubensky, but the relationship ended in tragedy when Lubensky was accidentally killed.

After a long, eventful life, Aunt May died of a heart attack just as Ben Reilly, the Spider-Man clone, came back into Spider-Man's life. Dealing with the clone left Peter with little time to mourn. Several years later, Peter discovered that the woman who had died in the hospital was a genetically altered actress who had been made up to look like Aunt May. The entire scenario turned out to have been an evil plot engineered by Norman Osborn to

AUNT MAY

Name

May Reilly Parker

Height 5' 5"

Weight 110 lbs

Eyes Blue

Hair White

Powers None

make Peter Parker suffer. Reunited with Peter and Mary Jane, Aunt May moved with them into Stark Towers, the Avengers' headquarters.

SECRETS

- Aunt May was once engaged to be married to Doctor Octopus.
- Aunt May recently has become romantically linked with the Avengers' butler, Jarvis.
- Nathan Lubensky suffered a heart attack and died protecting Aunt May from the Vulture.
- Aunt May is an active member of the Gray Panthers.

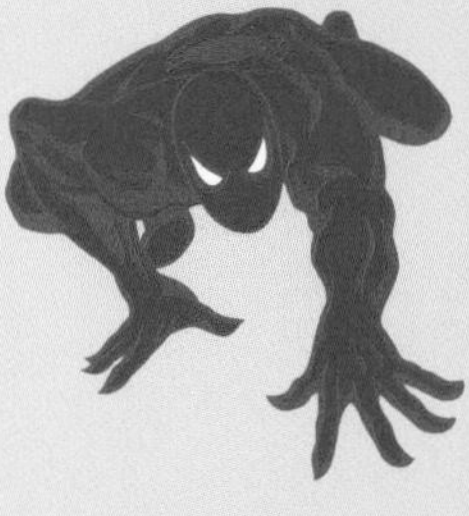

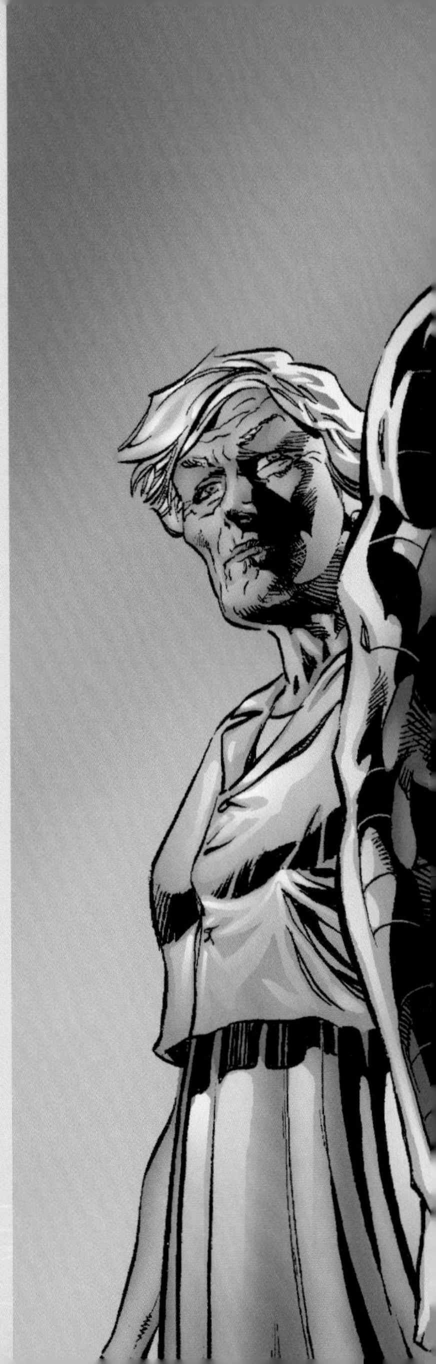

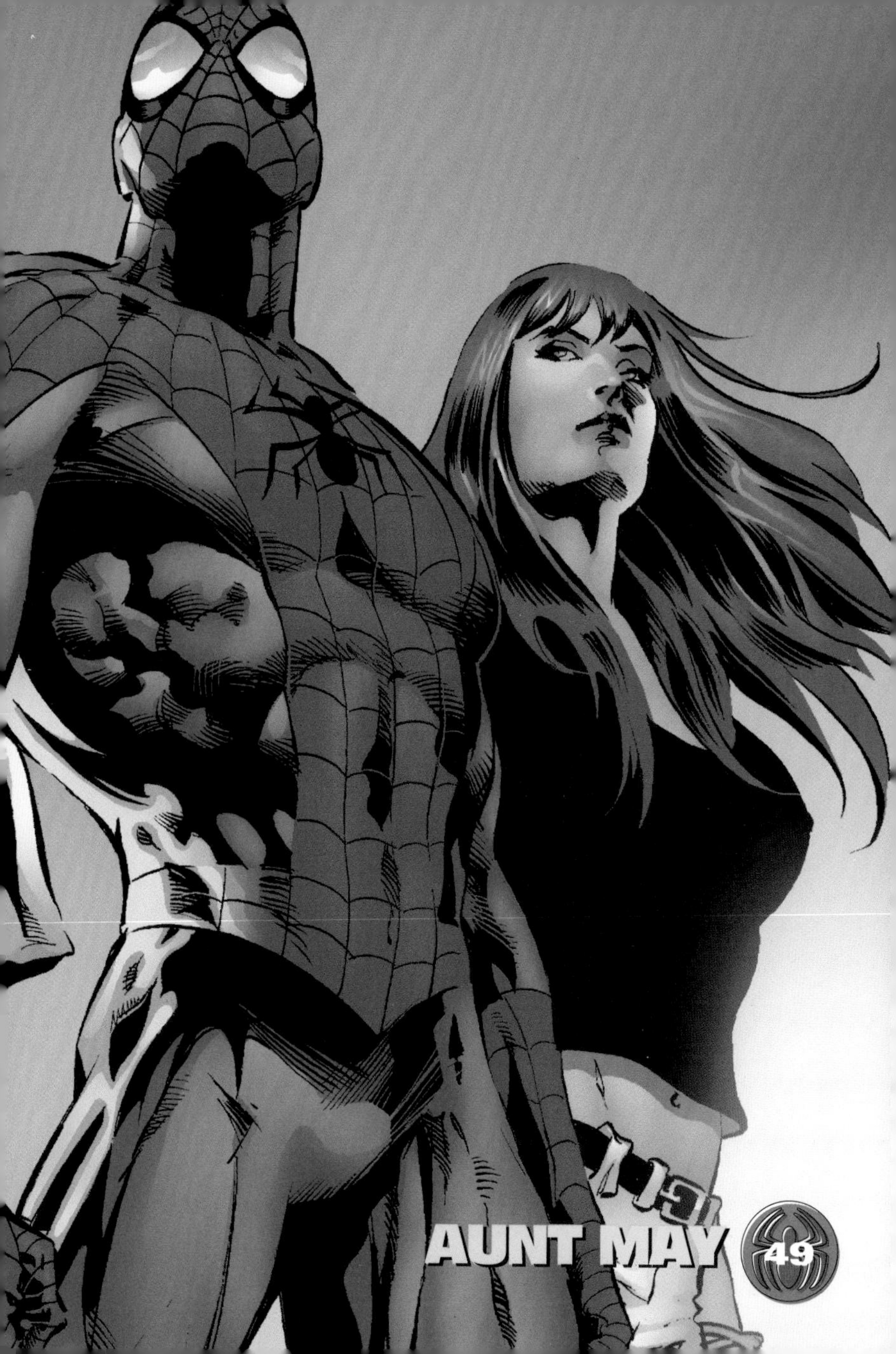

AUNT MAY

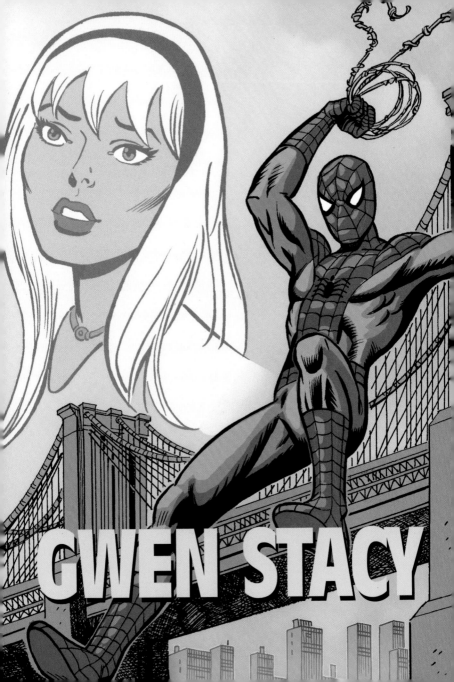

GWEN STACY

GWEN STACY

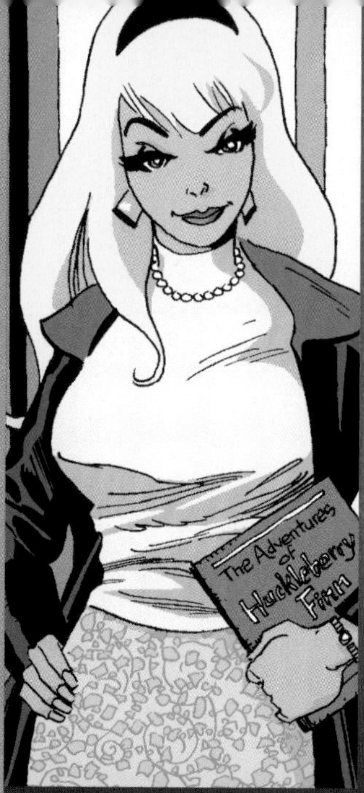
The Adventures of Huckleberry Finn

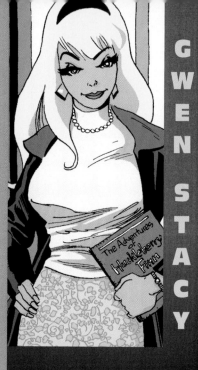

Peter Parker met Gwen Stacy, an attractive blonde science major, when they were both freshmen at Empire State University. Flash Thompson had tried to introduce Peter to Gwen and Harry Osborn, but Peter didn't pay Gwen any attention because he was too preoccupied with his own problems. Gwen felt insulted by Peter's arrogance, but the two eventually ironed out their misunderstandings and became friends. In time, the friendship blossomed into romance and Gwen became Peter's first true love.

Peter's life as Spider-Man also made romance difficult: missed dates and untold secrets bothered Gwen terribly. Nevertheless Gwen's father, retired police captain George Stacy, liked Peter and did all he could to keep the couple together.

When the Kingpin kidnapped Captain Stacy and Gwen, Spider-Man, with the help of a reformed Norman Osborn, rescued the two. Gwen visited Osborn to thank him for his help and, to her surprise, found herself attracted to the older man. They had a brief affair, which left Gwen pregnant with twins.

When George Stacy was killed during a battle between Spider-Man and Doctor Octopus, Gwen blamed Spider-Man for her father's death. She went to live with relatives in London to deal with the loss. She resumed her romance with Peter after returning to the United States, but when her pregnancy developed she once again fled to Europe on a pretense so that Peter would not learn of her affair with Norman Osborn. Gwen carried her twins to full term although her pregnancy only lasted seven months. She gave birth to a boy, Gabriel, and a girl, Sarah. Norman

Name Gwen Stacy

Height 5' 7"

Weight 130 lbs

Eyes Blue

Hair Blonde

Powers None

Osborn arranged for the twins to be cared for in Paris.

Gwen returned home hoping to marry Peter. She didn't tell him about the twins, but felt certain that once they were married he would overlook her brief affair and that they would raise the children as their own. Norman Osborn, who had once again become the Green Goblin, had different plans: he wanted to raise the children to become his evil successors.

Norman, in his Goblin guise, kidnapped Gwen and carried her to the top of the Brooklyn Bridge. Though ill, Spider-Man pursued them. The Green Goblin pushed Gwen off of the bridge and the best Spider-Man was able to do was catch her by one foot with a strand of webbing. When he pulled Gwen up, she was dead, her neck snapped due to the long fall. In the ensuing fight with Spider-Man, the Goblin was impaled by his own glider and for years to come Spider-Man and everyone else believed that the Green Goblin and Gwen Stacy had died on the same night.

Years later, Spider-Man learned that Norman Osborn had survived his impalement and fled to Europe, where he raised Gwen's two children. Owing to the enhanced Goblin blood in their veins, the twins aged much faster than ordinary humans. Spider-Man soon found himself engaged in a life-or-death struggle with Gwen's twins who had been told by Osborn that Spider-Man was the person who killed their mother. When the true circumstances of Gwen's death were revealed, Gabriel refused to believe it and became the Grey Goblin. Sarah realized that Peter wasn't lying and shot down her brother's glider.

SECRETS

- Gwen was killed by whiplash in her fall from the top of the Brooklyn Bridge.

- Peter recently used money he was paid to protect a corrupt mob boss named Forelli to establish a memorial library in Gwen Stacy's name.

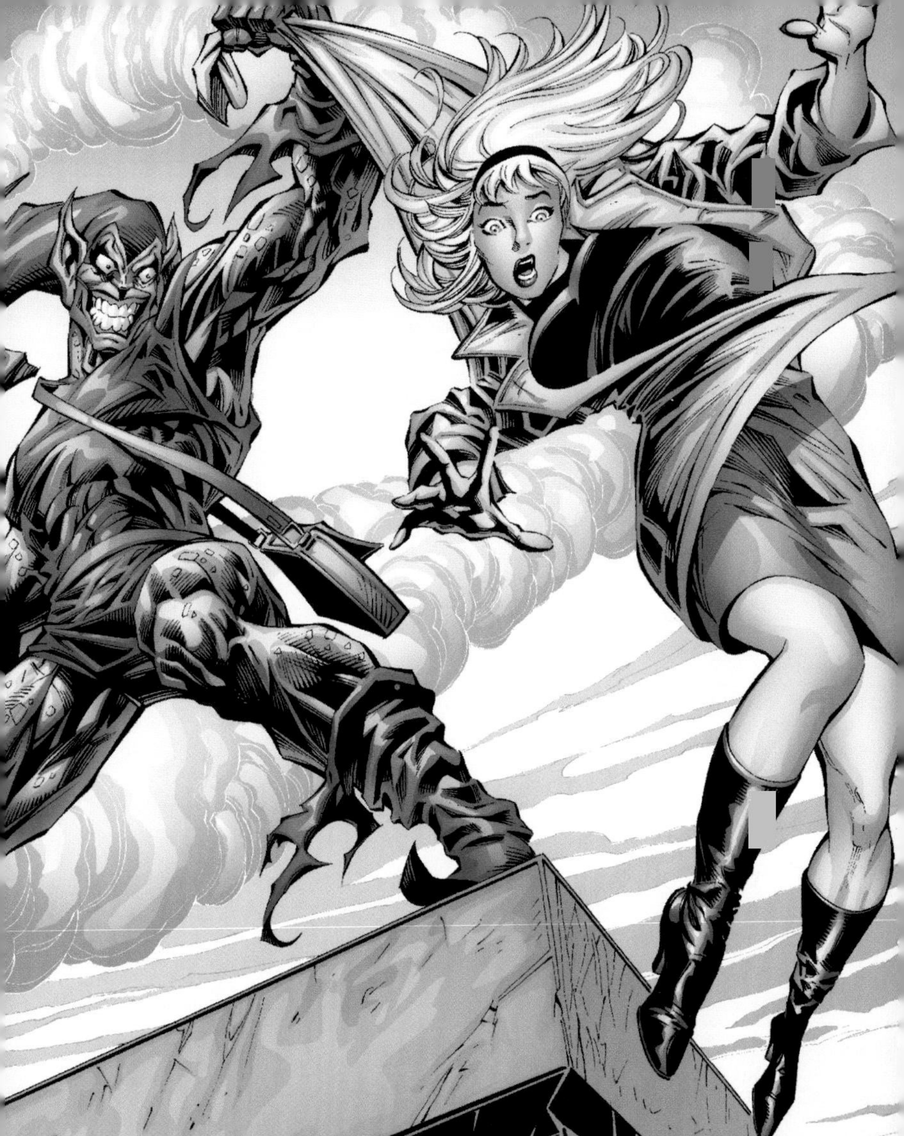

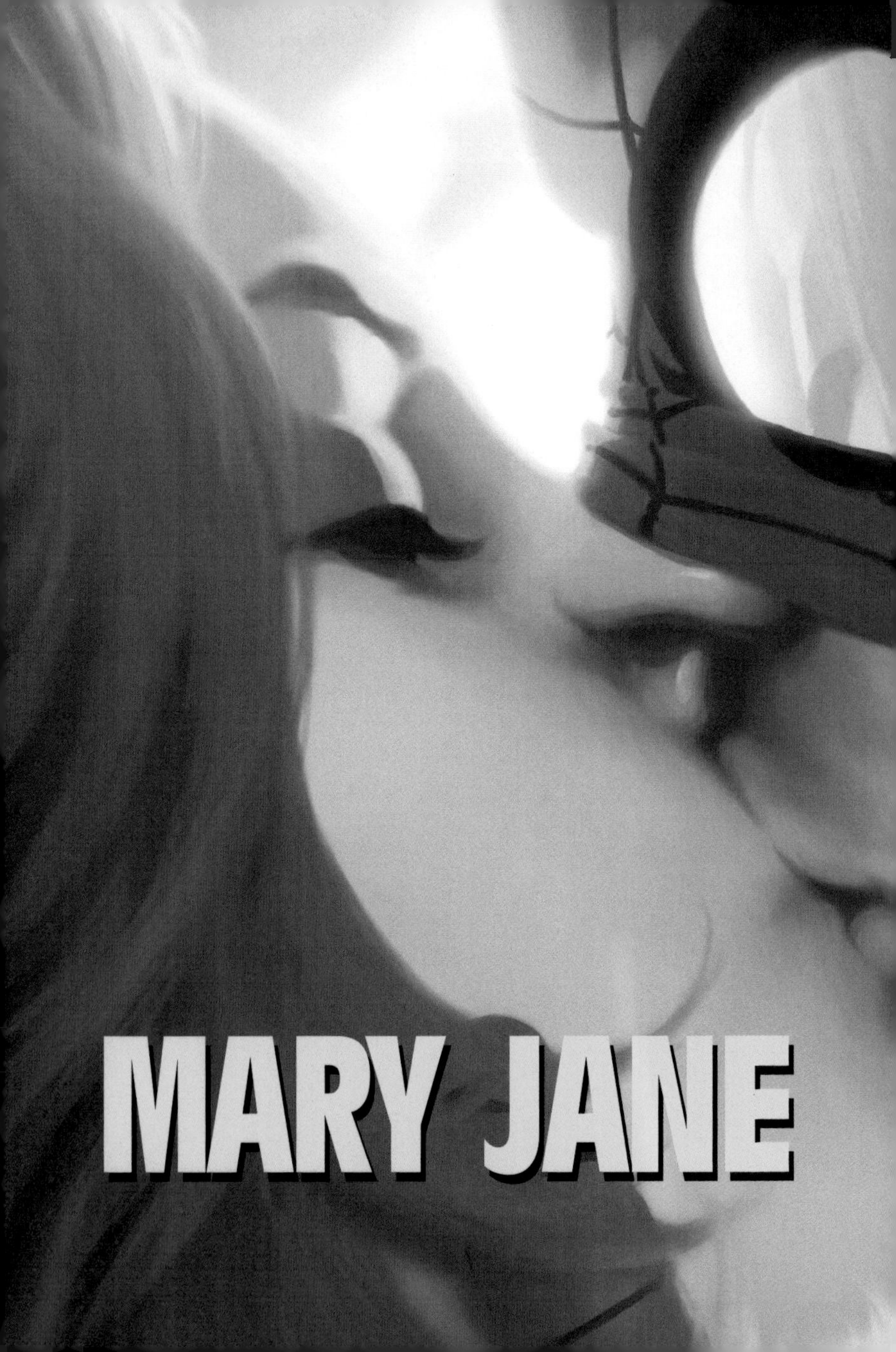
MARY JANE

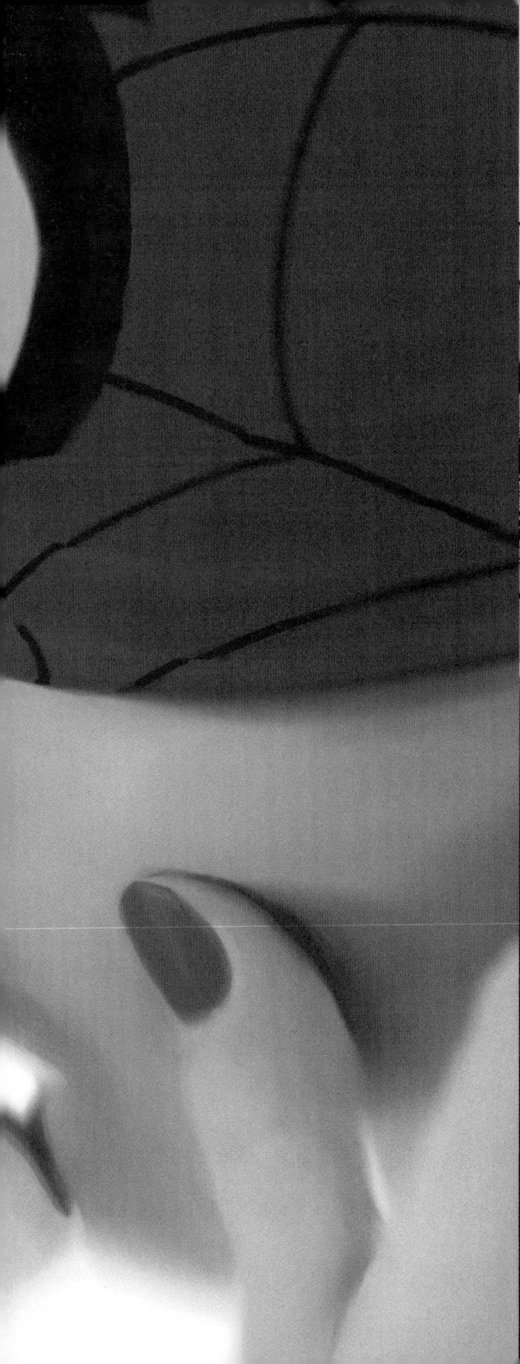

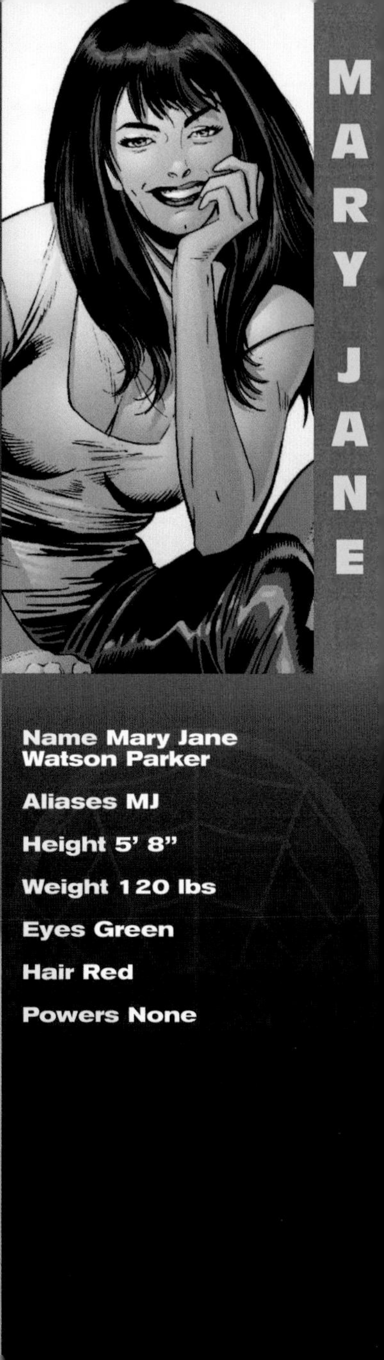

MARY JANE

Name Mary Jane Watson Parker

Aliases MJ

Height 5' 8"

Weight 120 lbs

Eyes Green

Hair Red

Powers None

Mary Jane "MJ" Watson came from a broken home. As a child, she was often despondent but swore never to let the world know of her unhappiness. Thus, while she often acted the life of the party outwardly, inside she tended to be miserable. One of the few pleasures in her teenage years was visiting her Aunt Anna Watson who lived in Forest Hills. She was amused by the efforts of her Aunt and her Aunt's best friend, May Parker, to fix her up with May's nephew, the bookish Peter Parker.

Like many teens of the time, Mary Jane was fascinated by the new TV sensation Spider-Man. Thus, she was shocked during one visit to see Peter enter the Parker home and, soon afterwards, Spider-Man exit. Mary Jane immediately realized that Spider-Man and Peter Parker were one and the same.

It wasn't until Peter Parker was in college and Mary Jane was living in her own apartment and embarked on a modeling career that the two met. Peter was stunned by MJ's good looks and bubbly personality. Mary Jane was pleasantly surprised by Peter's good humor and quiet self-confidence. Plus, she knew that he was Spider-Man.

Peter and Mary Jane remained friends, despite their mutual attraction. MJ didn't want to be tied down to anyone, and Peter was obviously very much in love with Gwen Stacy. That all changed when Gwen was killed by the Green Goblin. Mary Jane helped Peter manage his life during this difficult period. When Peter left on a trip for Europe, he kissed MJ goodbye, and with that kiss, it became apparent to both that they were falling in love.

After dating for months, Peter asked Mary Jane to marry him. Remembering her parents' strained relation-

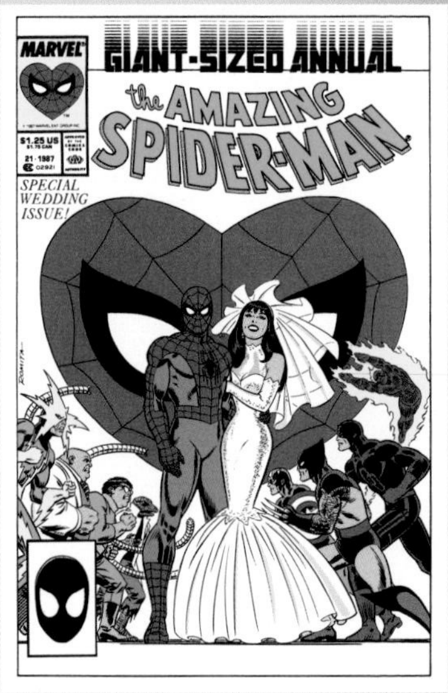
MARVEL
GIANT-SIZED ANNUAL
the AMAZING
SPIDER-MAN
$1.25 US
21 1987
SPECIAL
WEDDING
ISSUE!

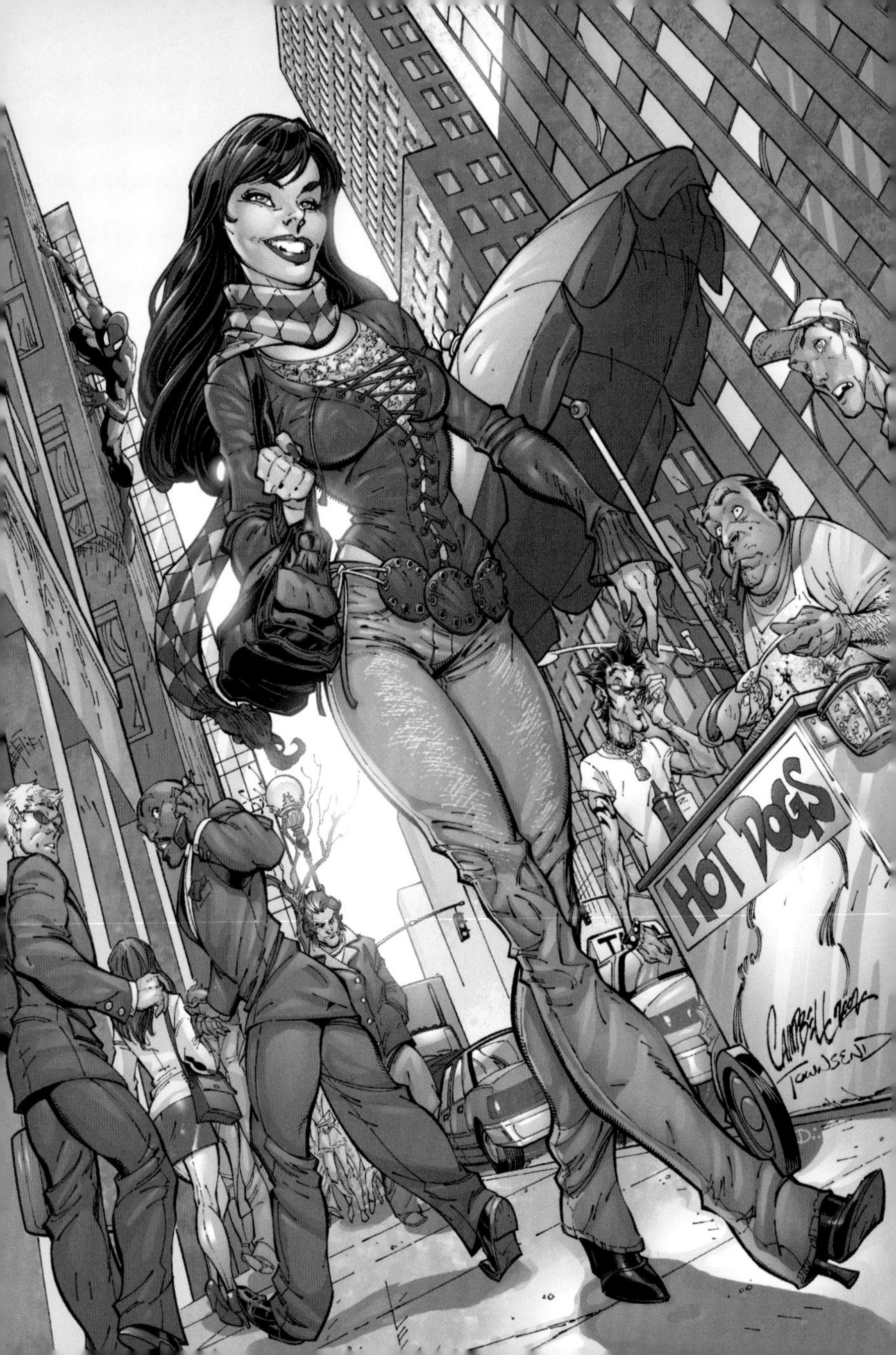
HOT DOGS
TOWNSEND

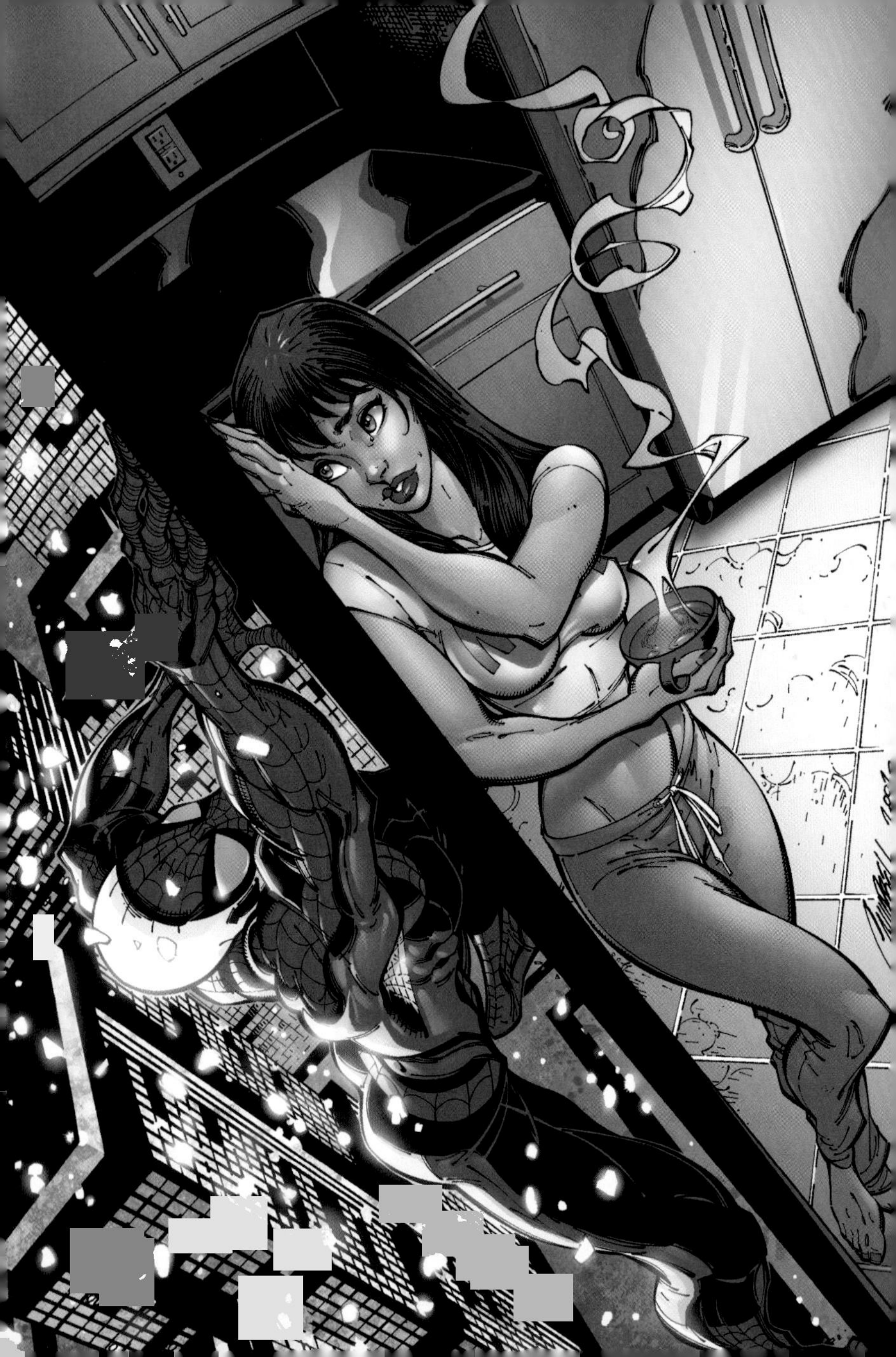

ship, MJ turned Peter down and moved to Florida to promote her modeling career. Peter remained in Manhattan and became involved with the Black Cat.

When Mary Jane finally returned, she could no longer listen to Peter's deceptions about his double-life and revealed to him that she knew he was Spider-Man. Afterwards, she told Peter the details of her own difficult life and this shared confession drew the two of them very close. When Peter proposed a few months later, Mary Jane accepted.

Being the wife of Spider-Man has had its good moments but more than its share of bad. Mary Jane lost the baby she had with Peter, believing the child was stillborn, when in reality it had been born healthy and was stolen by Norman Osborn. MJ was pursued by a stalker, who blew up a plane she was on, took her prisoner, and convinced everyone, including Peter, that she was dead.

Most recently she saw her husband killed, and then reborn.

MJ is focused on developing her acting skills. She knows that life with Peter Parker will never be easy, but she also knows it will be the best life she could ever imagine.

SECRETS

- Mary Jane was the only person Gwen Stacy told about her twins with Norman Osborn. Although Gwen swore her to secrecy, Mary Jane told Peter the whole story years later so that he could tell the twins the truth about their birth.

- When Mary Jane met Peter Parker, her first words to him were: "Face it, Tiger . . . you just hit the jackpot!"

- Mary Jane forced Peter to abandon his black Spider-Man costume because it reminded her too much of Venom.

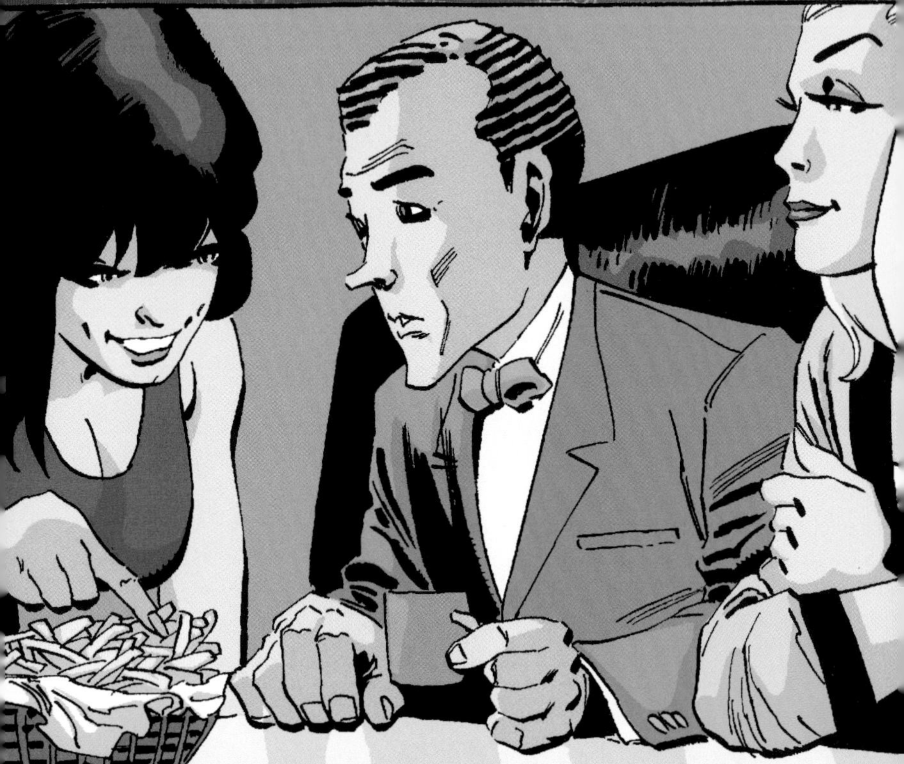

HARRY OSBORN

HARRY OSBORN

Harry Osborn was Peter Parker's first and closest friend. He was also one of Peter's worst enemies and tried to kill him more than once. In the end, Harry sacrificed himself to save Peter.

Harry is the son of ruthless businessman Norman Osborn. His mother, Emily, died before Harry was one. Norman had little time for his child and he was annoyed that Harry wasn't a brilliant student or a highly competitive athlete. Harry was not aware that his father's body had been permanently transformed by a chemical explosion, and that he masqueraded as the criminal mastermind the Green Goblin.

Harry graduated from Standard High and went to Empire State University as a science major. It was there that he and fellow science major Gwen Stacy met and befriended Peter Parker. Harry invited Peter to move into his apartment, which Harry's father was paying for. Peter repaid the favor by tutoring Harry.

Peter and Gwen started dating, and Harry started dating aspiring model Mary Jane Watson. Mary Jane, however, couldn't resist flirting with Peter, a habit that annoyed Harry. The pressure of school life, his father's extremely high expectations, and Mary Jane's actions pushed Harry to experiment with hard drugs. This angered Mary Jane and she broke off their relationship. When Harry blamed Peter for the break-up, Peter discovered that Harry had overdosed on LSD and got him medical attention.

Harry's drug problem so shocked his father that, for a while, Norman Osborn forgot that he was the Green Goblin. When Harry returned home, he was in such terrible condition that Norman's mind

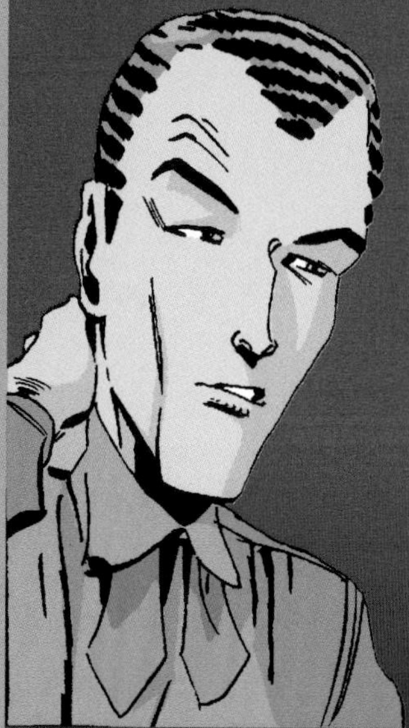

Name Harold "Harry" Osborn, The Green Goblin 2

Height 5' 10"

Weight 170 lbs

Eyes Blue

Hair Reddish brown

Powers
When he was the Green Goblin, using the Goblin formula created by his father, Harry had superhuman strength, agility, speed, endurance, and healing.

twisted and he once again became the Goblin. Angry at Spider-Man, the Goblin kidnapped Gwen Stacy and threw her off of the Brooklyn Bridge, killing her. Harry witnessed the entire fight between Spider-Man and the Green Goblin, and when he saw his father impaled on his Goblin Glider, Harry's mind snapped. When no one was near, he removed the Goblin costume from his father so that no one would know of his crimes. Harry then let Norman's body be taken to the morgue, not realizing that his father wasn't actually dead, only badly injured.

When Harry discovered that Peter Parker was Spider-Man, he put on the Goblin costume and attacked the web-slinger. However, he had no powers and was quickly defeated. Spider-Man removed the Green Goblin outfit from Harry before the police arrived to arrest him. The authorities didn't believe Harry's wild story that he was the Green Goblin, nor did they take seriously his claim that Peter Parker was Spider-Man.

Harry was put under the psychiatric care of Dr. Barton Hamilton, who cured Harry of his drug habit and got him to forget his adventure as the Green Goblin. After he returned home, Harry started seeing Liz Allen, whom Peter had known in high school. Liz was the daughter of wealthy hotel and restaurant owners, and also the stepsister of Mark Raxton, the Molten Man. Liz's activities on behalf of her stepbrother caused problems in her relationship with Harry, but when Norman Osborn was reported dead, Harry took control of the family business and eloped with Liz. After becoming the successor to his father and president of Osborn Industries, Harry moved to Long Island and then to a large house in Englewood, New Jersey, where he and Liz sought a more peaceful life in which to start a family. Liz gave birth to a son, Norman Harold Osborn, and Harry and Liz asked Peter and Mary Jane to be the child's godparents.

Shortly afterward, Harry began losing his mental stability and the Green Goblin persona reasserted itself. Using his father's notes, he made a new, more potent batch of Goblin serum that made Harry stronger than Spider-Man. As the Goblin, Harry kidnapped Mary Jane and took her to the top of the Brooklyn Bridge, the scene of Gwen Stacy's death. But Harry had once loved Mary Jane and found that he couldn't kill her.

Harry decided to kill all of his father's associates and invited them all to his townhouse rigged with explosives. He also planned to kill Spider-Man at the same time. However, he didn't foresee that Mary Jane and his son, Norman, would also attend the meeting. Harry raced inside and saved not only them, but Peter. Just as his friends started thanking him, Harry collapsed. The new goblin formula had turned toxic and Harry died moments later, just after apologizing to Peter and saying they were still best friends.

SECRETS

- As a young boy, Harry sabotaged the original Green Goblin formula because he was angry that his father was paying more attention to his work than to him.
- Once, while fighting the original Green Goblin, Spider-Man showed him Harry strung out on cocaine. The sight brought Norman Osborn back to his senses.
- Before his death, Harry paid the Chameleon to create android replicas of Peter's parents. These androids fooled Peter, who was devastated when he finally learned the truth about them.

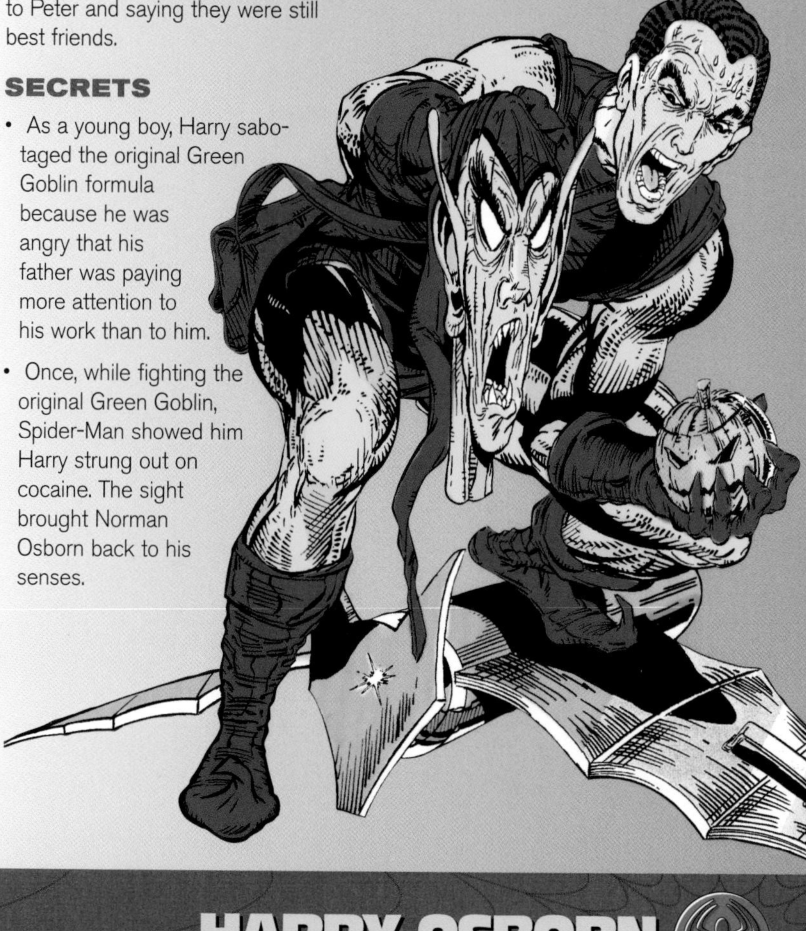

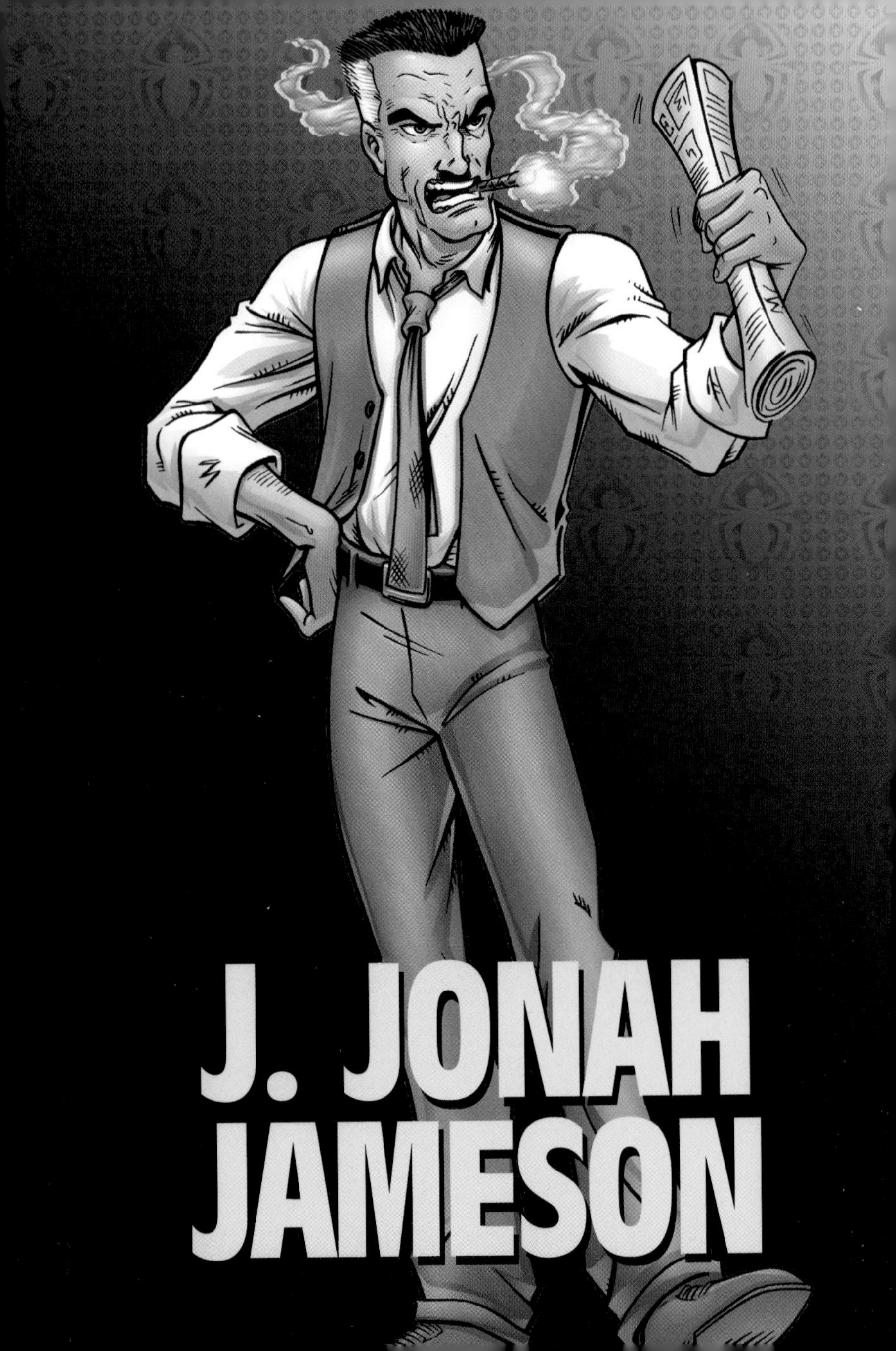

J. JONAH JAMESON

J. Jonah Jameson is the son of David and Betty Jameson. His father was an army officer and a decorated war hero who regularly beat up his wife and son. His actions convinced Jonah that, "No one's a hero every day of the week."

Jameson grew up interested in boxing and photography. He met his first wife, Joan, when they both joined the high school photo club. They were married after graduation. Jameson went into journalism and became a reporter working for the *Daily Bugle*. He served as a war correspondent for the *Bugle* in the European theater during World War II. After the war, he returned home and he and Joan became parents of a boy, John. When the United States entered the Korean conflict, Jameson traveled to Asia to cover the war for the *Bugle*. While he was gone, Joan was killed by muggers. Upon returning home, Jameson threw himself into his work and was promoted to chief editor of the Bugle. When the newspaper was put up for sale, Jameson cobbled together every cent he had and bought the paper

A strong supporter of civil-rights and labor unions, Jameson fought for what he believed in, often making enemies along the way. He was a brash, belligerent man, and because of his stubborn streak he refused to bend, no matter how much pressure was put on him. Distinguished by his mustache, flattop haircut, and ever-present cigar, he is a newsman as recognizable as anyone he writes about.

When Spider-Man first appeared, Jameson instinctively mistrusted him. He could not understand why any super hero would help people without being paid or reaping some

J. JONAH JAMESON

Name J. Jonah Jameson

Height 5' 11"

Weight 181 lbs

Eyes Blue

Hair Graying black, white at temples

Powers None

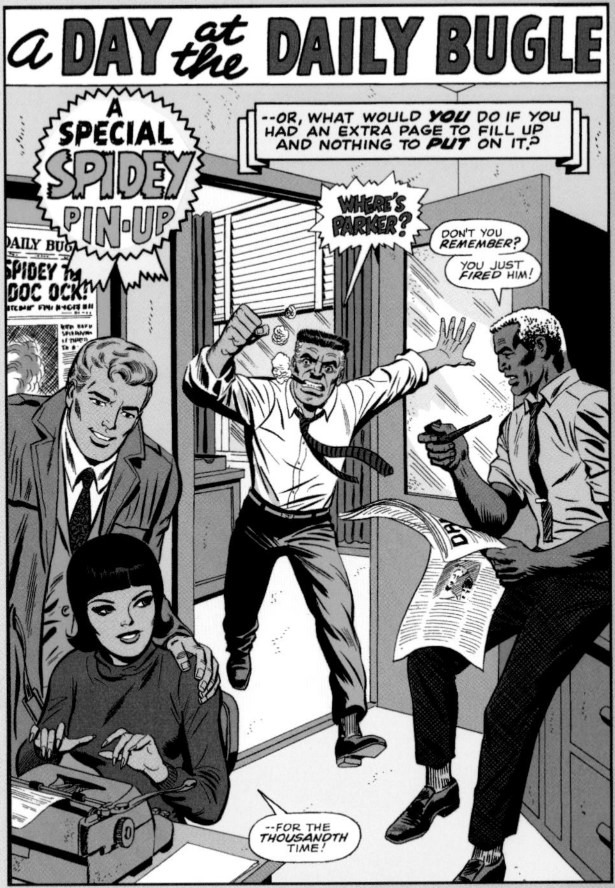
a DAY at the DAILY BUGLE
A SPECIAL SPIDEY PIN-UP
--OR, WHAT WOULD YOU DO IF YOU HAD AN EXTRA PAGE TO FILL UP AND NOTHING TO PUT ON IT?
WHERE'S PARKER?
DON'T YOU REMEMBER?
YOU JUST FIRED HIM!
--FOR THE THOUSANDTH TIME!

financial reward. Despite a lack of evidence, Jameson declared the web-slinger a crook and menace to society and labeled him Public Enemy Number One. He cannot accept that Spider-Man might do good for purely altruistic reasons and is convinced that somehow, some way, the web-slinger has an angle. Jameson is determined to find out what that angle is.

When Spider-Man rescued Jameson's son, John, from danger, Jonah accused Spider-Man of setting up the entire situation as a publicity stunt.

When scientist Spencer Smythe invented what he called Spider Slayer robots, Jameson used them to track down Spider-Man. Jameson hired detective Mac Gargan to find Spider-Man and subjected the detective to a series of lab experiments that transformed him into the villain known as Scorpion. Gargan went insane and attacked not only Spider-Man, but Jameson; as a result Jameson kept the full story of Scorpion off the pages of his newspaper for years.

Despite all of his protests about Spider-Man, Jameson covers the web-slinger's every action because he knows that stories about the super hero help sell papers. Where possible, Jameson wants Spider-Man on the front page. That's a boon to Peter Parker who sells his Spider-Man photos exclusively to the Bugle.

Some time after his first wife's death Jameson met Dr. Marla Madison, a brilliant scientist and daughter of an old friend. He needed her help in developing new Spider Slayer robots and the relationship that followed grew into romance. Jonah and Marla were married and adopted their niece, Mattie Franklin.

The story of Scorpion came back to haunt Jameson when the Hobgoblin tried to blackmail him with it. Rather than give into the super villain's demands, Jameson revealed the whole story of Scorpion's creation on the front pages of his newspaper. Immediately afterwards he stepped down as the newspaper's editor-in-chief, and awarded the job to his assistant, Joseph "Robbie" Robertson. Jameson remains involved with the paper as its publisher.

Jameson has been a strong supporter of the government's Superhuman Registration Act. However, he was caught totally by surprise and fainted when Spider-Man removed his mask to reveal the face of Peter Parker.

SECRETS

- Jameson returned to his hard-hitting days as a reporter when he investigated a waterfront extortion scheme. He interrogated Kingpin and risked his life to uncover the criminals, with some unexpected help from Spider-Man.

- Tied to a bomb with Spider-Man and sure they were both doomed, Jameson admitted that his obsession with the web-slinger had harmed him much more than it had Spider-Man. Afterwards, Spider-Man deactivated the bomb.

- The criminal known as Chameleon once imprisoned and impersonated Jameson, raising the level of newspaper attacks on Spider-Man to an all-time high.

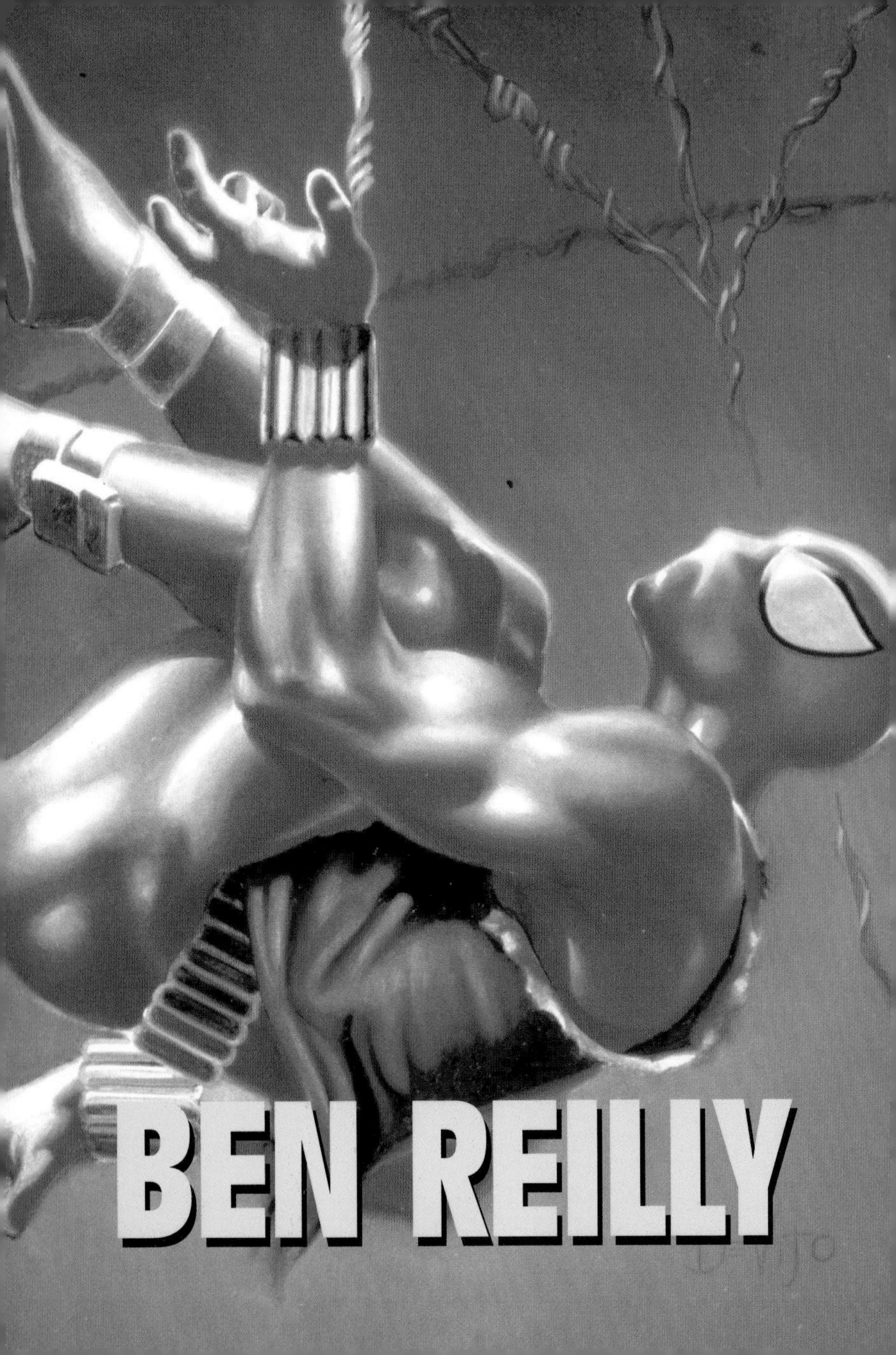
BEN REILLY

BEN REILLY

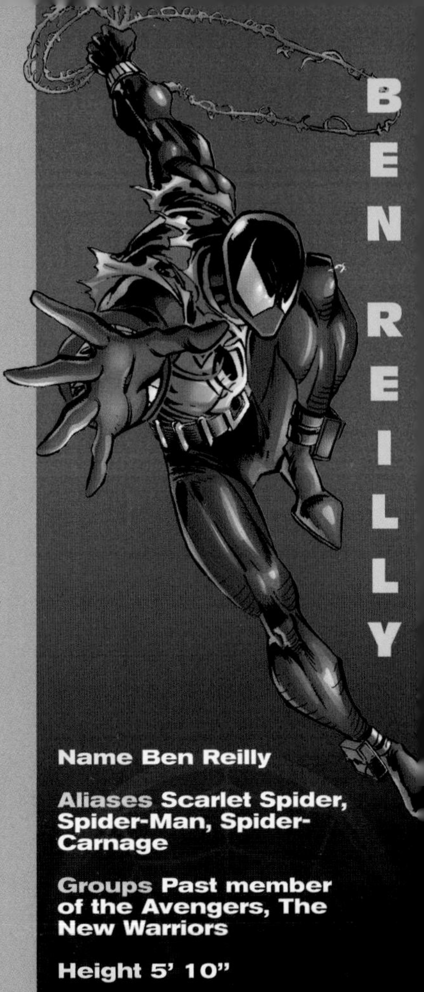

Name Ben Reilly

Aliases Scarlet Spider, Spider-Man, Spider-Carnage

Groups Past member of the Avengers, The New Warriors

Height 5' 10"

Weight 165 lbs

Eyes Hazel

Hair Brown (bleached blond)

POWERS

As Spider-Man's clone, Ben had the same spider-powers as Peter Parker. These included superhuman strength, speed, agility, and the ability to cling to surfaces. Ben's spider-sense was the same as Peter's, except that it could detect Venom.

Ben Reilly was the most genetically stable of the many clones of Spider-Man created by Professor Miles Warren, aka the Jackal. Warren created clones of Peter Parker and Gwen Stacy from tissue samples he had obtained from a class experiment. After many attempts, most notably the monstrous creature called Kaine, a failed clone of Peter, Warren finally succeeded in creating a clone that did not suffer cellular degeneration.

Jackal sent this new clone to fight Spider-Man in a deadly trap with a bomb, using Ned Leeds, a reporter at the Bugle, as bait. However, a clone of Jackal at the scene felt sorry for Ned and saved him, sacrificing itself. With Spider-Man and his clone both knocked unconscious, the real Jackal emerged, picked the person whom he thought was the real Spider-Man and injected him with a drug that simulated death. When the "other" Spider-Man woke, he dropped the dead body in a smokestack. Jackal then planted clone memories in the supposed dead body. What Jackal didn't realize was that the body he thought was the real Spider-Man was the clone. The deception was all part of a complex plot conceived by Norman Osborn and implemented by Jackal's assistant, Seward Trainer.

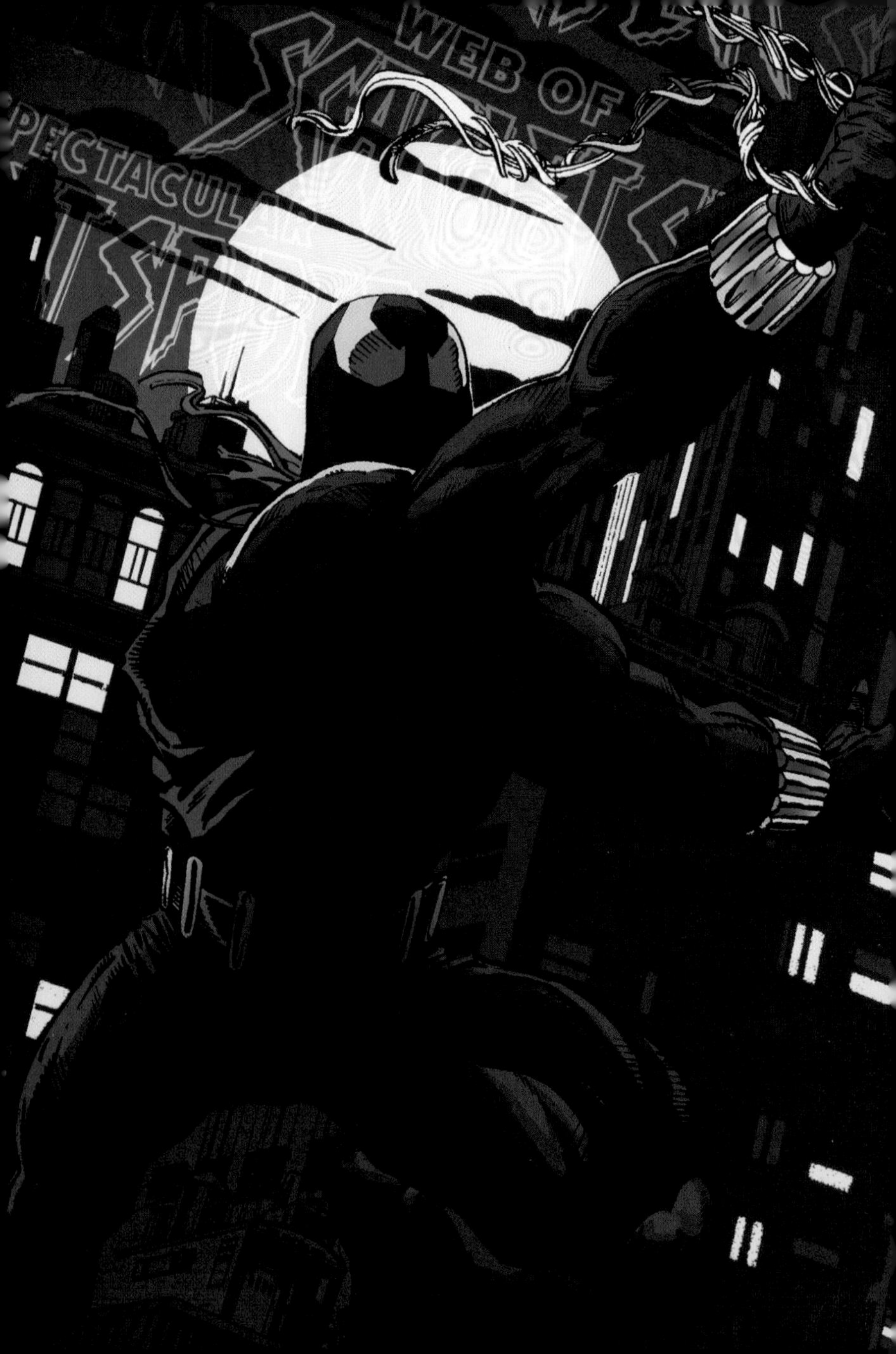
WEB OF
PECTACULAR

When the clone woke up in the smokestack, he believed himself to be the clone, not Spider-Man. He took on the name Ben Reilly, which it derived from the names of Uncle Ben and Aunt May's maiden name, and spent five years wandering through America. During this time, he met Janine, the girl who was to become the love of his life. However, Janine died shortly thereafter.

During his wanderings, Ben occasionally fought Kaine and a few other criminals. He also became friends with Seward Trainer, not realizing the man was actually Jackal's assistant. He stayed away from New York and Spider-Man until he learned that Aunt May was very sick.

Upon returning to Manhattan, Ben learned that Venom also had returned. Realizing he had to do something, Ben designed an all red costume with a blue hooded sweatshirt and took the name the Scarlet Spider to fight the villain. Ben's return also revived Jackal from suspended animation. Believing that Ben was the real Spider-Man, Jackal told Peter Parker that Parker was actually the Spider-Man clone. Seward Trainer, continuing his work for Norman Osborn, corroborated what the Jackal had told Peter. Working together, Peter and Ben stopped the Jackal's plan to release the carrion virus.

Ben and Peter soon formed a strong bond. They treated each other as brothers and introduced Ben to everyone as Peter's cousin. When Mary Jane became pregnant, Peter turned the Spider-Man name over to Ben. Ben, meanwhile, established his own life, and took a job in a coffee shop.

In the months that followed, Ben battled Kaine several times until the disfigured clone finally turned itself in to the police. He also encountered Janine who had faked her death after killing her father. She also turned herself in to the police.

Ben never doubted that he was the real Spider-Man and he gave his life to save Peter in a fight with the Green Goblin. Ben's body dissolved into dust right after he was killed, proving to everyone he, not Peter, was the clone.

SECRETS

- Ben Reilly saw Trainer as a father figure, and he trusted Trainer completely.

- Spider-Man's last words to Ben were: "Rest easy . . . brother."

- Peter Parker, Kaine, and Ben Reilly all had the same fingerprints.

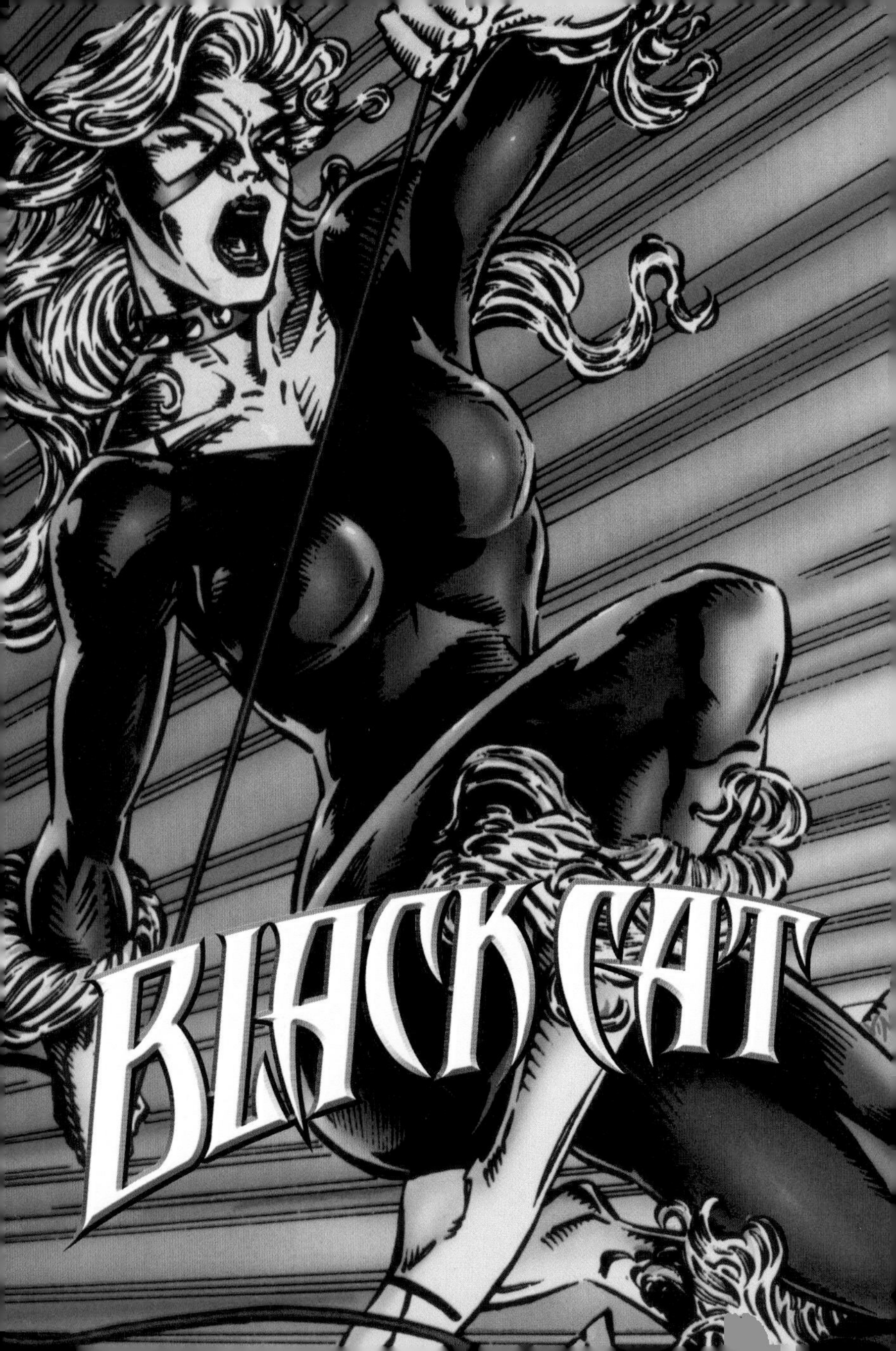
BLACK CAT

POWERS

Originally, Black Cat had no super powers, but Kingpin's scientists endowed her with a "bad luck" power that somehow affected probability fields, causing unusual coincidences to beset her enemies. After Dr. Strange removed this power, Black Cat developed infrared vision, inhuman balance and agility, and cat-like claws. She has since lost those powers.

F elicia Hardy, also known as the Black Cat, was a reformed burglar and one-time girlfriend of Spider-Man who believed in living life to its fullest and not worrying about consequences. Her father, famous cat burglar Walter Hardy, taught her to excel in anything she tried. During her freshman year of college, she was raped by a date. Felicia decided she would kill her rapist, and she trained exhaustively in gymnastics, acrobatics, and various fighting techniques. When she set out to avenge the crime, she discovered her rapist had been killed in an auto accident.

As a result, Felicia focused all of her training into becoming a cat burglar like her father. After amassing a fortune, she decided to free Walter Hardy from prison. That's when she took on the masked identity of the Black Cat and met Spider-Man. Spider-Man prevented Felicia from committing the crime, and over time, the two became romantically involved.

After a particularly dangerous encounter with the Kingpin and Doctor Octopus in which Felicia was almost killed, Peter decided to remove his Spider-Man mask and

BLACK CAT

Name Felicia Hardy, Black Cat

Aliases Cat, 'Licia, Felicity Harmon

Height 5' 10"

Weight 120 lbs

Eyes Green

Hair Platinum blonde

reveal his face to her. Felicia was disappointed. She saw no reason for Peter's civilian identity; she was in love with the super hero, not the ordinary man. Still, she cared for him a great deal and worried that she was becoming a burden on him since she had no super powers to protect herself from harm. When Spider-Man was gone during the Secret Wars, Felicia went through a process that gave her super powers. However, the power she gained was a "bad luck" aura that affected everyone she knew, including Spider-Man. Tired of being jinxed, Peter finally broke up with Felicia.

Still, Spider-Man felt responsible for Felicia's troubles and he consulted with Dr. Strange, who removed Felicia's bad luck aura and gave her cat-like powers and abilities instead. Peter's budding relationship with Mary Jane Watson angered Felicia and she tried several times to ruin Spider-Man's life before finally coming to terms with her own problems. When the Chameleon tricked Spider-Man into losing his powers, the Black Cat came to Peter's aid. She sacrificed her powers so that he could regain his.

At present, the Black Cat relies on equipment she bought from her friend, the Tinkerer, as substitutes for her lost powers. She helped Spider-Man and other heroes fight Carnage during the monster's rampage in Manhattan. Plus, she helped Spider-Man battle the menace of two Lizards.

SECRETS

- Felicia dated Flash Thompson in hopes of making Peter Parker jealous. Then, she found herself falling in love with Flash, who dropped her.

- The Black Cat has miniature grappling hooks hidden in her gloves that enable her to swing from building to building like Spider-Man.

- Felicia is the only person who calls Spider-Man by the nickname, "Spider."

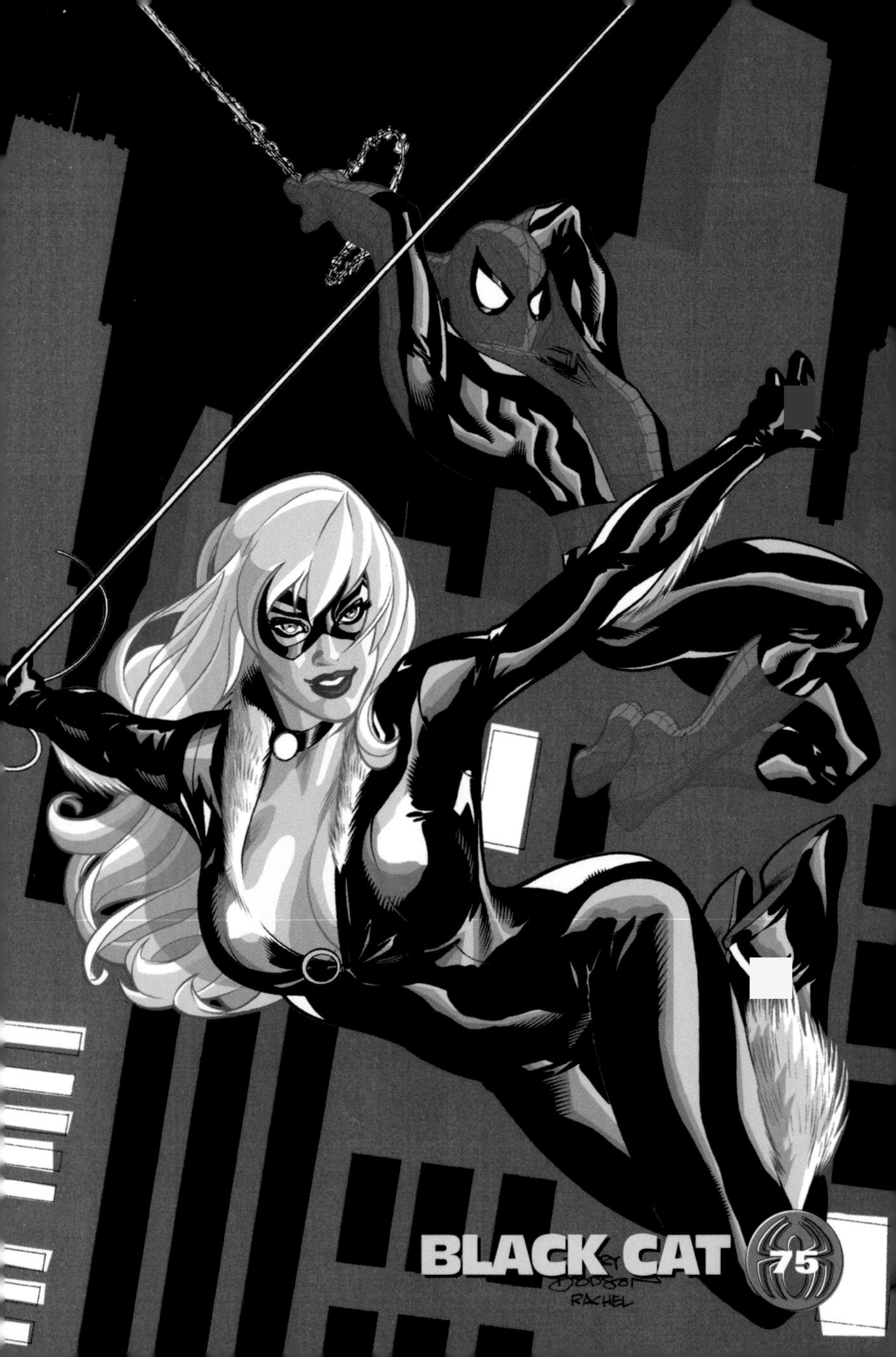
BLACK CAT
75

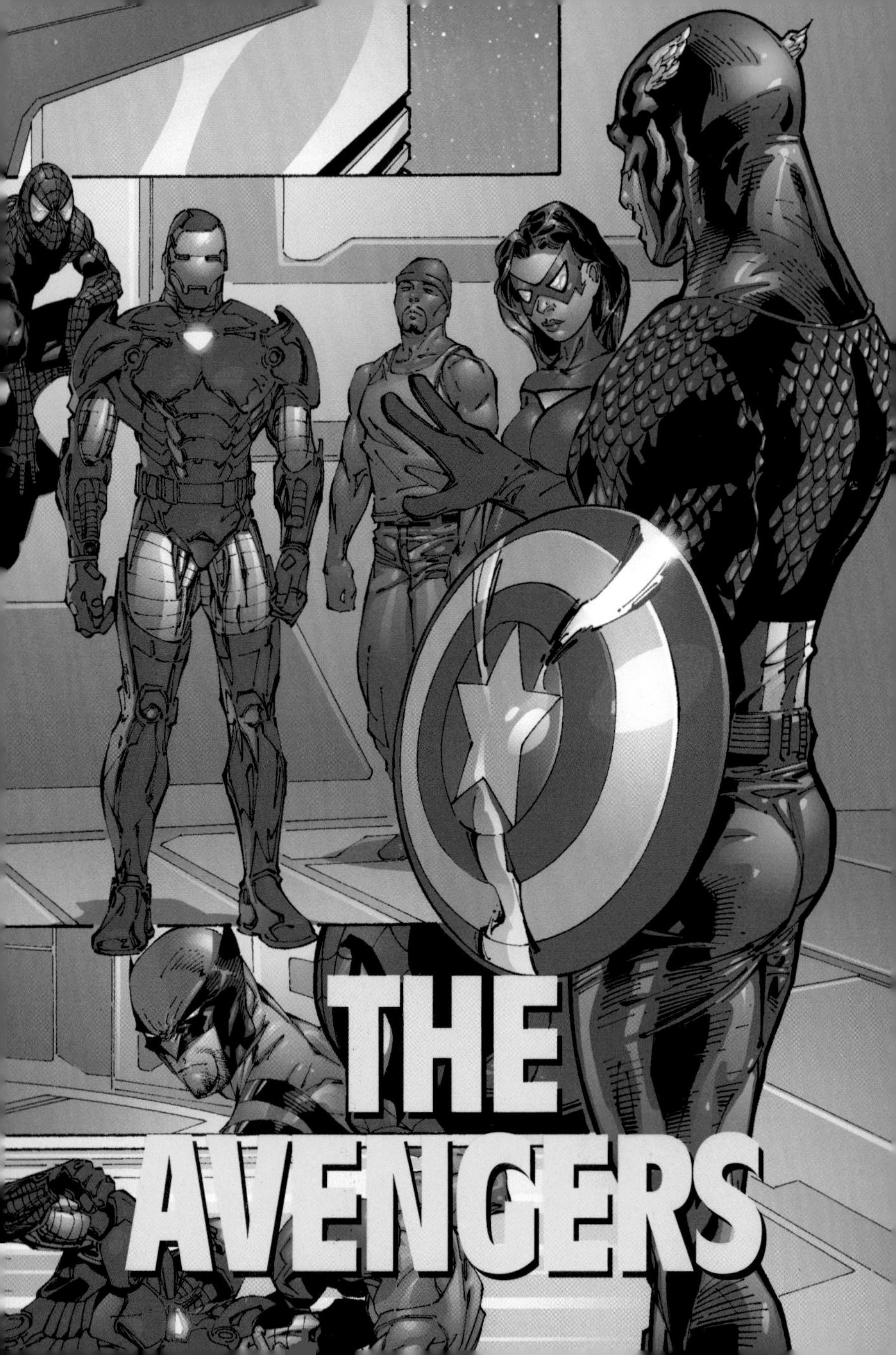
THE
AVENGERS

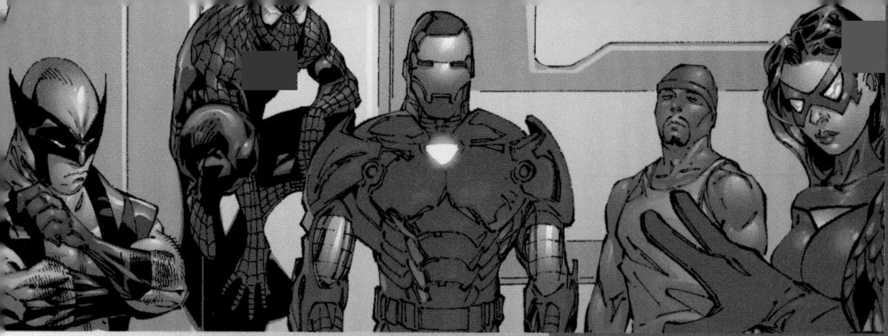

THE AVENGERS

The Avengers originally formed as a super hero team to protect Earth from menaces that could not be combated otherwise. Over the years, membership changed as super heroes, mutants, and crime-fighters joined and quit. The original Avengers were finally destroyed by one of their own when the mutant, the Scarlet Witch, turned against the team and killed several of its members. Their headquarters was destroyed and the remaining team disbanded.

Several months later, Captain America, Iron Man, Spider-Man, Luke Cage, Spider-Woman, Daredevil, and Sentry teamed up after a mass breakout from the super prison known as the Raft. With forty super villains on the loose, Captain America invited his six allies to help reform the Avengers and track down the escapees. Daredevil and Sentry turned the offer down, but the others joined. Wolverine also joined a short time later. When Spider-Man was threatened by the Sinister Twelve, the Avengers saved him.

Recently, the United States government passed a law that all super heroes had to register with the authorities and reveal their secret identities. Both Iron Man and Spider-Man believe the law is a good idea. Captain America does not.

Current team includes Captain America (Steve Rogers), Iron Man (Tony Stark), Luke Cage, Spider-Woman (Jessica Drew), Spider-Man (Peter Parker), Wolverine (James Howlett), Sentry (Robert Reynolds), Ronin (Maya Lopez)

SECRETS

- Jarvis, the butler at the Stark mansion, is the only person to have stayed with the Avengers for all of their incarnations.
- Stark Tower was intended to be Tony Stark's new home, but when the new Avengers team assembled, Stark gave it to them to serve as their headquarters.

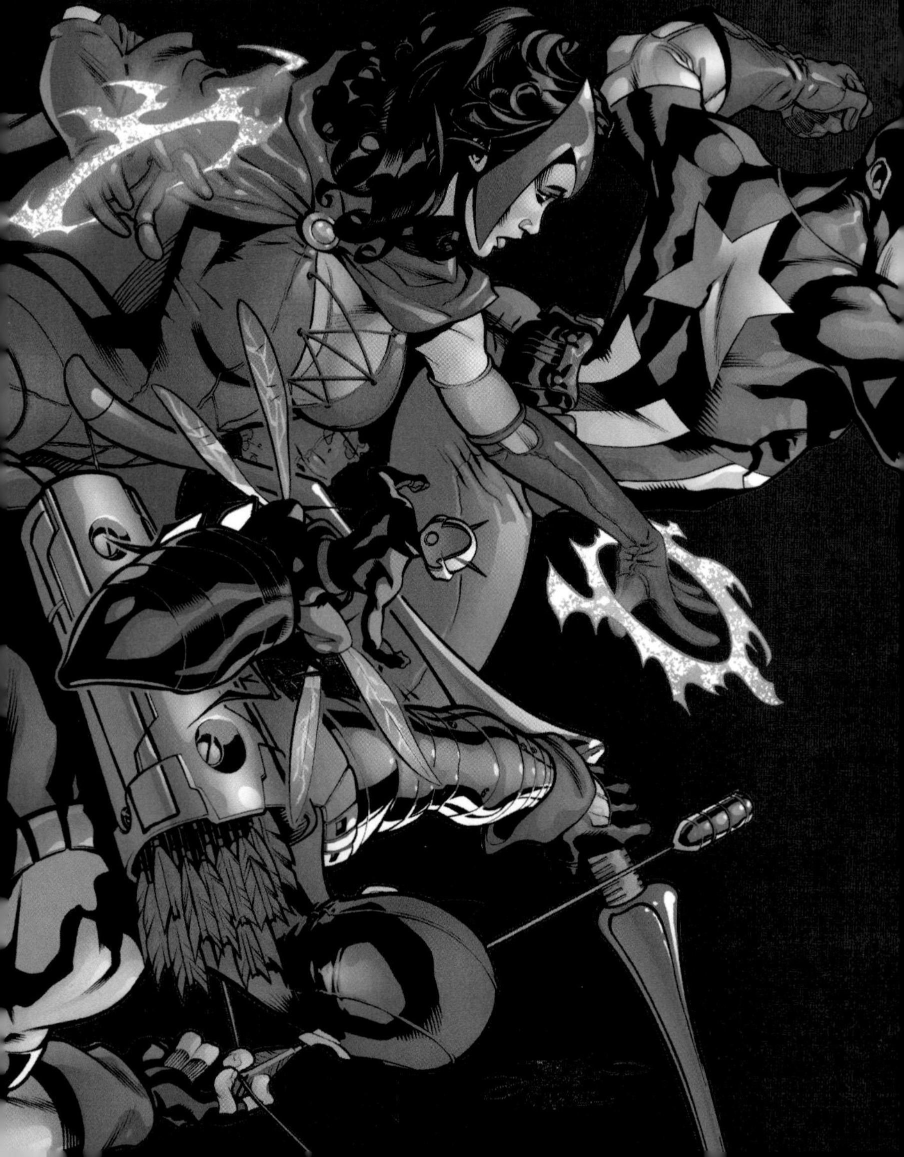

- More than sixty different super heroes have been members of the Avengers at some time during the team's history

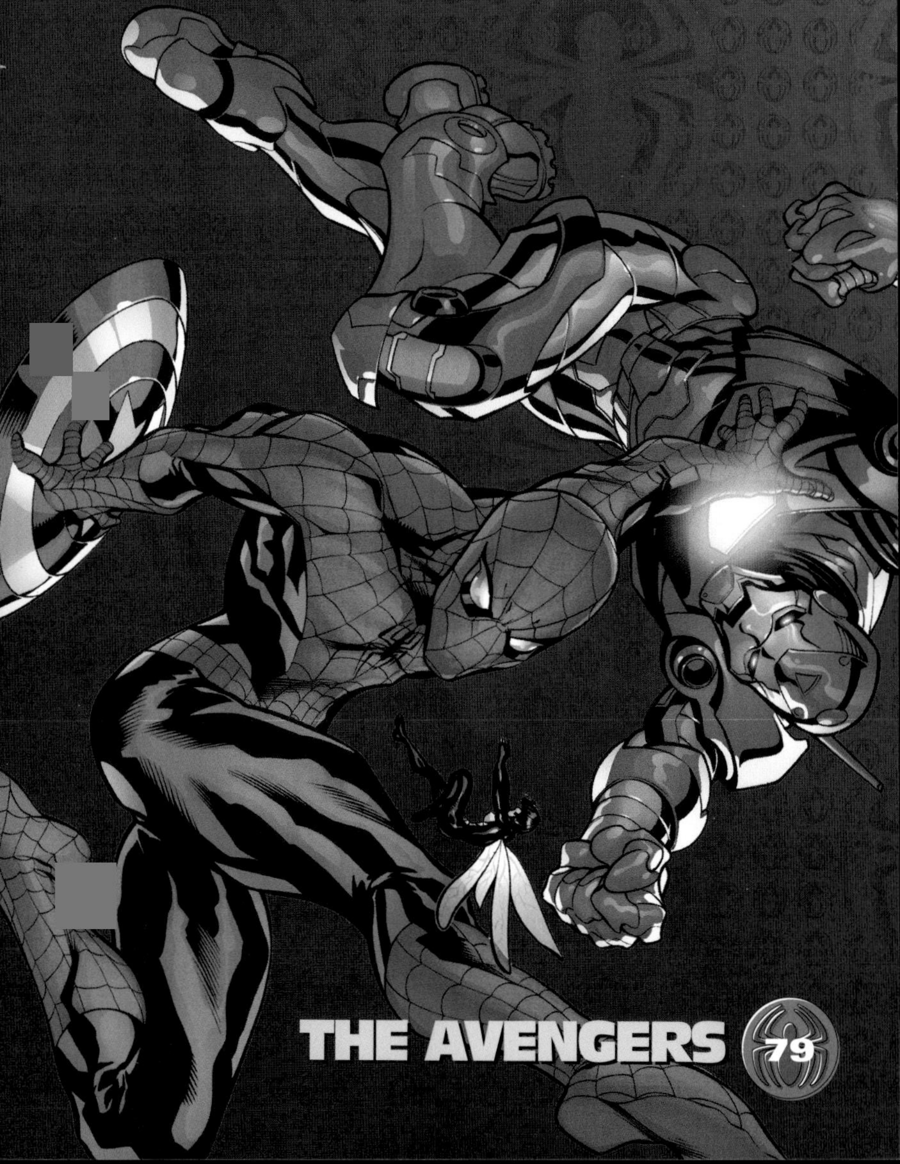

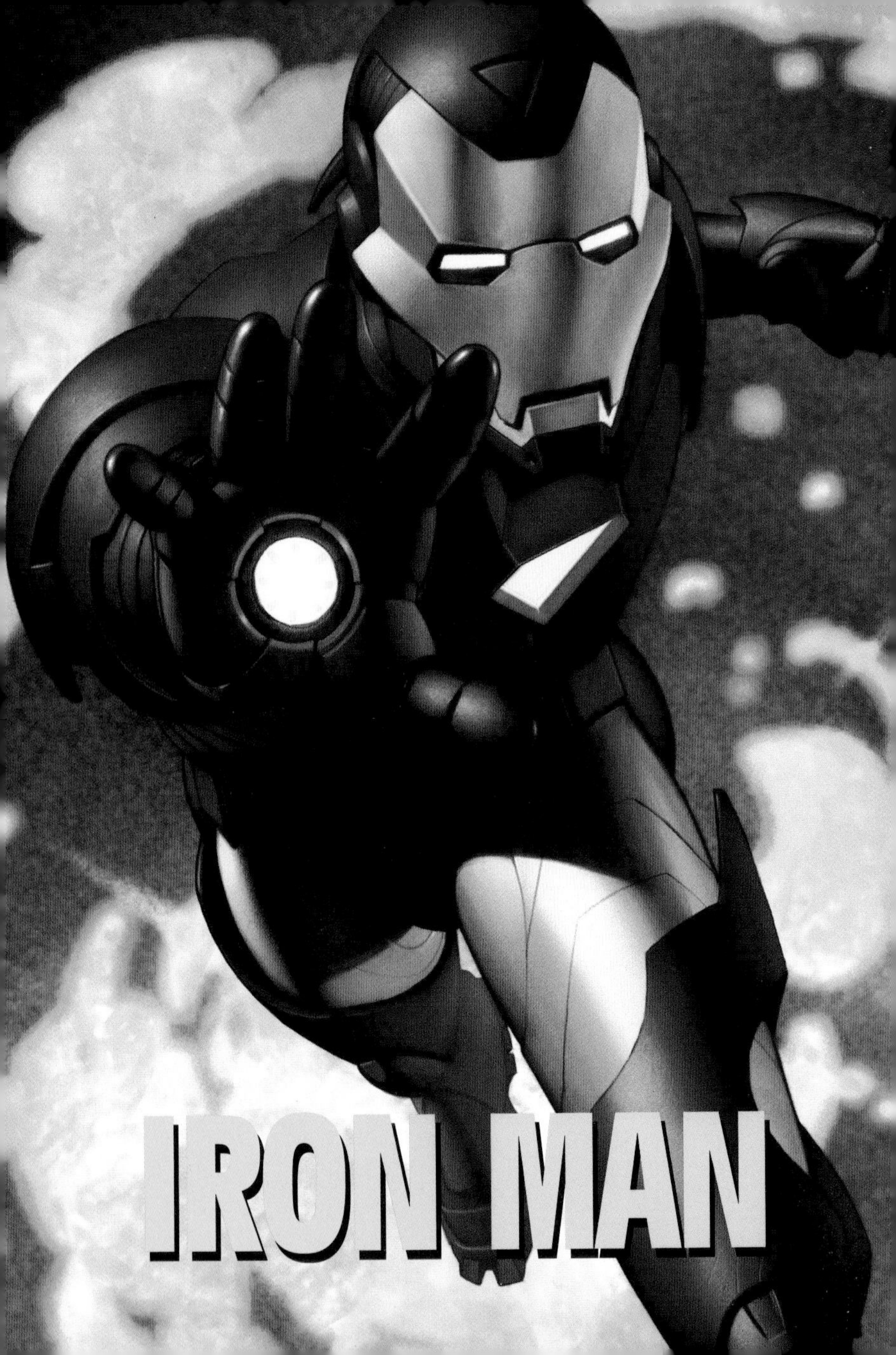
IRON MAN

POWERS

Originally Tony Stark had no powers of his own, and he depended on his armored suit for all of his abilities. Recently, he injected himself with a powerful techno-organic virus to save his life. The virus bonded Stark's armor to his body, making it possible for him to store the inner layers of his armor inside the hollows of his bones. He controls the armor by brain waves. Stark also can remotely connect to various communications systems such as satellites, cell phones, and computers throughout the world. The armor has boosted his reaction time to super speed, and his healing factor can re-grow entire organs.

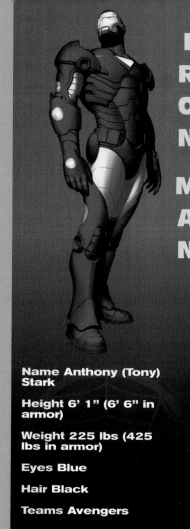

Anthony "Tony" Edward Stark was born with extremely high intelligence. At the age of fifteen, he was admitted to the electrical engineering department at MIT. He graduated at the top of his class. At twenty-one, he inherited Stark Enterprises after his parents died in an automobile accident. Badly wounded by shrapnel in Vietnam, Tony and fellow scientist Dr. Ho Yinsen built an armored suit that would keep him alive. This suit was the first of many that Tony would wear in years to come in the guise of Iron Man. Each armored suit was a vast improvement over its predecessor, complete with numerous weapons and gadgets that helped Tony become one of the leading super heroes of his time.

Early in his career as Iron Man, Stark helped to organize the super hero group the Avengers. Original members of the team included Thor, Ant Man, the Wasp, and the

IRON MAN

Name Anthony (Tony) Stark

Height 6' 1" (6' 6" in armor)

Weight 225 lbs (425 lbs in armor)

Eyes Blue

Hair Black

Teams Avengers

Hulk. Over the years, the team has gone through many changes in personnel, but it has remained a potent force in the fight for justice.

SECRETS

- Tony Stark's most desperate battle wasn't with a super villain, but his fight with alcoholism.

- Tony Stark's armor became so sophisticated that it achieved sentience. When Stark had a heart attack, the armor sacrificed itself to create an artificial heart for its creator.

- The cybernetic interface of Stark's early armored suit caused his nervous system to malfunction. The problem became so bad that Stark had to fake his own death and enter suspended animation in order to survive.

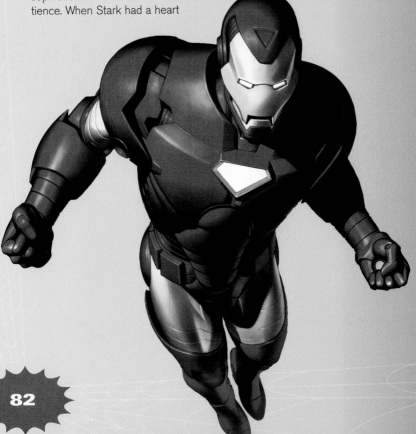

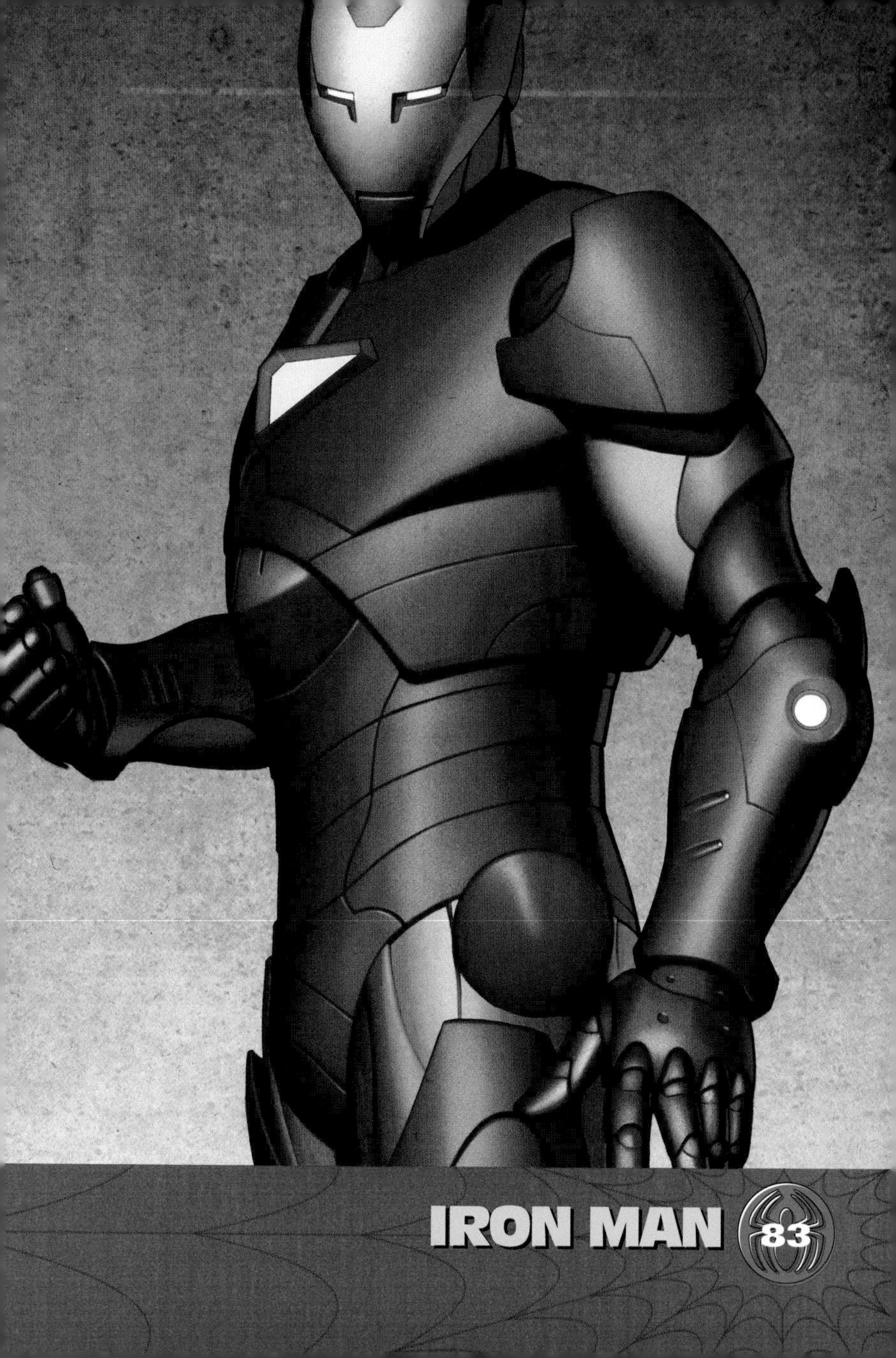

IRON MAN

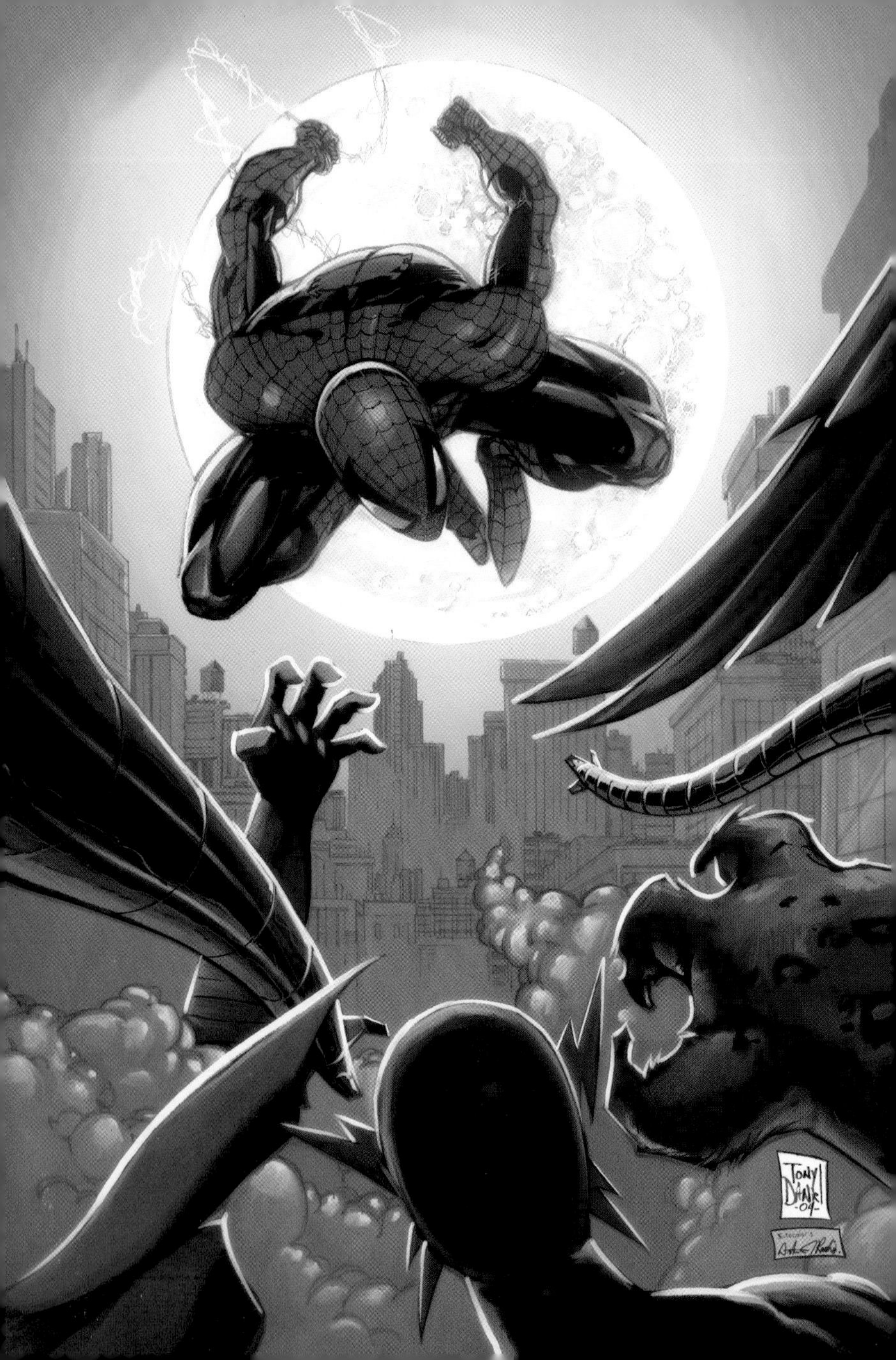

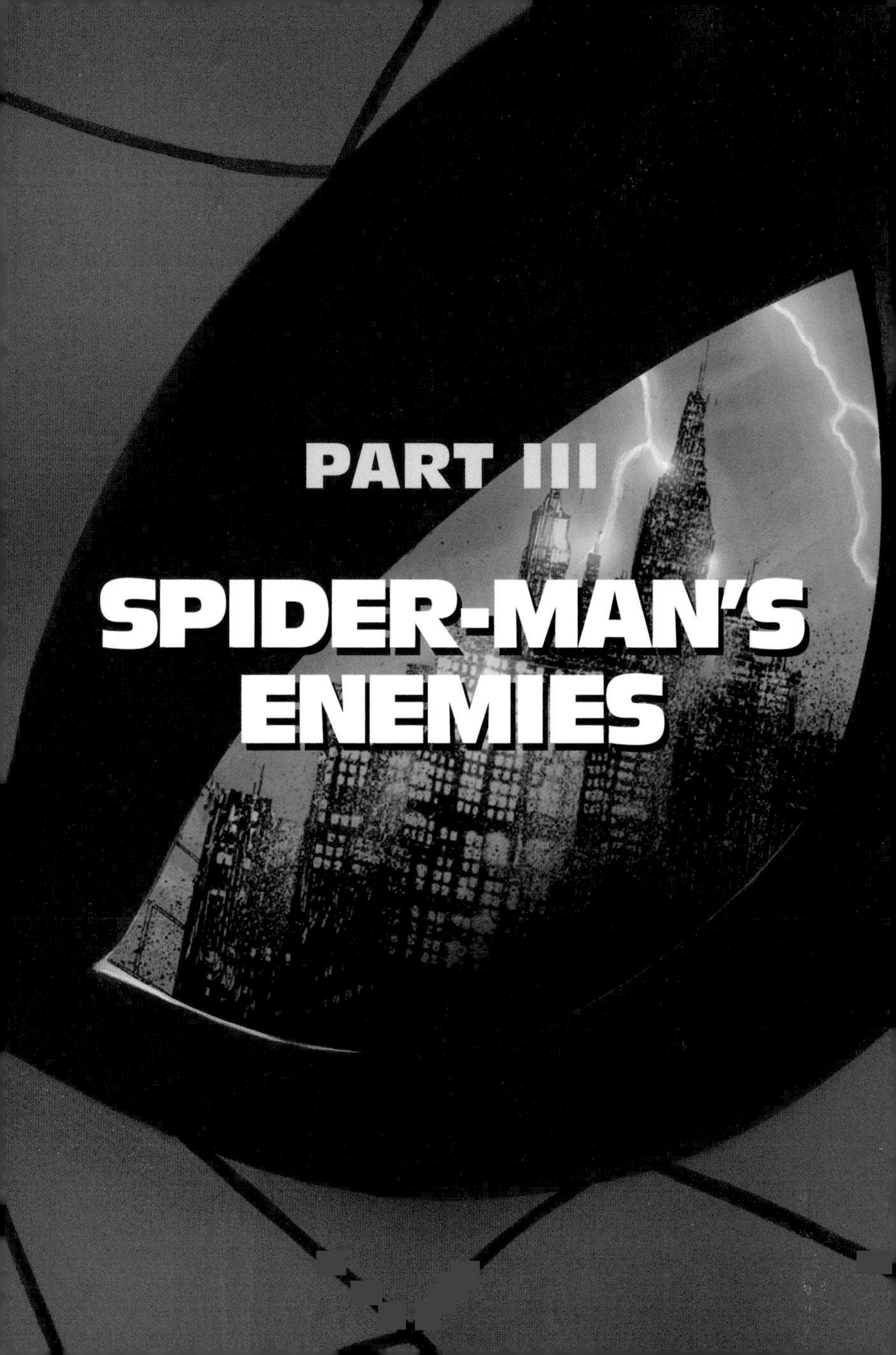

PART III

SPIDER-MAN'S ENEMIES

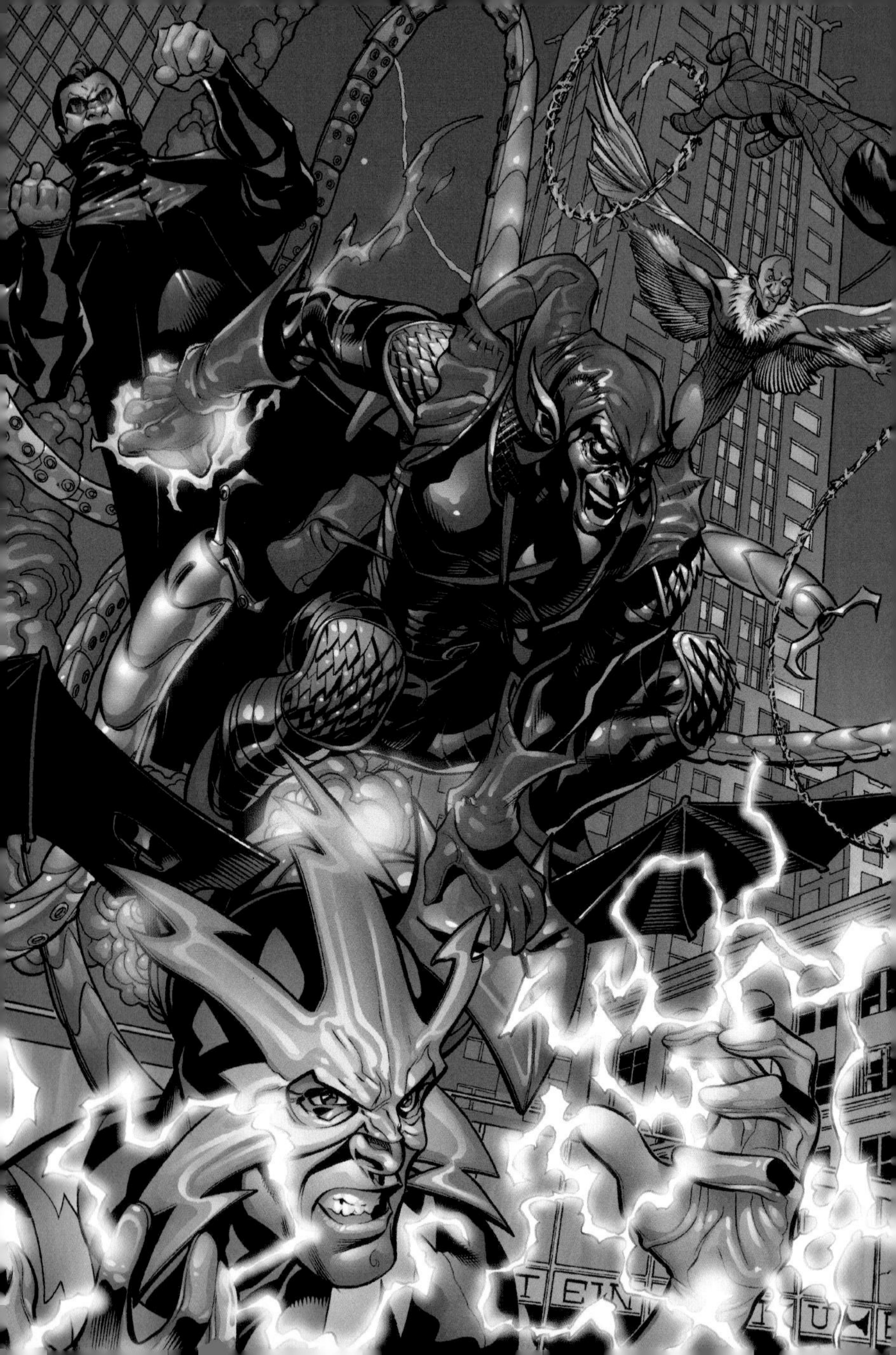

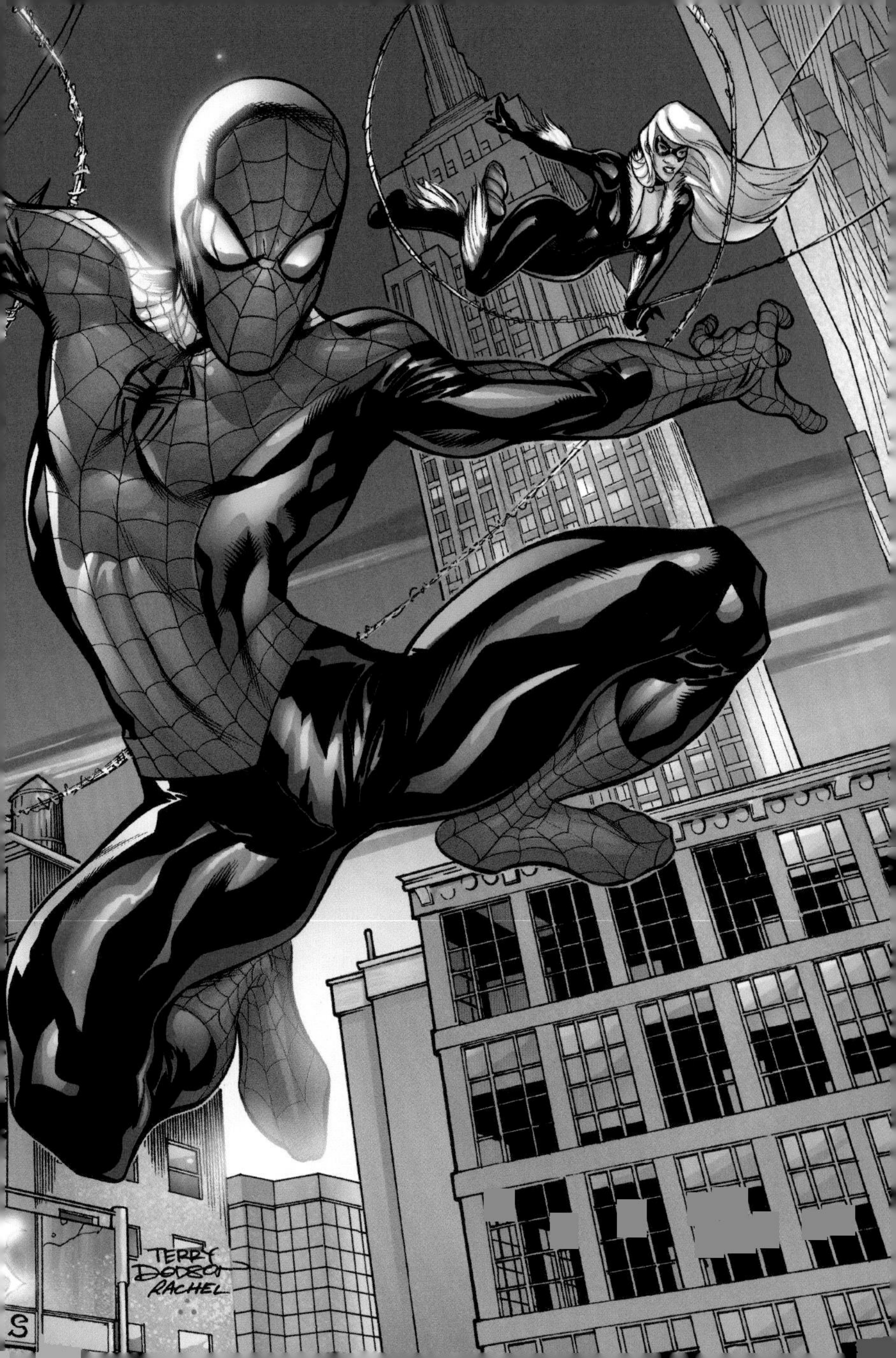
TERRY
DODSON
RACHEL

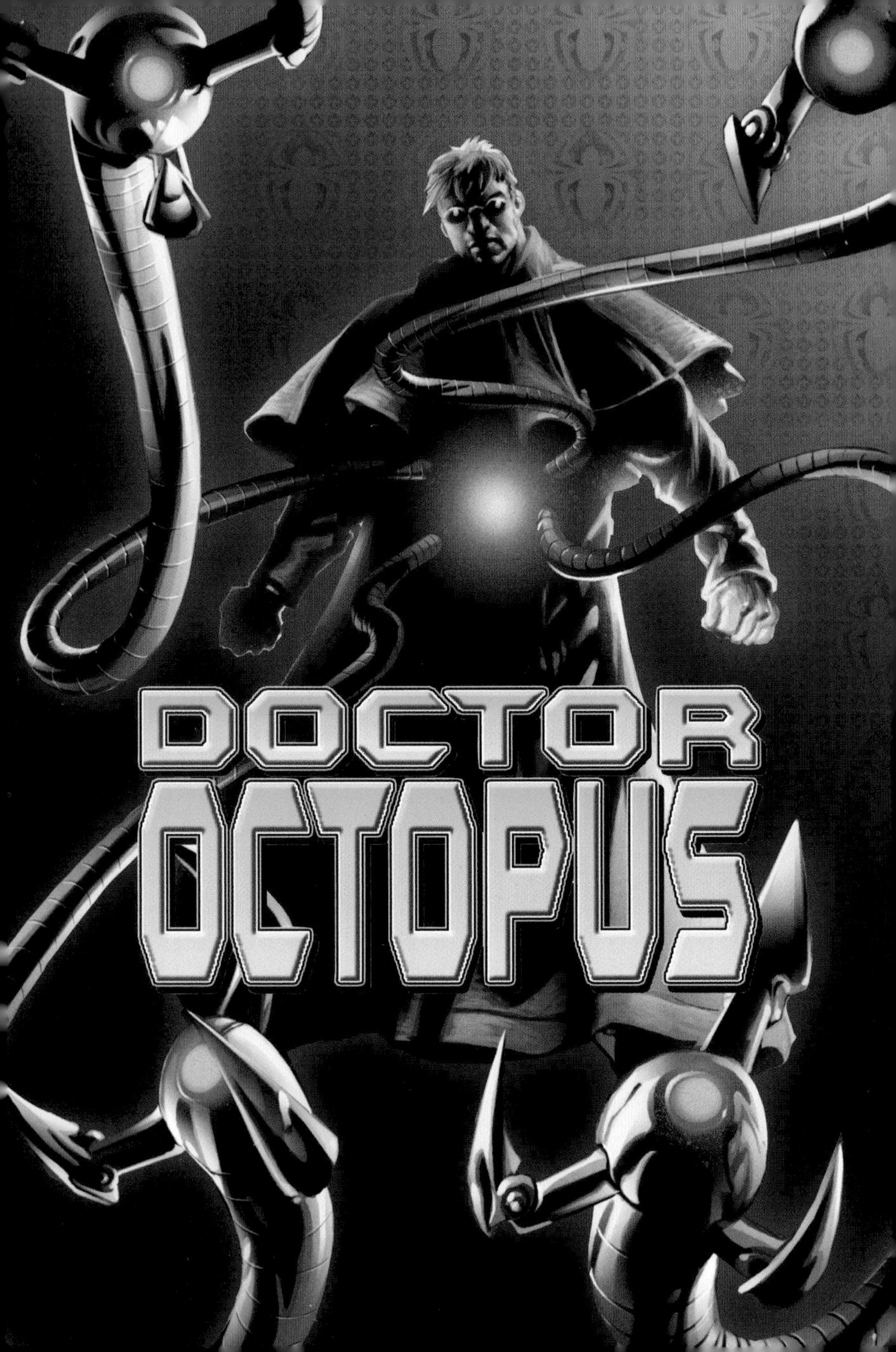
DOCTOR
OCTOPUS

POWERS

Doctor Octopus is linked mentally with his four tentacles, which are made out of adamantium steel, the world's strongest metal. With them, he can lift up to twenty tons if properly balanced and braced. These tentacles are capable of highly precise craftsmanship as well as lifting heavy objects. Each tentacle ends in a three-pronged, razor-sharp, metal claw. Doctor Octopus is able to use his tentacles to move rapidly over any sort of terrain and to climb walls. He has also developed control over his tentacles to the point where he is able to battle multiple enemies at the same time.

Doctor Otto Octavius was one of the top research scientists in the United States and a specialist in the fields of atomic energy and nuclear radiation. A brilliant inventor, he designed a set of four extremely advanced artificial limbs similar to "waldos" used in laboratories to handle dangerous materials from a distance. The powerful limbs were radiation-resistant and attached to a harness that Octavius wore around his body.

An accidental radiation leak at a nuclear power plant caused an explosion that fused the four mechanical arms to Octavius's body. The radiation also affected Octavius's brain, giving him mental control over the four tentacles but also turning the dedicated scientist into a megalomaniacal criminal who became known as Doctor Octopus, or "Doc Ock."

Doctor Octavius was overweight and had eyesight so poor that he needed extremely powerful eyeglasses. With his four mechanical arms, however, Doctor Octopus was

Name Otto Octavius

Aliases
Doc Ock; formerly
Master Planner,
Bowery Bum, Master
Programmer

Groups
formerly Sinister Six,
Masters of Evil

Height 5' 9"

Weight 245 lbs.

Eyes Brown

Hair Brown

DOCTOR OCTOPUS

more powerful than Spider-Man. In their first fight, he beat Spider-Man so badly that the web-slinger actually considered giving up his career as a crime fighter.

Over the years, Doctor Octopus battled Spider-Man numerous times and became known as one of the web-slinger's most dangerous enemies. He served as leader of the original Sinister Six, a group of villains he recruited to destroy Spider-Man, and he helped to reorganize the group with some new members after their defeat by Spider-Man. He also founded his own version of the criminal organization known as the Masters of Evil.

When Octavius attacked and badly wounded Spider-Man's one time girlfriend, Black Cat, the infuriated web-slinger tracked down Doctor Octopus and gave the criminal mastermind the worst beating of his life. Traumatized by the attack, Doctor Octopus became terrified of spiders and Spider-Man. Later, when New York City was threatened by a nuclear plant meltdown, Spider-Man was forced to "throw" a fight with Doctor Octopus so that the criminal genius would regain his confidence and help shut down the reactor.

A teenager named Oliver Osnick ran away from home after stealing from his father equipment much like that used by Dr. Octopus. Oliver wanted to serve as Doc Ock's assistant, but one fight with Spider-Man convinced him that would be a terrible mistake.

When Otto Octavius was killed by an evil clone of Spider-Man known as Kaine, his student, Carolyn Trainer donned his tentacles and for a brief period became the new Doctor Octopus. She later helped the criminal organization, the Hand, in resurrecting Octavius, and when he returned to life, yielded his equipment to him.

Doc Ock also fought an egotistical scientist named Carlyle, who used Octavius's original blueprints to build his own set of tentacles and a harness to use them. Octopus defeated Carlyle by ripping open his harness and destroying his control mechanisms. Involved in a plot to kidnap a foreign diplomat, Doctor Octopus was captured by Spider-Man and sent to prison. At present, he remains incarcerated.

SECRETS

- Though the four tentacles were once surgically removed from Dr. Octopus's body, he still was able to control them telepathically from a great distance.

- Octavius was recently involved in a plot to use prosthetic limbs as mind-control devices, but his scheme was thwarted by Spider-Man.

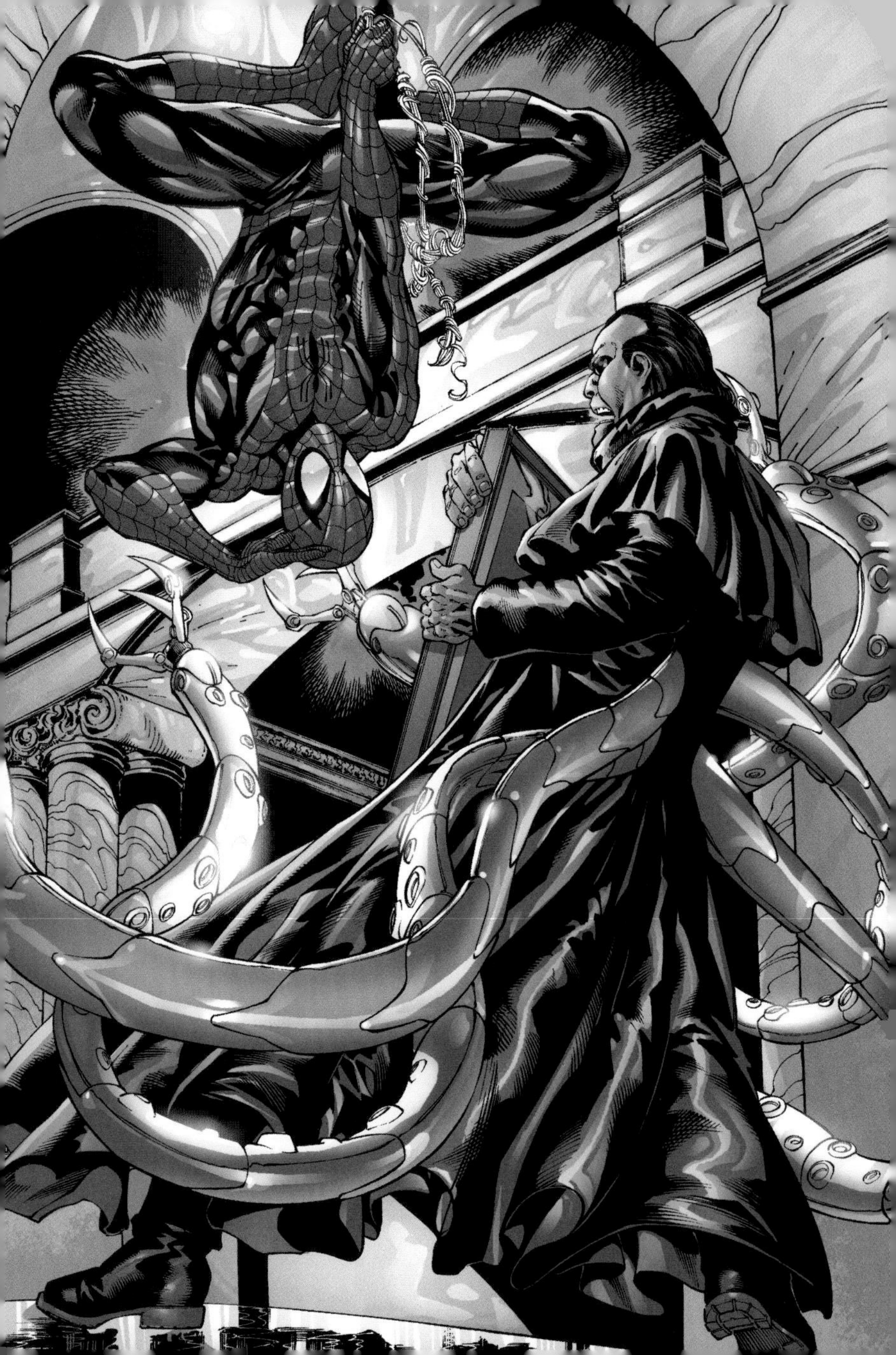

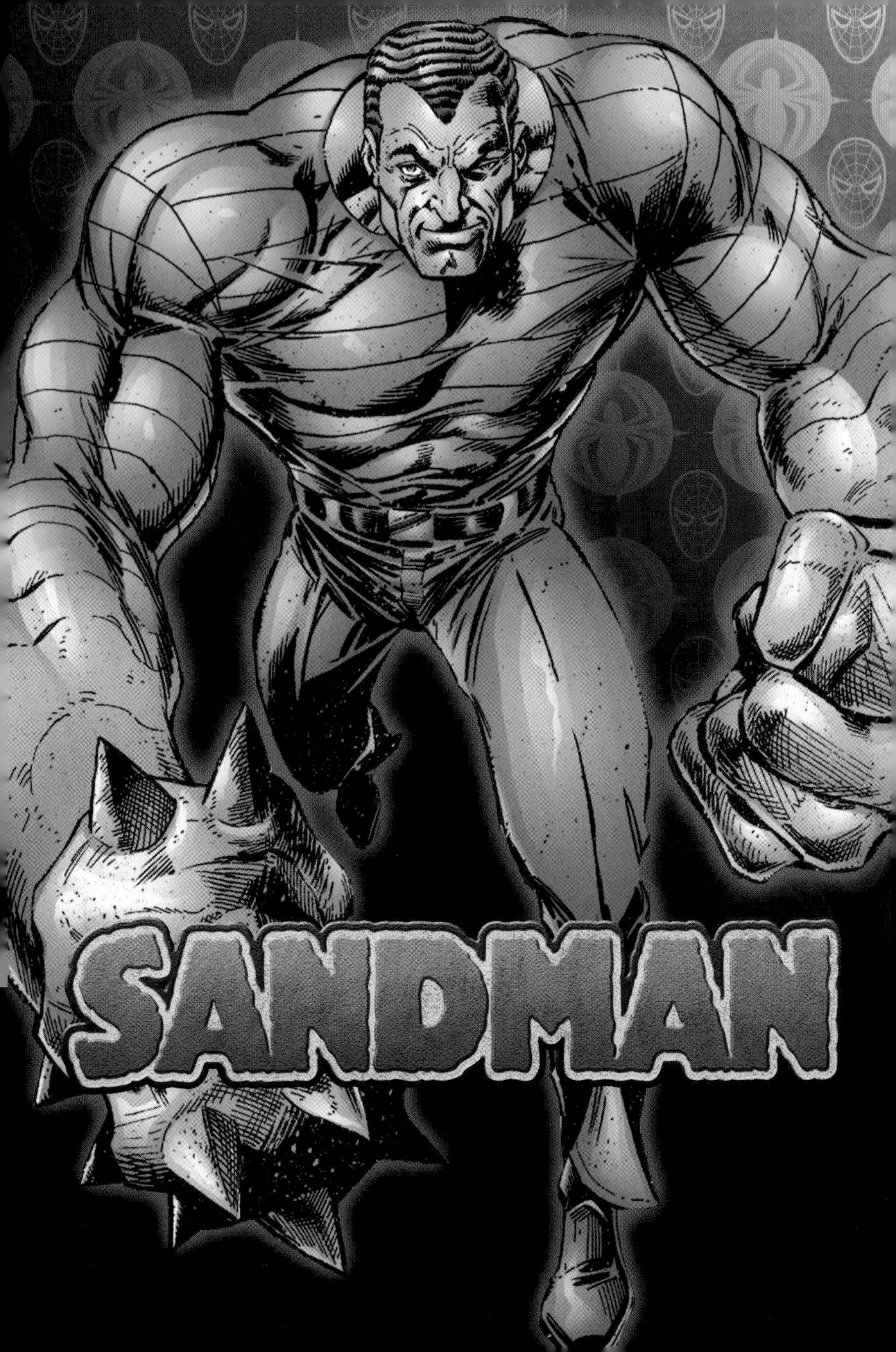
SANDMAN

POWERS

Sandman possesses the ability to convert all or part of his body into a sand-like substance by mental command. Because his brain can control all the particles of sand in his body, with conscious effort, he can shape the sand into any form. He can also harden or soften his sand structure so that he can be hard as stone or soft as sand, and he can also move his sand body in any direction at a high speed. At high temperatures above 3400 degrees Fahrenheit Sandman fuses into glass. Sandman can absorb sand from the beach to grow larger. None of this villain's powers can be explained by ordinary science.

William Baker (also known as Flint Marko) was a career criminal who spent most of his adult life in prison. After being released from jail, he went berserk when he learned his girlfriend had left him for another crook. Caught by the police, Marko faced a stiff sentence. He escaped before he could be convicted and hid out at a nuclear generating plant near Savannah, Georgia. Marko was on the beach when the reactor's steam system exploded, bombarding him with a huge dose of radiation that somehow bonded his body with the sand on the beach and transformed him into a near invulnerable criminal. Marko renamed himself Sandman and during his reign of crime he fought Spider-Man, the Incredible Hulk, and the Fantastic Four.

Marko's criminal career went into decline when he joined forces with Hydro-Man and a weird accident welded the two together to form a mud monster. The

SANDMAN

Name William Baker

Aliases Flint Marko, Sylvester Mann, Quarryman

Group Affiliation Former member of Sinister Twelve, the Sinister Six, the Frightful Four, the Outlaws, and the Wild Pack; reserve member of the Avengers.

Height 6' 1"

Weight 240 lbs-450 lbs

Eyes Brown

Hair Brown

creature was captured, but scientists had no idea what to do with it. Before the substance could be disposed of, the two crooks separated back into their original forms.

Badly shaken, Marko decided to leave crime behind and use his powers to help people. He even went so far as to become a reserve member of the Avengers. However, a criminal mastermind brainwashed him into believing he had faked his conversion, and Sandman once again turned to crime.

Recently, Sandman was poisoned by a bite from Venom and his body started dissolving slowly. Determined not to die without a fight, Sandman tried one last time to defeat Spider-Man. However, he was so weak that he was unable to do much. Barely alive, he asked Spider-Man to say goodbye to his mother. With those words, Sandman was washed away into a Manhattan storm drain. But not even Venom could destroy Sandman. After merging with Jones Beach, Sandman returned to his original self, once again evil.

SECRETS

- In their first fight, Spider-Man defeated Sandman by sucking him into a vacuum cleaner.

- Venom joined the Sinister Six to make sure no other super villain would kill Spider-Man. He turned on the five other members of the group, poisoning Sandman as part of his plot.

- Though Sandman's real name is William Baker, he almost always uses the alias, Flint Marko.

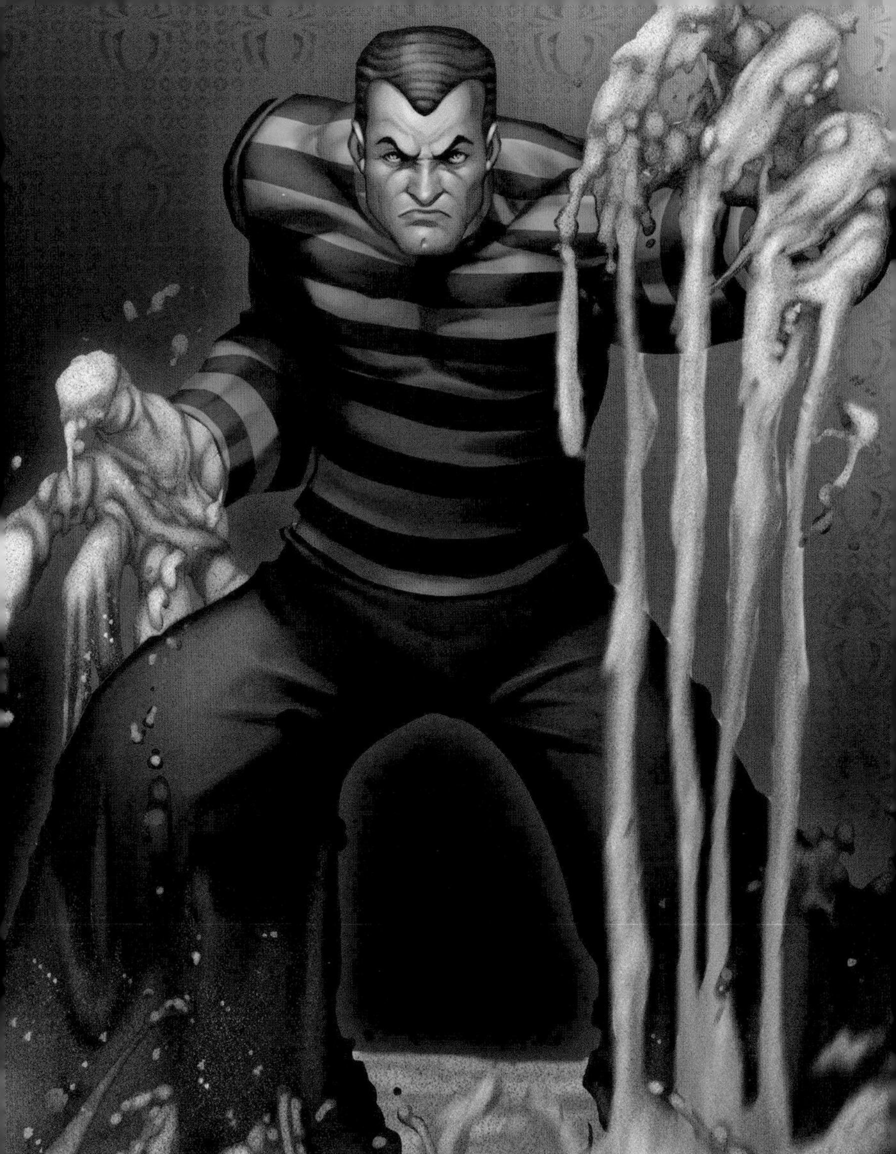

SANDMAN

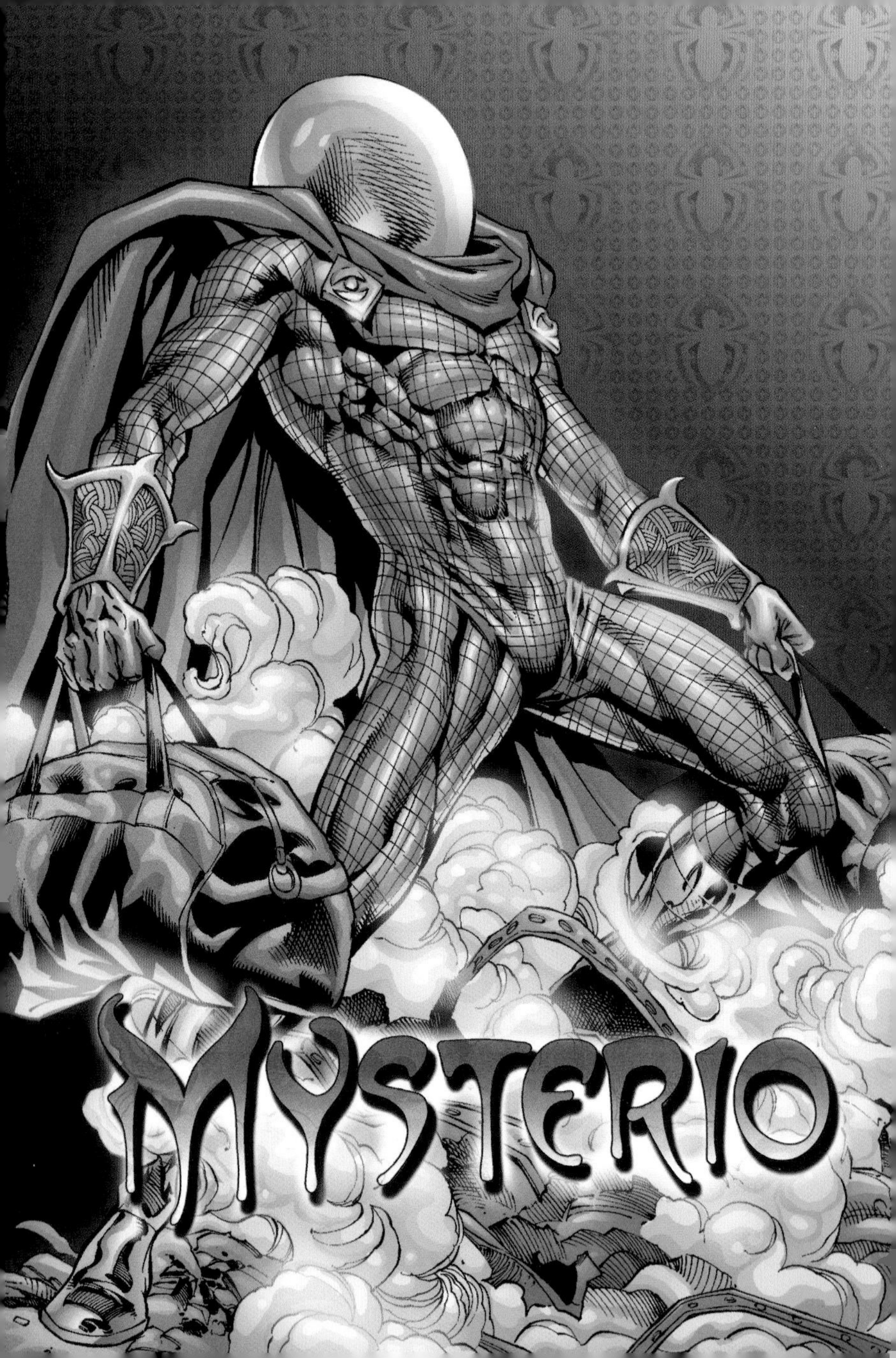
MYSTERIO

Quentin Beck, a Hollywood special-effects maestro, dreamed of becoming famous in the film industry. But, he wasn't good looking enough to be an actor and lacked the skill of a director. Concerned that his career in film would take him nowhere, Beck decided to become a super villain. He reasoned that the fastest way to make a reputation was to defeat Spider-Man and invented the persona Mysterio. Having no actual super powers, Beck spent several months preparing his equipment to defeat the web-slinger. Although he used a special nerve gas to dull Spider-Man's spider-sense and a chemical toxin to dissolve his webbing, Spider-Man was still able to defeat Mysterio and send him to jail.

Mysterio returned to plague Spider-Man with a number of well-planned schemes. He faked the death of Aunt May, disguised himself as a psychiatrist in an attempt to persuade Spider-Man he was losing his mind, and even joined the Sinister Six in a team effort to destroy the web-slinger. All of these attempts failed.

Mysterio was granted an early release from prison when it was discovered he was suffering from lung cancer and a brain tumor caused by his equipment. Reading the newspapers, he concluded that the current Spider-Man was a clone and instead decided to attack the hero known as Daredevil. His evil scheme succeeded in eliminating a number of Daredevil's closest friends, but eventually the super hero realized that Mysterio was behind the deaths. Mysterio hoped that Daredevil would kill him, ending his life in grand style, but Daredevil knew that letting Mysterio live

M Y S T E R I O

Name Quentin Beck

Aliases Nicholas Macabes, Rudolph Hines, Gerdes, Doctor Ludwig Rinehart

Group Affiliation formerly in Sinister Six

Height 5' 11"

Weight 175 lbs.

Eyes Brown

Hair Black

Powers None

was a much worse punishment. Mysterio then killed himself.

After Beck's suicide, his friend, Daniel Berkhart, took on the persona of Mysterio for several appearances with the Sinister Six.

SECRETS

- Mysterio once built a number of elaborate traps in an amusement park to convince Spider-Man he was only six inches high.

- Calling himself Rudolph Hines, Beck started a new TV network called "Mystery Vision," which sent addictive subliminal messages to viewers, hooking them on the station.

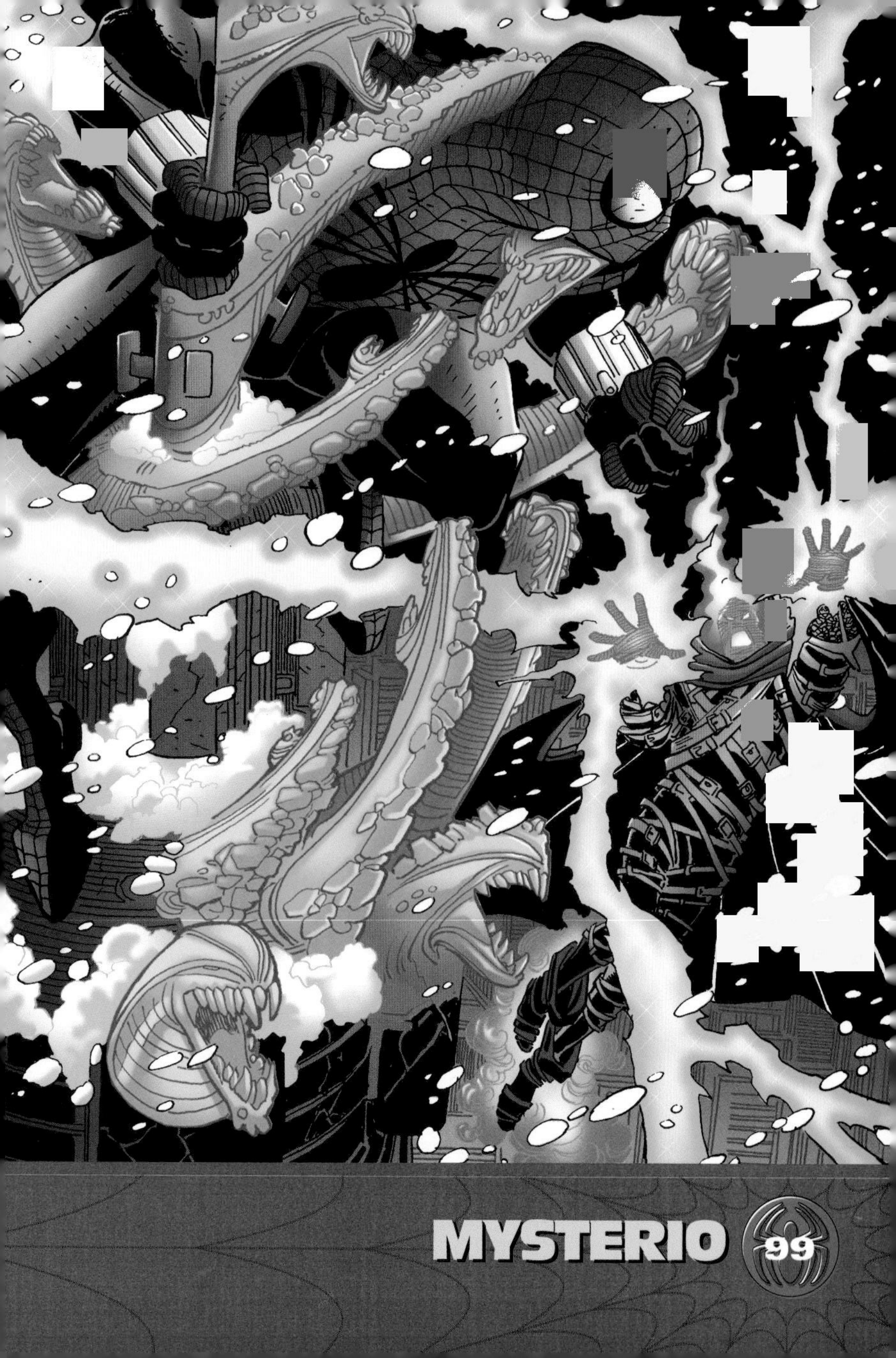

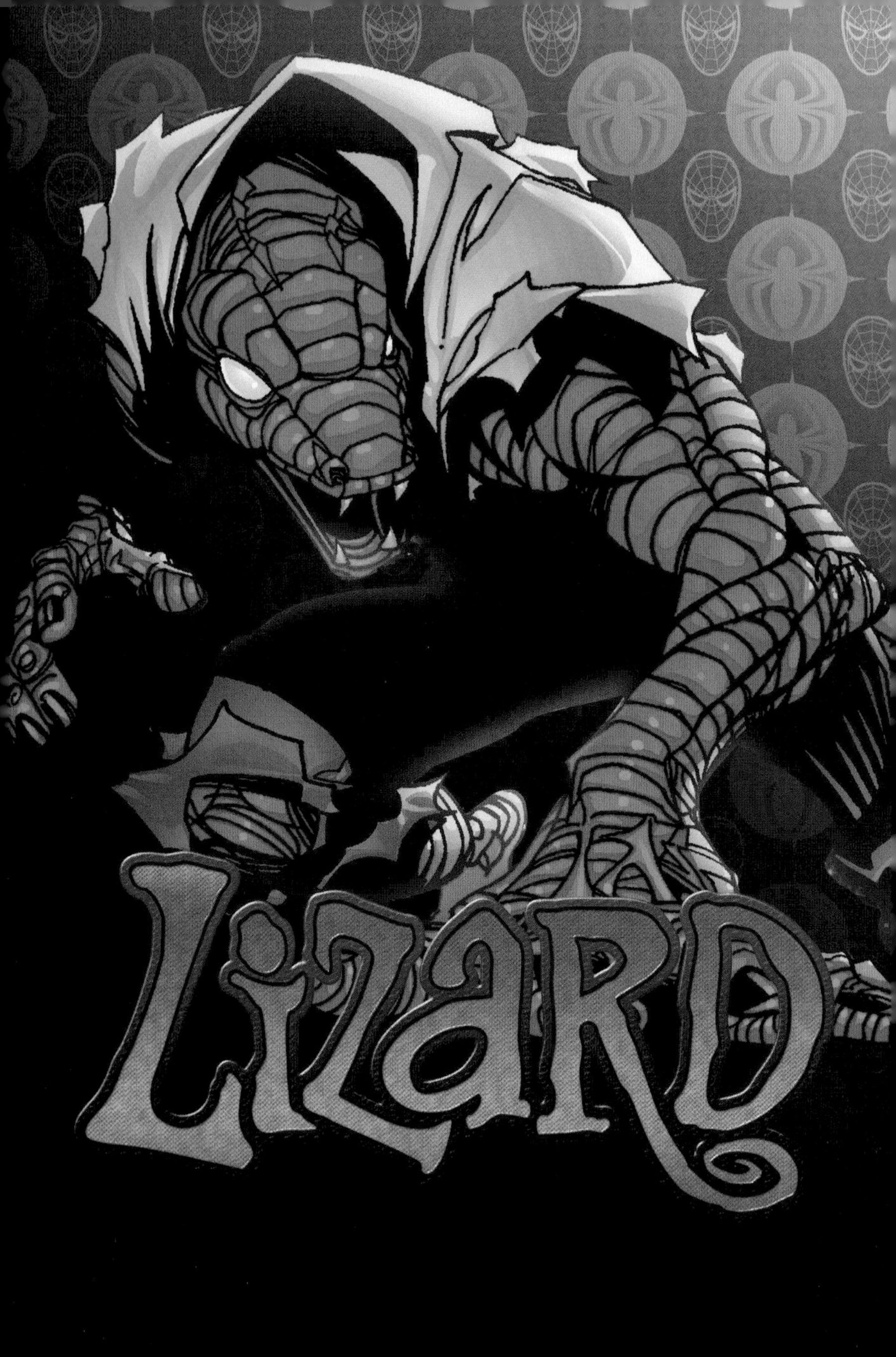
LIZARD

POWERS

Lizard has superhuman strength, speed, agility, and reflexes that match those of Spider-Man. His rough skin makes him very difficult to injure. He can also regenerate parts of his body, growing a new tail or limb as needed. Lizard's tail is extremely strong and can move incredibly fast. He can climb walls like a lizard and has telepathic control of all reptiles within a mile of his location. Lizard grows sluggish in cold temperatures. Recently Lizard has gained the power to emit pheromones that make humans behave violently.

Doctor Curtis Connors lost his right arm while working as a medic in the army. After his tour of duty, Connors returned home and set out to find a method of regenerating lost limbs. Working on his own with reptiles and amphibians, he developed a serum that reproduced their regenerative powers in humans. Connors decided to try the potion on himself, and it transformed him into a semi-intelligent, man-sized lizard who plotted a reptile take over of the world.

Spider-Man was able to defeat Lizard by out-thinking him and using an anti-venom to transform him back into kindly Dr. Connors. However, any major stress attack transformed the scientist back into his evil doppelganger.

In his human form, Connors has helped Spider-Man solve major medical and scientific problems. No matter what form he took, Connors never attacked his wife or son. However, his wife, Martha, died from years of exposure to industrial toxic waste,

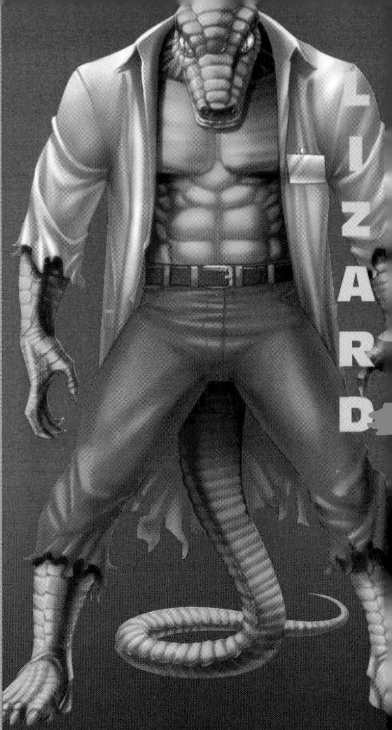
LIZARD

Name
Dr. Curtis Connors

Group Affiliation
formerly the Sinister Twelve

Height
6' 8" as Lizard;
5' 11" as Connors

Weight
510 lbs as Lizard;
175 lbs. as Connors

Eyes
Red as Lizard;
Blue as Connors

Hair
None as Lizard;
Brown as Connors

leaving Connors a single parent. The stress of raising his son and retaining his human persona made his life doubly difficult. At present, Connors in Lizard form lives in the Manhattan sewer system.

SECRETS

• Connors developed a formula to save Aunt May's life after Peter Parker gave her radioactive blood during a blood transfusion.

• One of Lizard's plans to take over the world had him poisoning the water supply to turn the entire population into his mindless slaves.

• Connors once cut off a piece of his tail to experiment on it, and the section grew into a second Lizard, one without any of Connors's human traits.

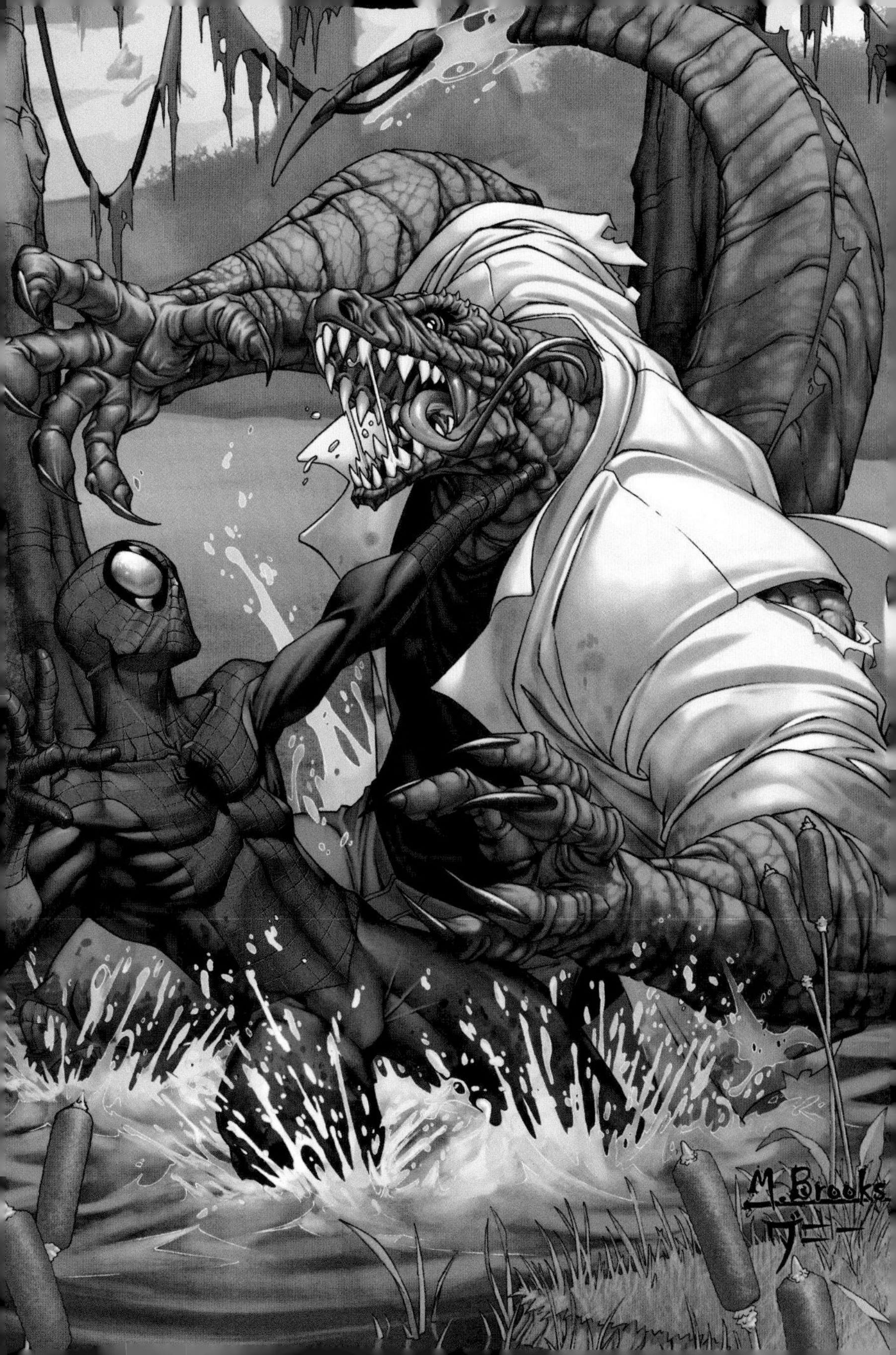
M. Brooks

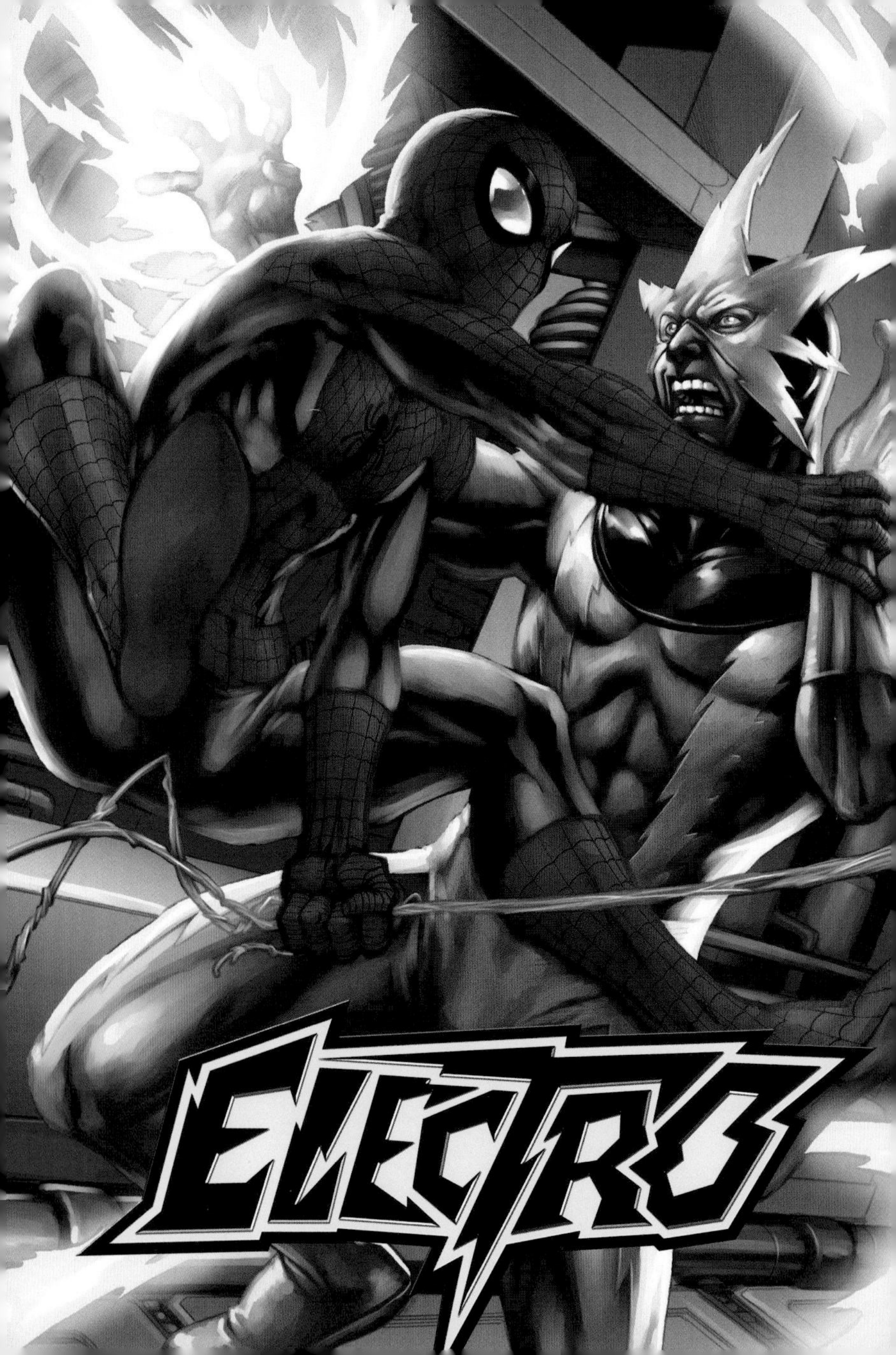
ELECTRO

POWERS

Electro is a living electrical capacitor, powered by the micro-fine rhythmic muscle contractions that normally regulate body temperature. He can generate electrostatic energy at a rate of about 1,000 volts per minute and store up to 1,000,000 volts, allowing him to emit lightning arcs from his fingertips at speeds of up to 1,100 feet per second, achieving a maximum distance of about 100 feet. He can also override electrically powered devices and manipulate them mentally, travel along conductive surfaces such as power lines at speeds as fast as 140 mph, and create electrostatic "bridges" to travel varying distances. Using his full powers, he can disrupt Spider-Man's ability to cling to walls. When fully charged, Electro is extremely sensitive to anything that can cause his abilities to short-circuit, especially water.

Maxwell Dillon was raised by an over-protective mother after his father abandoned them. Although Max had ambitions to become an electrical engineer, his mother convinced him he wasn't smart enough for college so he took a job working as a lineman for the electric company. One day, while repairing a powerline still on its spool, Max was hit by lightning. The freak accident didn't kill him—rather, it changed him into a human electric generator. Max became the criminal, Electro.

Early in Electro's career, J. Jonah Jameson published an article in the Daily Bugle saying the criminal was merely Spider-Man in disguise. Looking to prove the piece false, Spider-Man fought Electro but was nearly

ELECTRO

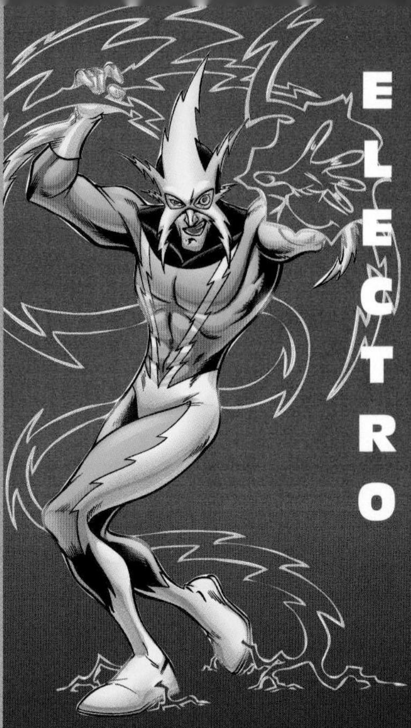

Name
Maxwell "Max" Dillon, Electro

Group Affiliation
formerly Sinister Six, Sinister Seven, Sinister Twelve, Frightful Four, Emissaries of Evil

Height 5' 11"

Weight 165 lbs

Eyes Blue

Hair Reddish-brown

killed when he touched him and received a massive electric shock. Spider-Man had to use a fireman's hose to defeat the villain.

Electro fought Spider-Man numerous times after that, on his own and as a member of the criminal organization the Sinister Six. Several times he tried to seize control of New York City's power grid, but each time he was defeated by Spider-Man. Disgusted with himself, Electro jumped into the Hudson River and, to all appearances, electrocuted himself.

Electro survived, however, and again joined with the Sinister Six in their attempts to kill Spider-Man. When the Sinister Twelve was organized, he joined that group as well. They failed when Spider-Man summoned the Avengers and the Fantastic Four for help.

Recently, Electro was hired to break into the maximum-security prison built to hold super villains and free one of the prisoners. He was responsible for a huge prisoner break that resulted in forty-two major criminals escaping. The prison break inspired a number of super heroes to re-form the Avengers. The new Avengers team quickly captured Dillon and put him in jail, where he now resides.

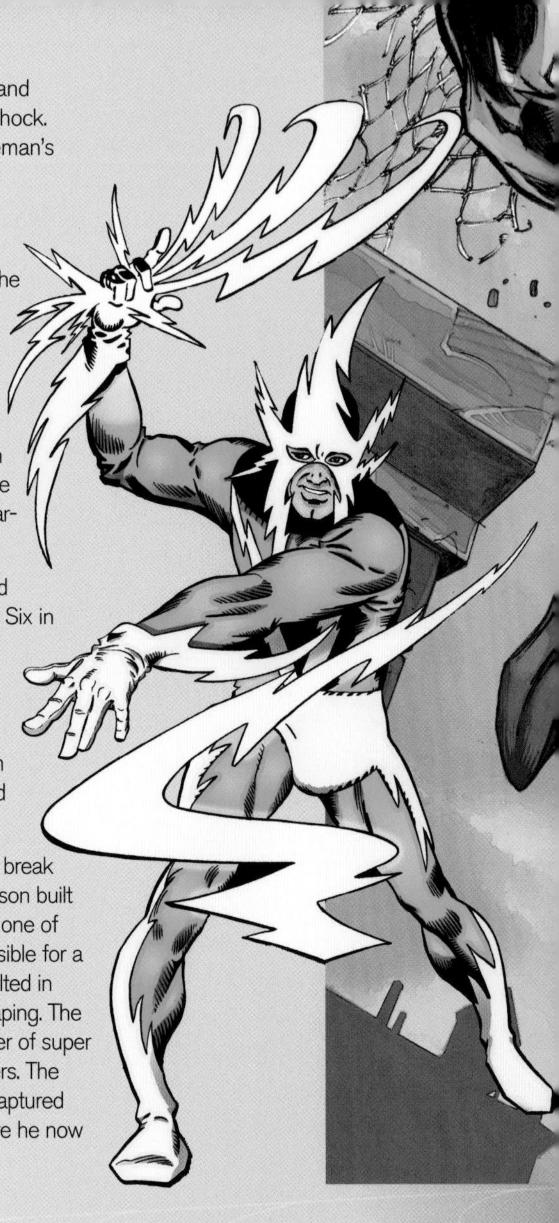

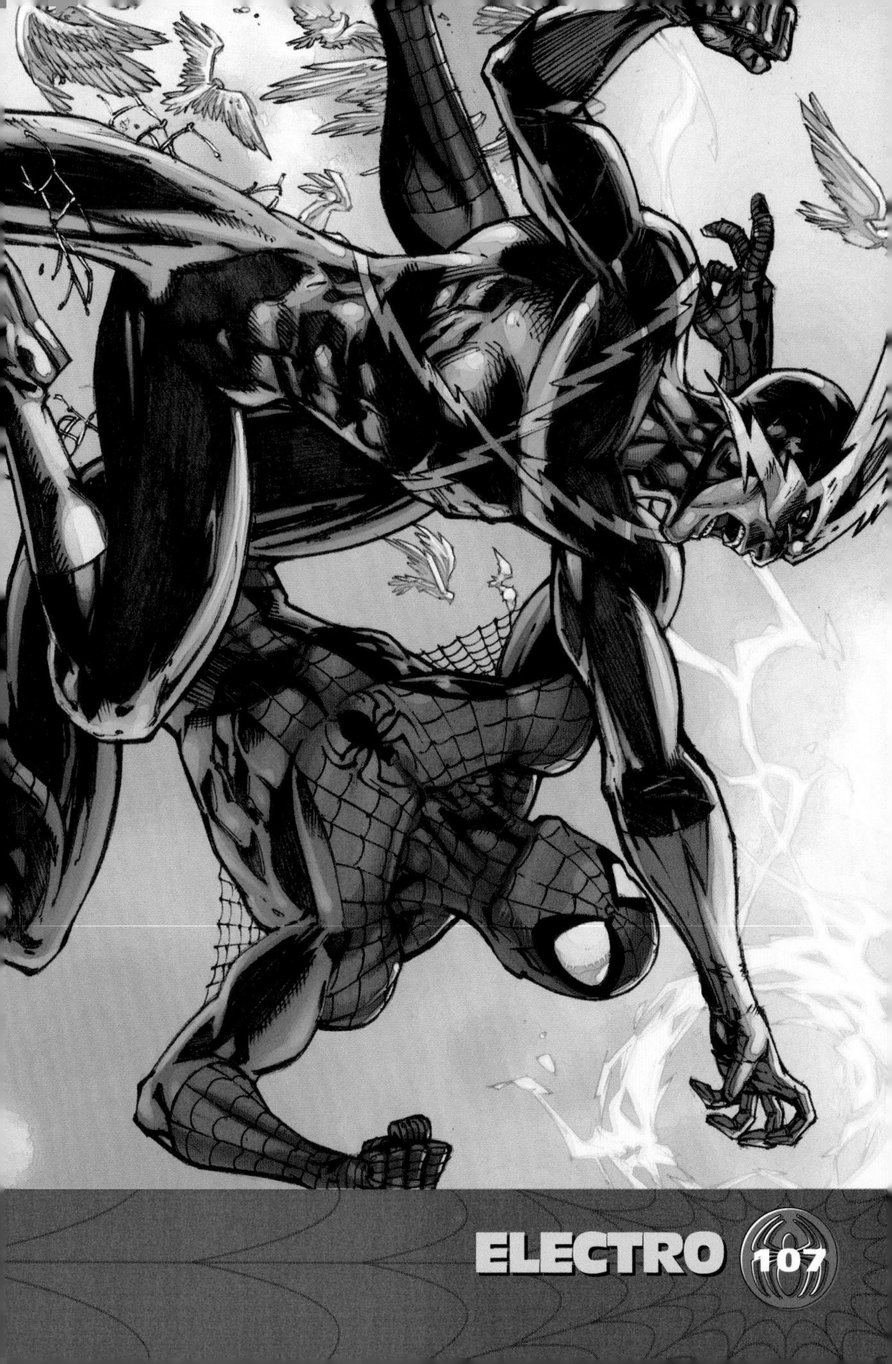

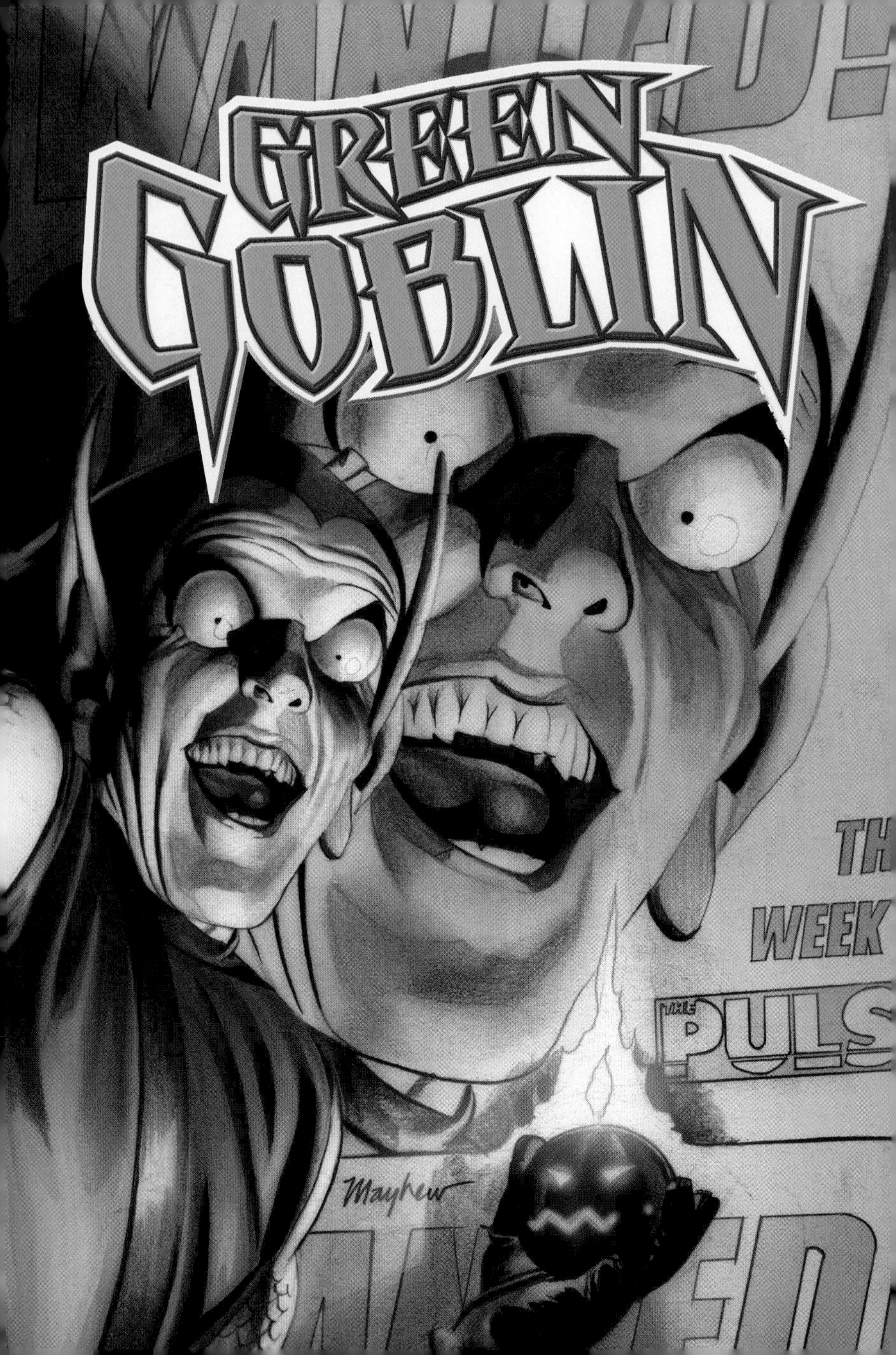
GREEN GOBLIN
TH
WEEK
THE PULS
Mayhew

POWERS

Super-human strength, speed, reflexes, stamina, durability, and a regenerative healing factor.

The original Green Goblin was the alter ego of millionaire industrialist, Norman Osborn. Osborn founded a major technology firm with Dr. Mendell Stromm. Seeking total control of the company, Osborn framed Stromm for embezzlement. During a search of the scientist's papers, Osborn discovered the notes for an experimental super-strength intelligence-enhancing formula. When Osborn mixed up the formula, it turned green and exploded in his face. The exposure to the liquid transformed Osborn, making him super strong, super intelligent, and quite insane.

Osborn donned a bizarre goblin costume and named himself the Green Goblin. Deciding that he was going to take over the organized crime in Manhattan, he reasoned that the best way to prove he deserved the job was by defeating Spider-Man. Osborn built the Goblin glider, a bunch of hand-grenades in the shape of pumpkins, razor-sharp Razor-bats, and gloves that shot energy blasts from their fingers. With these weapons, he set out to eliminate Spider-Man.

After losing several battles to Spider-Man, Osborn came up with a gas that suppressed the web-crawler's spider sense. Trailing him without his being aware, the Goblin discovered that Spider-Man was actually Peter Parker. Osborn took Parker prisoner and revealed his own identity and plans to take control of the New York

GREEN GOBLIN

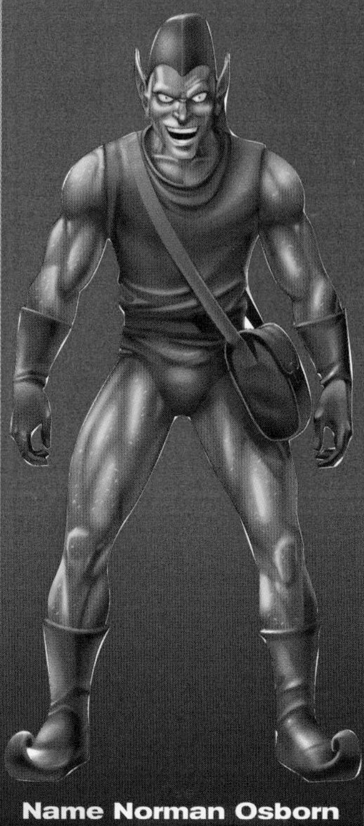

Name Norman Osborn

Alias Green Goblin

Group Affiliation Order of the Goblin (leader), formerly the Cabal of Scrier (leader), Sinister Twelve, Hellfire Club

Height 5' 11"

Weight 185 lbs

Eyes Blue

Hair Reddish-brown

underworld. Peter escaped and when the two fought he defeated the Goblin. Osborn lost his memory, and with his costume and laboratory destroyed, the Green Goblin was no more.

From time to time, Osborn's memory manifested itself again, and the Goblin was resurrected. But each time, Spider-Man managed to defeat the Goblin and Osborn returned to sanity. In the meantime, Peter became close friends with Harry Osborn, Norman Osborn's son. Through that friendship Norman Osborn learned that Peter loved Gwen Stacy, with whom he had once had an affair and fathered twins. Reverting to the Green Goblin one more time, Osborn took Gwen captive, and before Spider-Man could stop him, threw her off the Brooklyn Bridge, killing her.

Spider-Man and the Goblin fought in a battle to the death. Osborn tried to stab Spider-Man with the tip of his Goblin Glider but instead impaled himself. Harry Osborn had watched the entire fight and blamed Spider-Man for the death of his father. Before the police came to remove the body, Harry took off the Goblin suit from his dad so no one would know he was the infamous criminal. Harry didn't know that his father wasn't dead, only wounded, owing to the power of the Goblin serum in his

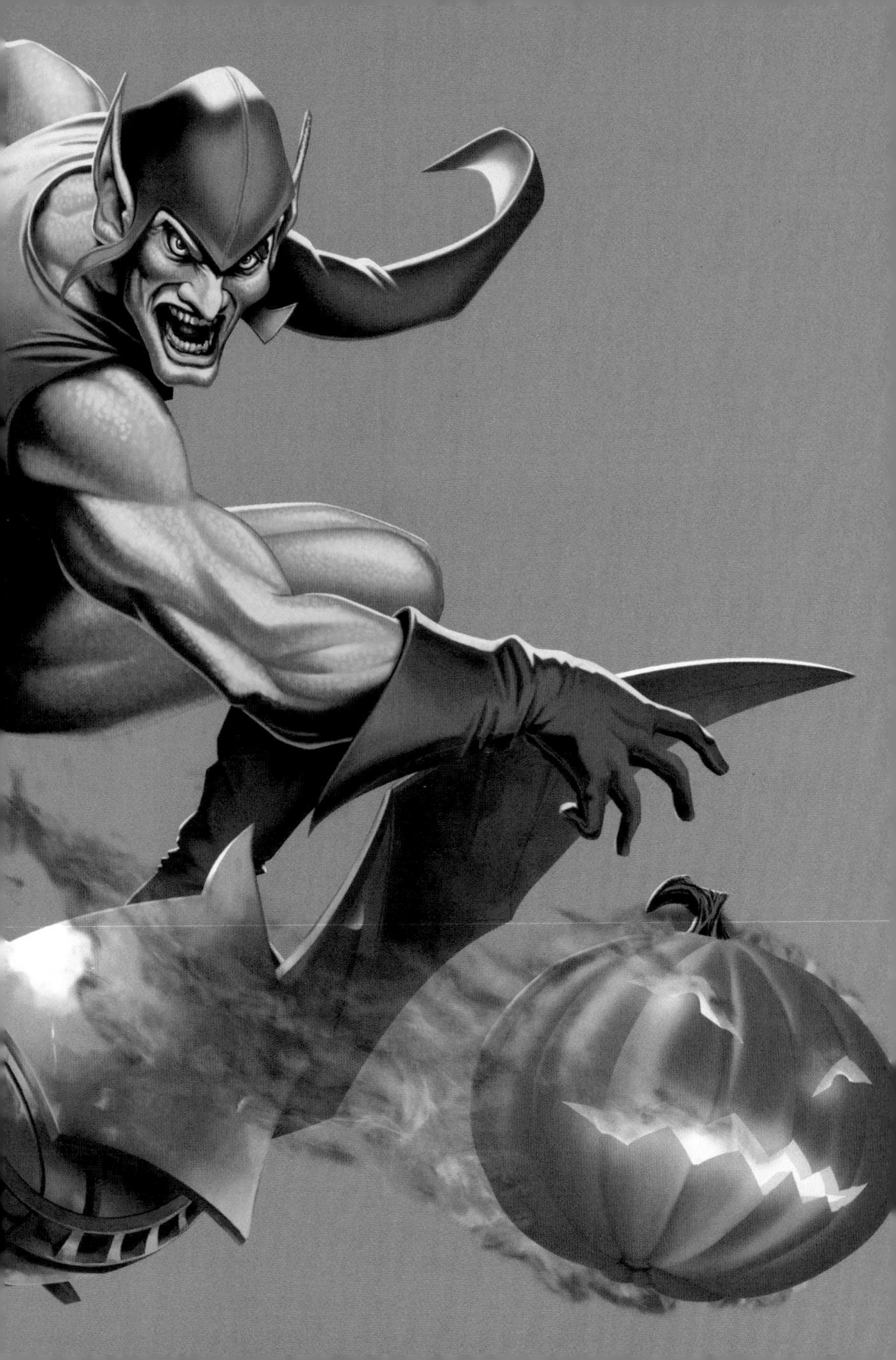

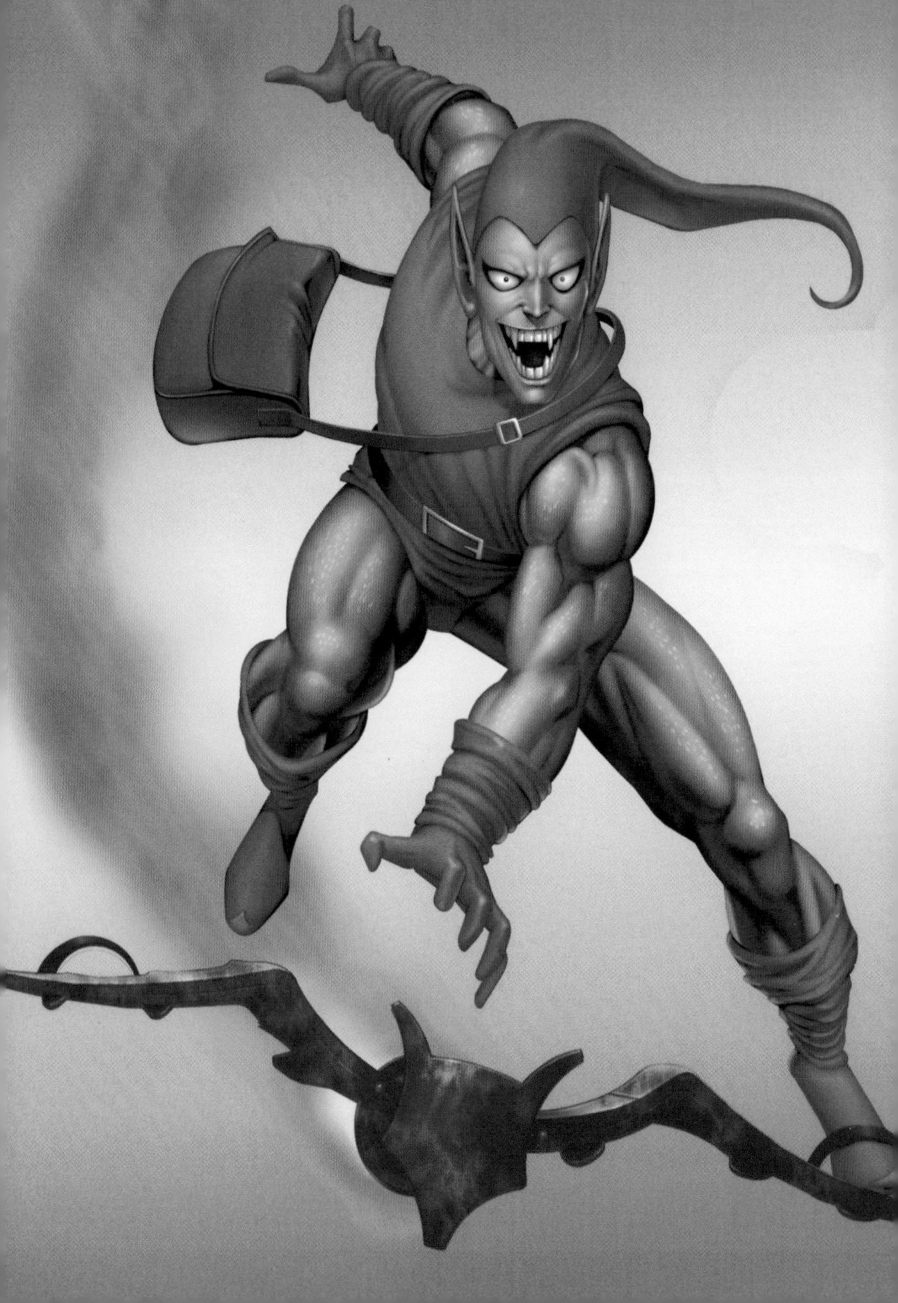

veins. At the morgue, Norman Osborn substituted another corpse for himself, and then fled to Europe to live in secrecy for years while plotting his revenge.

Harry Osborn, in an effort to avenge his "dead" father, became the Green Goblin, although the Goblin serum eventually killed him. Dr. Barton Hamilton, who was Harry's psychiatrist, tried to become the Green Goblin but failed and died. Roderick Kingsley, another millionaire, found a cache of Norman Osborn's Goblin equipment and became the Hob-goblin, an underworld crime lord.

Years later, Norman Osborn resurfaced and used a genetic construct of the Green Goblin to convince the public he was no longer a fearsome criminal. When the simulacra quickly self-destructed, Osborn realized he had to come up with another plan to get his revenge on Parker. His new scheme was to make Peter his heir and force him to become the Green Goblin. This bizarre plot involved brainwashing Peter and killing many of Peter's long time friends. The plan didn't succeed, but Spider-Man declared a truce between himself and Osborn.

When the Goblin murdered one of the reporters for the *Daily Bugle*, an investigation revealed to the nation that Norman Osborn was the Green Goblin. After a major battle in Manhattan between the Goblin, Luke Cage, and Spider-Man, the Goblin was captured and sent to prison.

Working from behind bars, Osborn put together a plan that forced Spider-Man to help him escape in return for the release of Aunt May, who had been abducted by the Scorpion. Osborn assembled the Sinister Twelve to destroy Spider-Man. They were defeated but the Green Goblin is still at large.

SECRETS

- Working in secret, Norman Osborn manipulated Empire State University professor Miles Warren in an attempt to convince Peter Parker that he was a clone.

- While hiding in Europe, Norman joined the secret Cabal of Scriers, moving up in the organization until he took it over.

- Harry Osborn bribed the coroner so that any autopsy of the body of his father would not show any trace of the "Green Goblin formula" in Norman's blood.

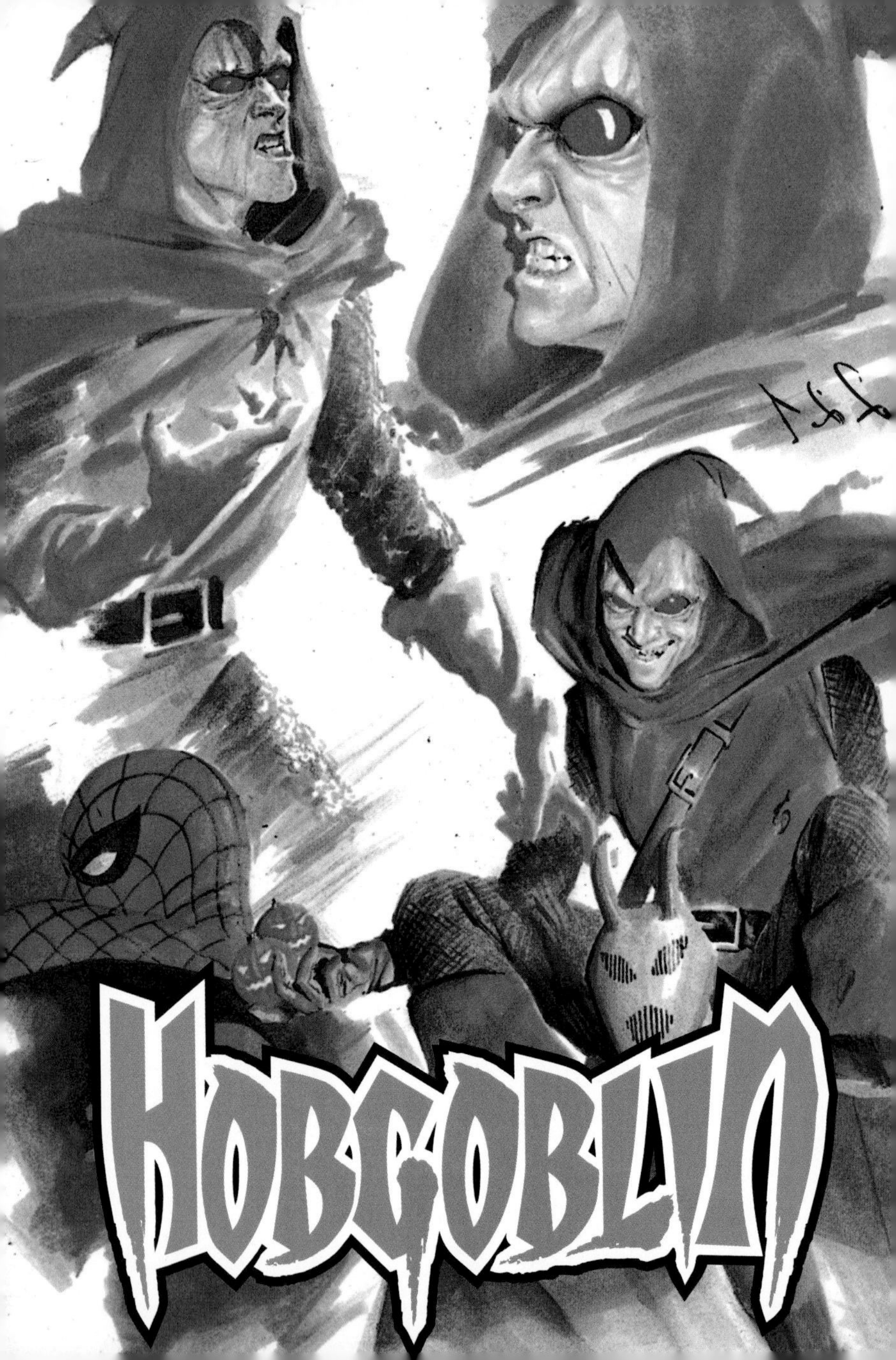
HOBGOBLIN

POWERS

As a result of taking an improved version of the Green Goblin formula, Hobgoblin (Roderick Kingsley) had super strength, super speed, incredible stamina, and enhanced reflexes. Because he had been in top physical condition for years before swallowing the potion, Kingsley was actually stronger than the original Goblin.

R oderick Kingsley was a millionaire fashion designer who had become wealthy through deceptive business practices. Mary Jane Watson was one of his employees. Anxious to avoid humdrum business affairs, Roderick had his identical twin brother go to work in his place. George Hill, a criminal associate of Kingsley's, discovered the secret lair of Norman Osborn, the Green Goblin, who supposedly had died some years before. He told Roderick of his discovery, hoping for a reward. Kingsley killed Hill to keep the discovery secret.

After studying the Goblin lair and learning all of the secrets of the Green Goblin, Kingsley decided to use the discovery to further his career. Using Osborn's equipment and files, Kingsley became the Hobgoblin. With the information in Osborn's files, he started blackmailing important people. He also tried to buy Osborn's company and merge it with his own business. Inevitably, he came into conflict with Spider-Man. Realizing that the one advantage Spider-Man had over Hobgoblin was his super-powers, Kingsley sought to duplicate Osborn's goblin formula, but with no success.

Kingsley finally managed to re-create the formula, but remembering that it had driven

Name
Roderick Kingsley

Height 5' 11"

Weight 185 lbs.

Eyes Blue

Hair Gray

HOBGOBLIN

Osborn crazy, he used the mixture on Lefty Donovan, a minor crook working for him. Using a form of brainwashing, Kingsley forced Donovan to put on the Hobgoblin costume and fight Spider-Man. Kingsley watched from a distance, taking notes. When Spider-Man defeated Donovan, Kingsley killed the crook before he could reveal any secrets. Believing the formula a success, Kingsley then took it himself.

Despite his newfound super powers, Hobgoblin was still unable to beat Spider-Man. Worse, he had attracted the attention of the crime boss known as the Kingpin. Plus, he was being followed by *Daily Bugle* reporter, Ned Leeds, who had discovered his hideout. A master plotter, Kingsley believed that he could resolve both problems with a single solution.

Kingsley kidnapped Ned Leeds and brainwashed him into becoming the third Hobgoblin. Although Ned had no super powers, Kingsley made sure the reporter only appeared in situations where super powers wouldn't be needed. Using Ned, he worked with the Kingpin's son, Richard Fisk, on a plan to topple the crime boss. When that plan failed, Kingsley tried to frame Flash Thompson as Hobgoblin. That scheme failed due to the intervention of mercenary Jason Philip Macendale, who was trying to find the secret of the original Green Goblin formula.

Macendale hired the super villain assassin the Foreigner to kill the Hobgoblin. When the Foreigner killed Ned Leeds everyone, including Spider-Man, believed Hobgoblin was dead. Feeling safe and secure, Roderick Kingsley retired to Europe.

Jason Macendale then took up Hobgoblin's identity. Concerned that authorities might discover his identity through Macendale, Kingsley returned to New York to deal with the impostor. Kingsley killed Macendale while he was in police custody and resumed the identity of the Hobgoblin. Still anxious to defeat Spider-Man, Kingsley kidnapped Betty Brant and tried to use her as bait for a trap. The trap failed, Kingsley was captured and unmasked, and Ned Leeds's name was cleared.

When Norman Osborn returned to America, denying he had ever been the Green Goblin, Kingsley sought to use his information about the Green Goblin to make a deal for his release from prison. Claiming he owned secret diaries written by Osborn, Kingsley offered the information to the DA in return for his freedom. Kingsley gambled on the fact that Osborn couldn't run the risk of being exposed. Soon afterwards, the Green Goblin broke him out of prison. In a complex game of deception, Spider-Man and Kingsley's twin brother, Daniel, were taken prisoner, after which Osborn revealed that he knew all along that Roderick had been lying. He had broken Hobgoblin out of jail just to let him know that he had secretly bought out Kingsley's corporation. In a rage, Hobgoblin attacked the Green Goblin. A huge fire erupted, and everyone, including Spider-Man and Daniel Kingsley, escaped. Roderick Kingsley escaped, too, retrieving several million dollars he had stashed away in foreign accounts and moving to a small island in the Caribbean.

SECRETS

- Roderick Kingsley became a master of hypnosis and mind control with the help of hallucinogenic drugs.

- Jason Philip Macendale was originally known as the costumed villain, Jack O'Lantern.

- Roderick Kingsley's first crime as Hobgoblin was to blackmail various members of his own country club.

HOBGOBLIN 117

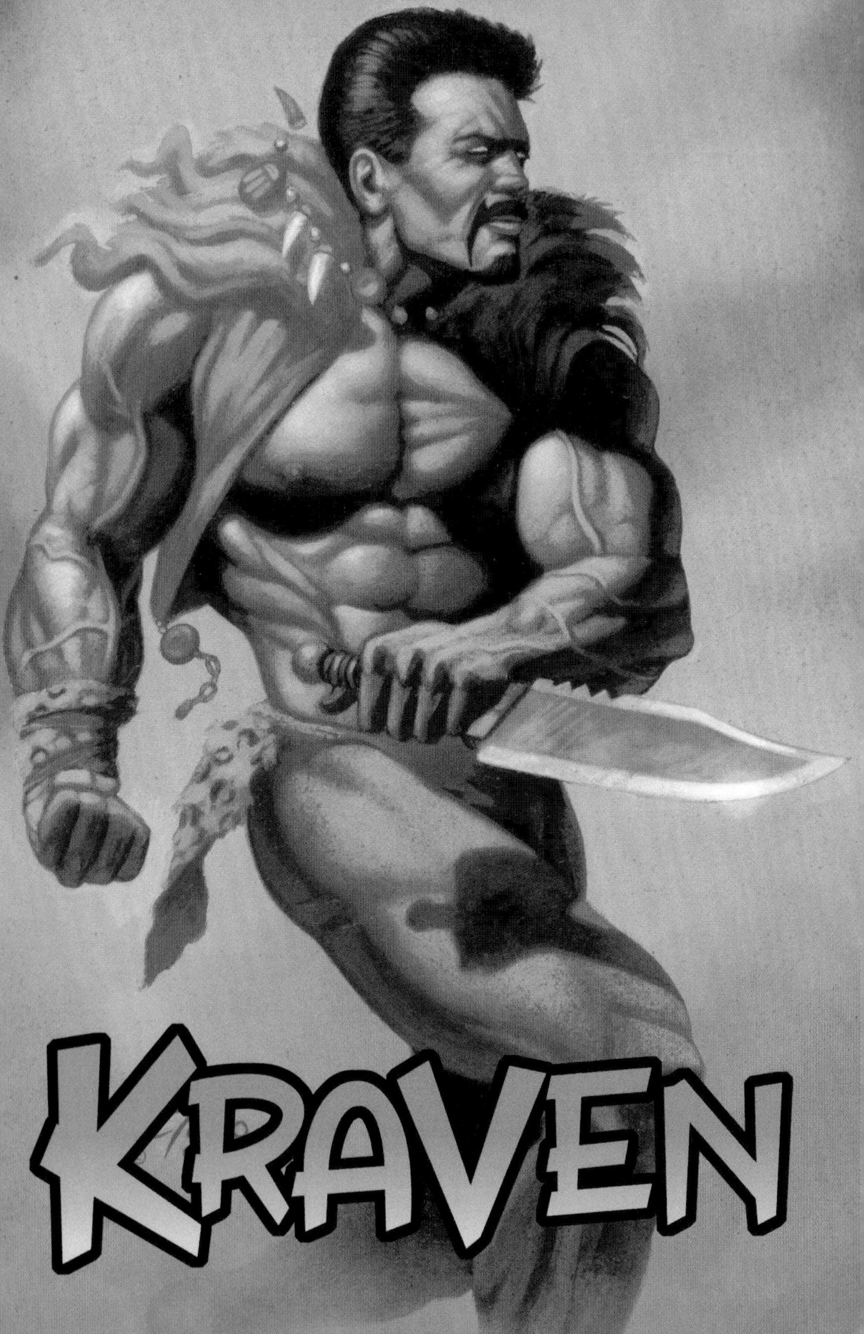
KRAVEN

POWERS

By ingesting certain mystical potions Kraven developed superhuman strength that made it possible for him to lift several tons in the air. He also developed super human speed, and running up to sixty miles an hour for short distances. These potions also slowed his aging process. At the time of his death he was over 70 years old, but appeared to be in his prime. His agility, reflexes, stamina, and endurance were also enhanced. Kraven constantly used these potions to maintain his superhuman physique. Even without their help, he was in top physical condition.

Sergei Kravinoff was one of the last aristocrats before the Russian Revolution of 1917. Anxious to prove his innate worth and nobility, he became the world's greatest big game hunter. Like many great hunters, he sought increasingly more challenging prey, and decided to hunt the only animal that could match his intellect: a human. As his ultimate prey, Kraven chose Spider-Man.

Kraven was a brilliant hunter and tracker, as well as an expert fighter and a master of nearly all types of weapons. As a big game hunter, he knew all the secrets of wild animals. Combining brains and brawn, he was one of Spider-Man's most dangerous opponents.

After being defeated a number of times by Spider-Man, Kraven gave up the hunt. However, his girlfriend, Calypso, fooled him into thinking that Spider-Man had freed his caged animals and goaded Kraven into resuming his battles with the

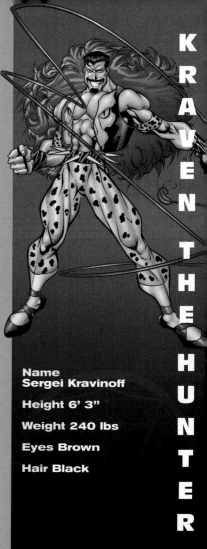

**K
R
A
V
E
N

T
H
E

H
U
N
T
E
R**

Name
Sergei Kravinoff

Height 6' 3"

Weight 240 lbs

Eyes Brown

Hair Black

web-slinger. When Calypso drugged Spider-Man with a hallucinogenic dart, Kraven refused to fight him, believing it would not be honorable.

In his final hunt, Kraven shot Spider-Man and buried him. He then put on Spider-Man's black costume and tried to prove that he could be as great a hero as Spider-Man. In the guise of Spider-Man, Kraven defeated the genetically altered being known as Vermin, who Spider-Man had only been able to stop with the help of Captain America.

Spider-Man, who had only been shot with a tranquilizer dart, dug himself out of his grave and pursued Kraven, but the hunter refused to fight. He felt he had nothing more to prove, and that he had regained his honor. Kraven released Vermin, and while Spider-Man fought the monster, Kraven took his own life.

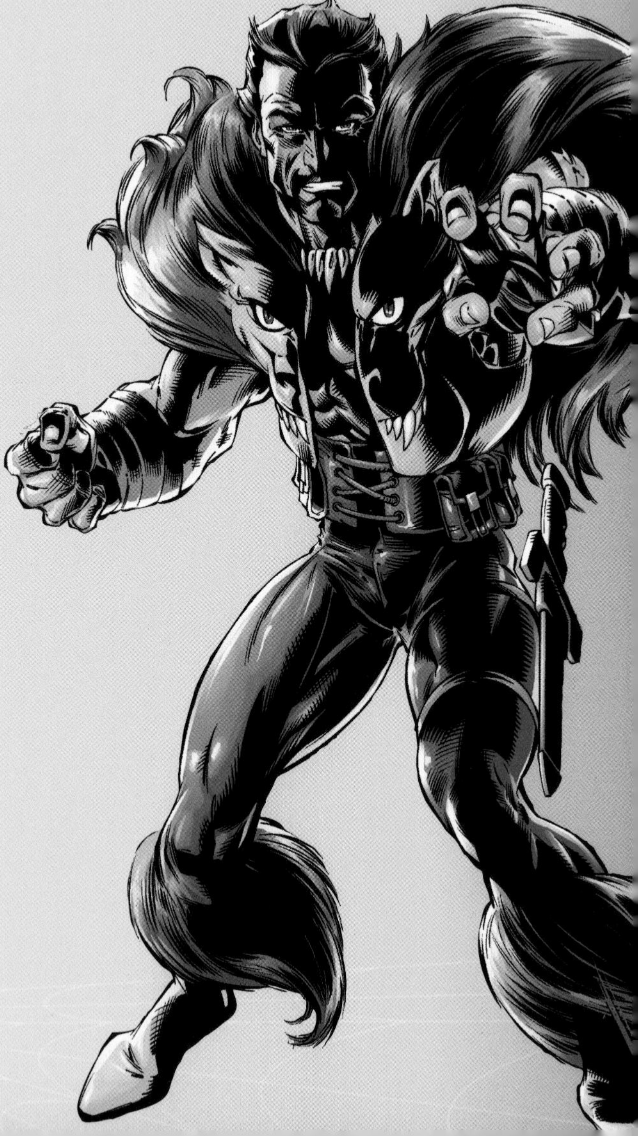

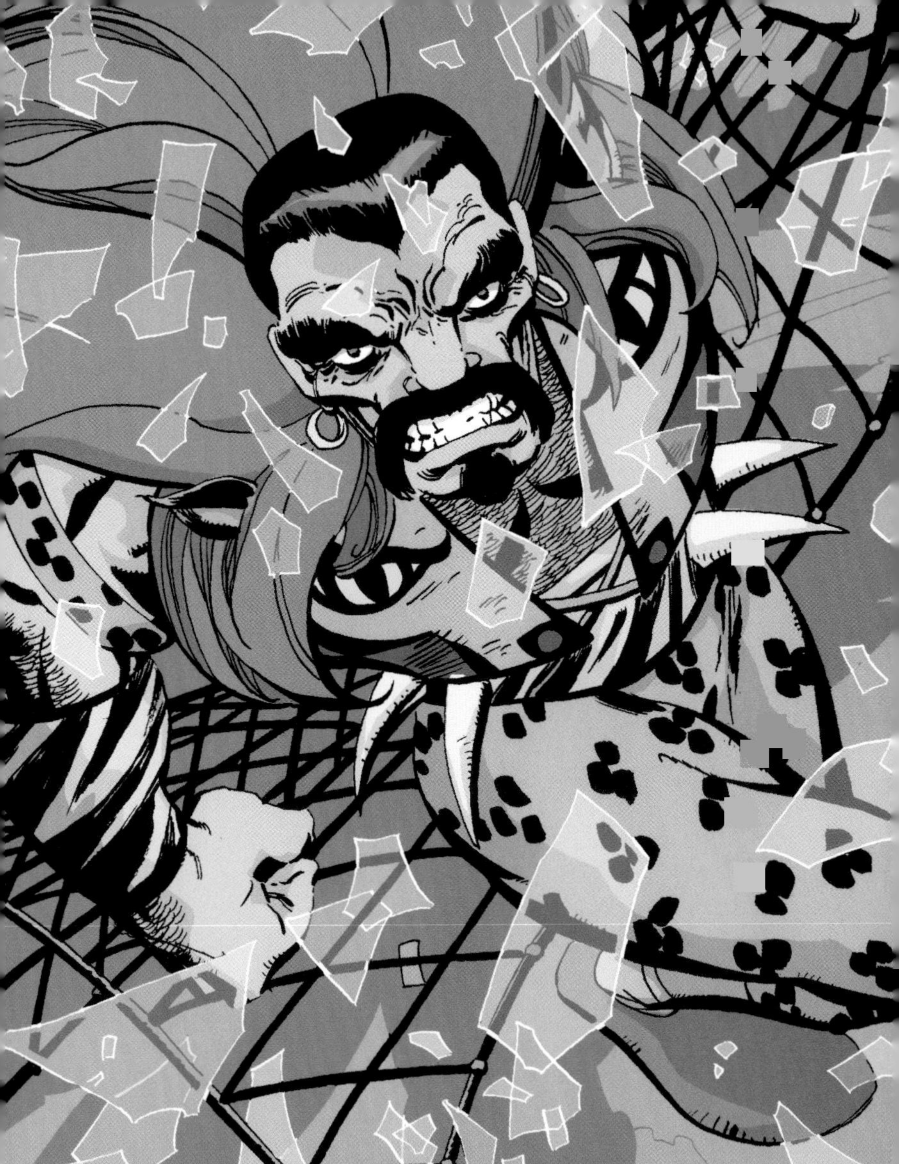

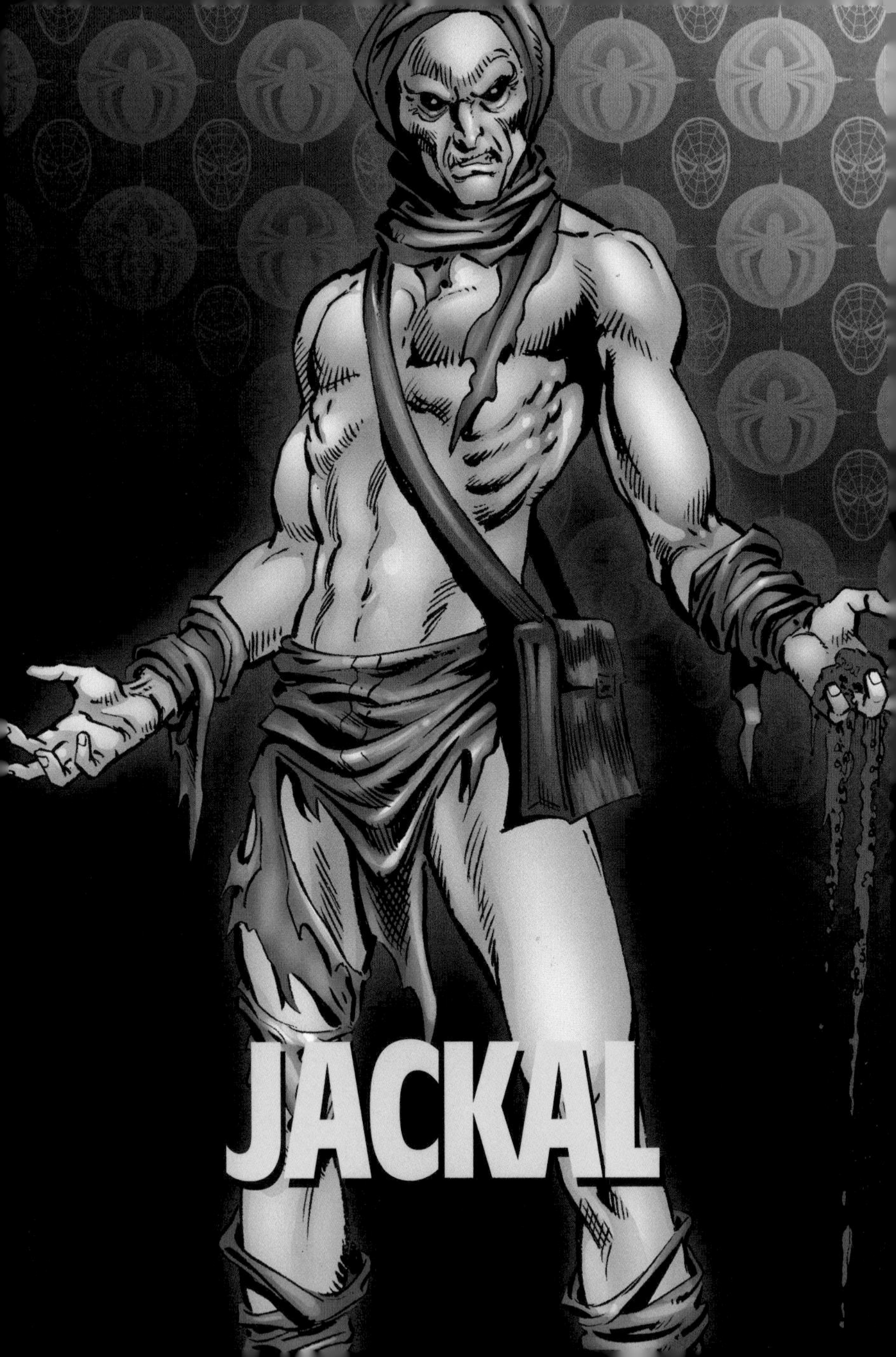

JACKAL

POWERS

After his regeneration, Miles Warren had the strength, speed, and agility of a jackal, but increased to super human levels.

Miles Warren was once a professor of biochemistry at Empire State University. Before that, he studied genetics with the being known as the High Evolutionary, but was dismissed for being unstable. At ESU, Warren fell in love with one of his students, Gwen Stacy. When Gwen was killed by the Green Goblin, Warren came up with the idea of cloning humans. Warren's lab partner Anthony Serba rejected the idea, so Warren killed him. The murder drove Warren insane and he developed an alternate personality, the Jackal, whom he blamed for the crime.

Working with a Scrier, a member of a secret order controlled by the Green Goblin, Jackal tried to grow clones of Gwen Stacy and Peter Parker. His early attempts proved unsuccessful but after much hard work he managed to create duplicates of both. In a battle with Spider-Man, Jackal was seemingly killed as was the Parker clone.

Years later, Spider-Man learned that both Jackal and the Parker clone had survived. The Parker clone, using the name Ben Reilly, had been wandering across the country. When he read that Aunt May was dying, he returned to Manhattan, became close friends with Peter Parker, and took on the identity of the Scarlet Spider. It was then that Jackal returned from suspended animation and claimed that Peter was the clone and Ben the real person. This subterfuge was all a plot by Norman Osborn to

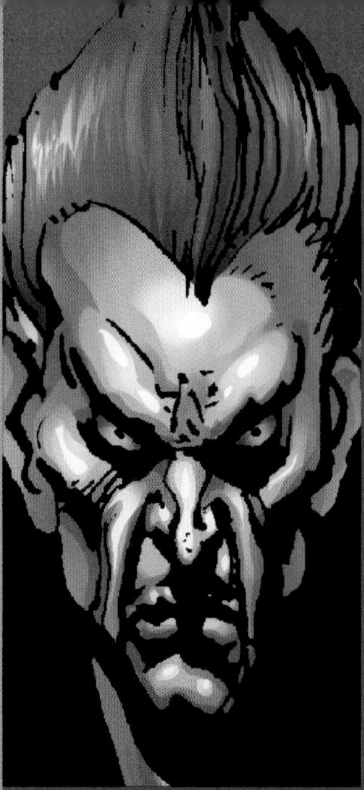

JACKAL

Name
Dr. Miles Warren

Height 5' 10"

Weight 175 lbs.

Eyes Green

Hair Gray

put an end to Peter's career as Spider-Man. The truth finally came out when Ben died heroically saving Peter and then turned to dust, proving he was the clone.

Jackal came up with a plan to kill millions of people and replace them with clones he could control. He died before he could put his scheme into action, falling off a skyscraper trying to save the life of the Gwen Stacy clone.

SECRETS:

- Jackal was a genius in the field of genetics. His cloning technique was a hundred years ahead of modern science.

- Jackal once tried to manipulate the Punisher into killing Peter Parker.

- Warren genetically mutated his own body by mixing his DNA with that of a jackal.

124 JACKAL

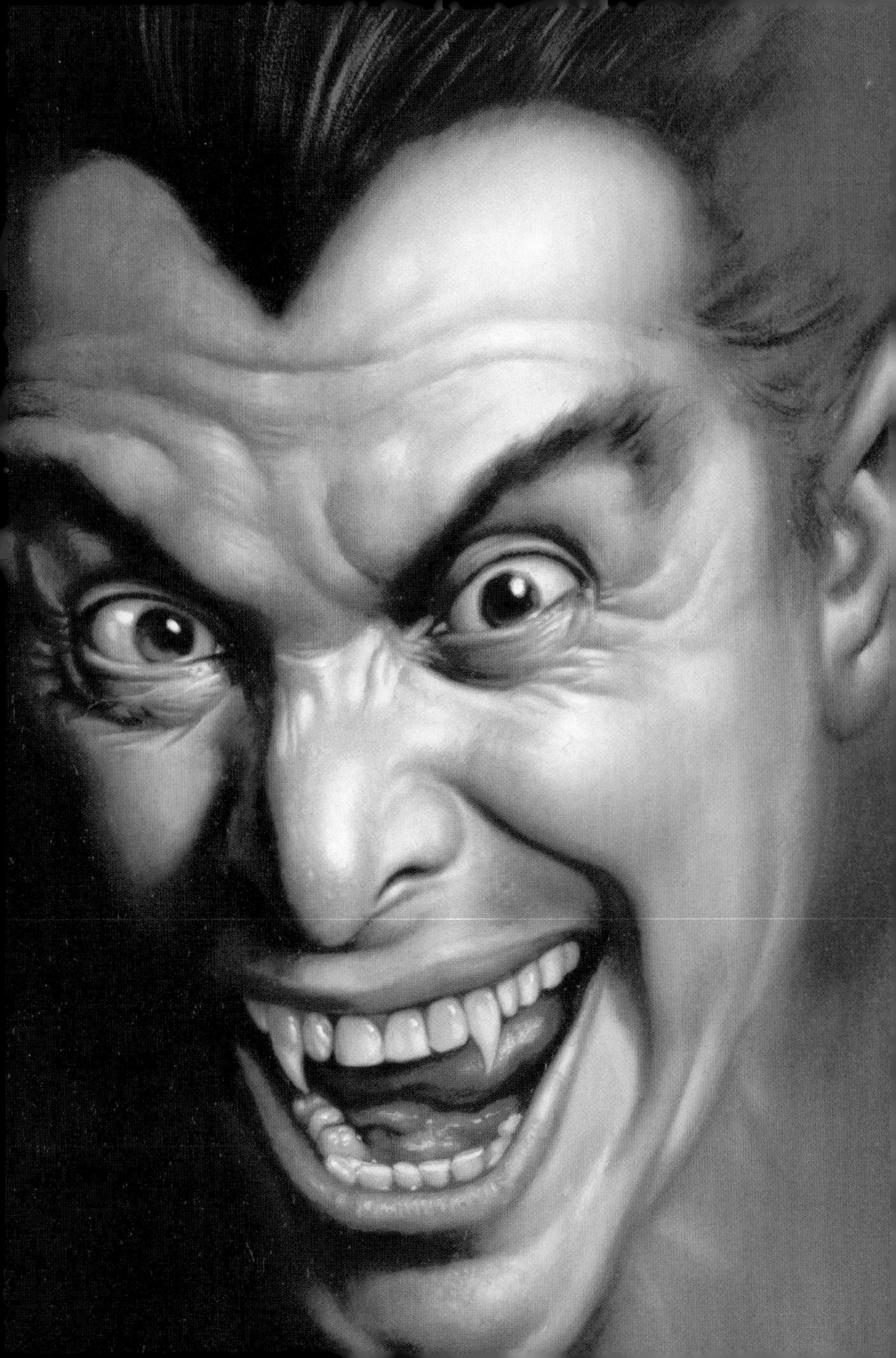

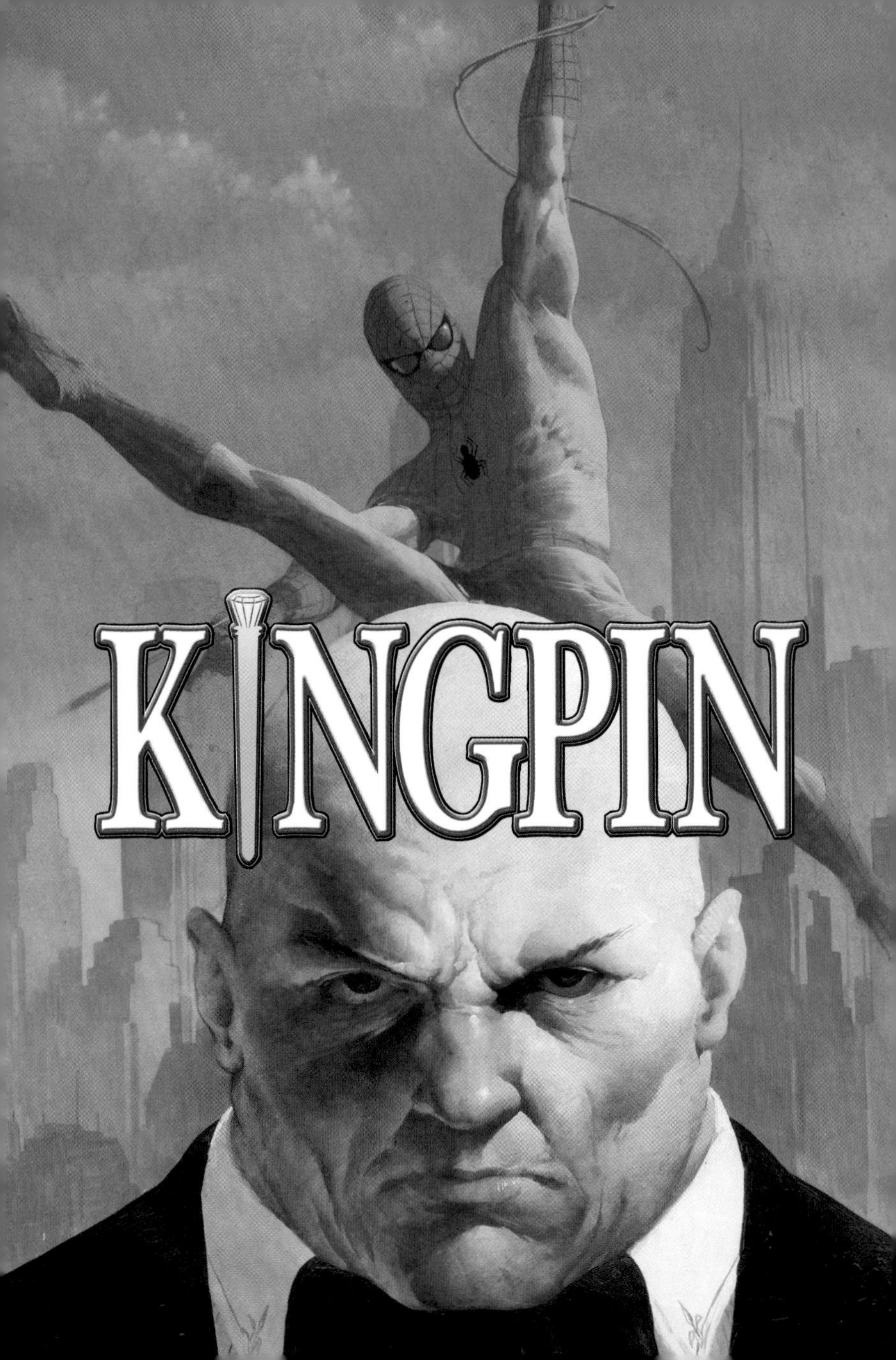
KINGPIN

As Kingpin, Wilson Grant Fisk is the cold-blooded leader of New York's criminal underworld. He maintains his image as a high-powered, legitimate businessman while engaging in numerous illegal activities including drug-running, murder, smuggling, and more. For many years, he had no criminal record.

Fisk weighs 450 pounds but that is all muscle. He is in top condition and a dangerous fighter. Wilson Fisk grew up in a poor neighborhood where he was taunted by the other children because of his huge size. Tired of being pushed around, Fisk built himself up into a powerhouse. Soon, he was the leader of his own gang. Mafia gang leader Don Rigoletto recognized Fisk's leadership skills and strength and hired the big man as his bodyguard. After a few years, Fisk killed the Don and took over his criminal empire.

Fisk was not viewed in a favorable light by other major New York crime organizations, especially the Maggia and HYDRA. The two cartels combined to eliminate his gang. Fisk retired to Japan, starting a spice business and biding his time. He eventually returned to New York and took control over all the city's criminal organizations.

Fisk married a woman named Vanessa and had a son named Richard. When Vanessa found out that Fisk was a crime lord, she threatened to leave him unless he gave up his empire. Fisk moved back to Japan, but gang wars in New York lured him out of retirement.

Richard, Fisk's son, initially disapproved of his father's criminal dealings and took on the identity of the Rose to destroy the

KINGPIN

Name Wilson Grant Fisk

Aliases The Brainwasher, Harold Howard

Group Affiliation Leader of a coalition of East Coast non-Maggia criminal organizations, former manager of Las Vegas HYDRA faction,

Height 6' 7"

Weight 450 lbs

Eyes Blue

Hair None

Powers None

Kingpin. However, Richard soon yielded to the temptation of crime. Combining forces with Fisk's second-in-command, Samuel Silke, Richard took over the Kingpin's empire. In a stunning betrayal, Vanessa killed Richard and fled the country, taking Fisk's remaining cash with her.

Recently, Fisk was captured by the FBI and put in prison. Though in jail for life, Fisk still schemes to break free and reassemble his criminal empire.

SECRETS

- Fisk wore a Kevlar bulletproof vest beneath his coat and carried a walking stick equipped with a laser.

- Richard Fisk never knew that his father was a crime lord until he was in college.

- During the course of his criminal career, Kingpin employed a number of deadly assassins including Elektra, Bullseye, Jack O'Lantern, and Typhoid Mary.

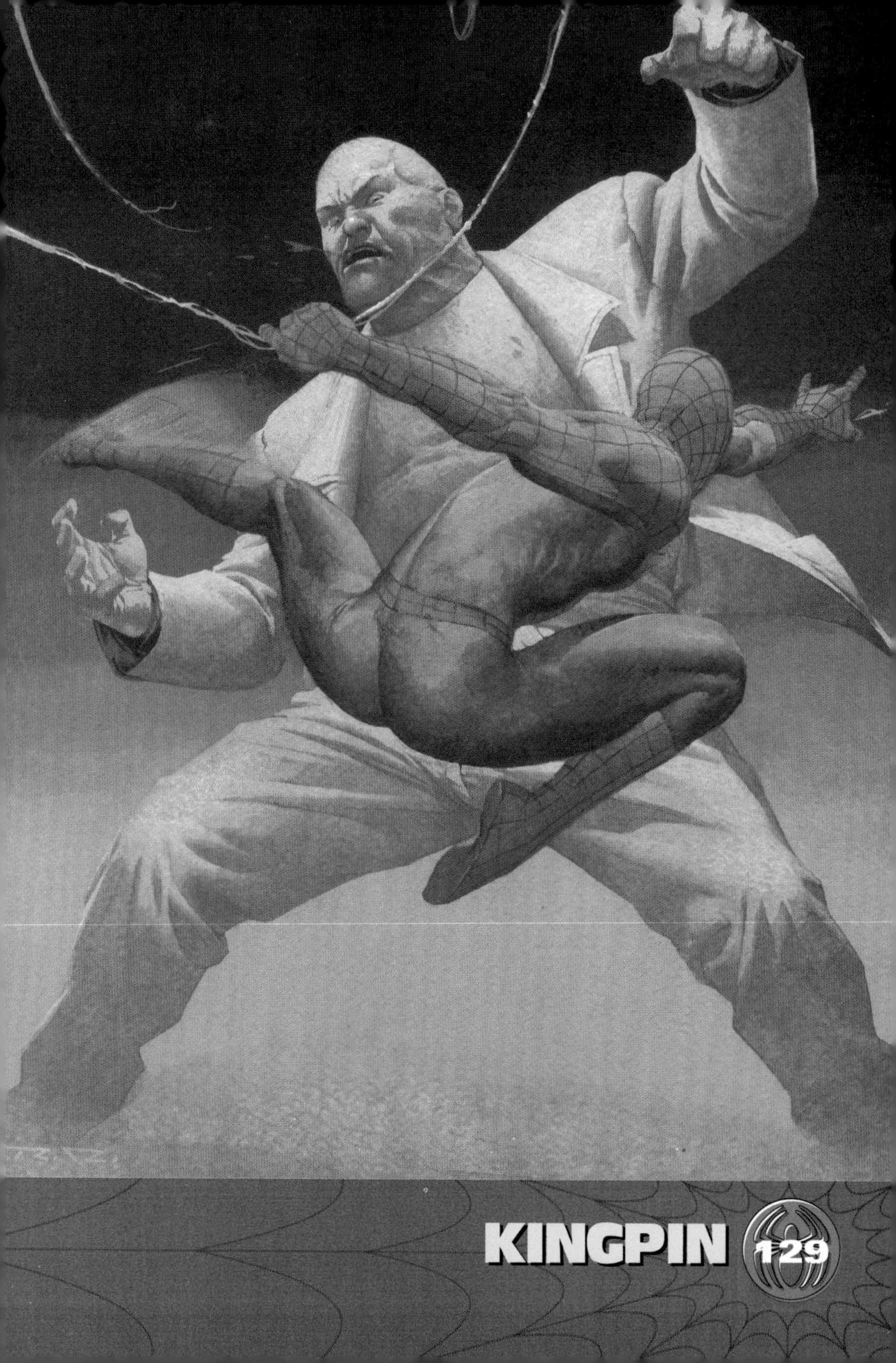

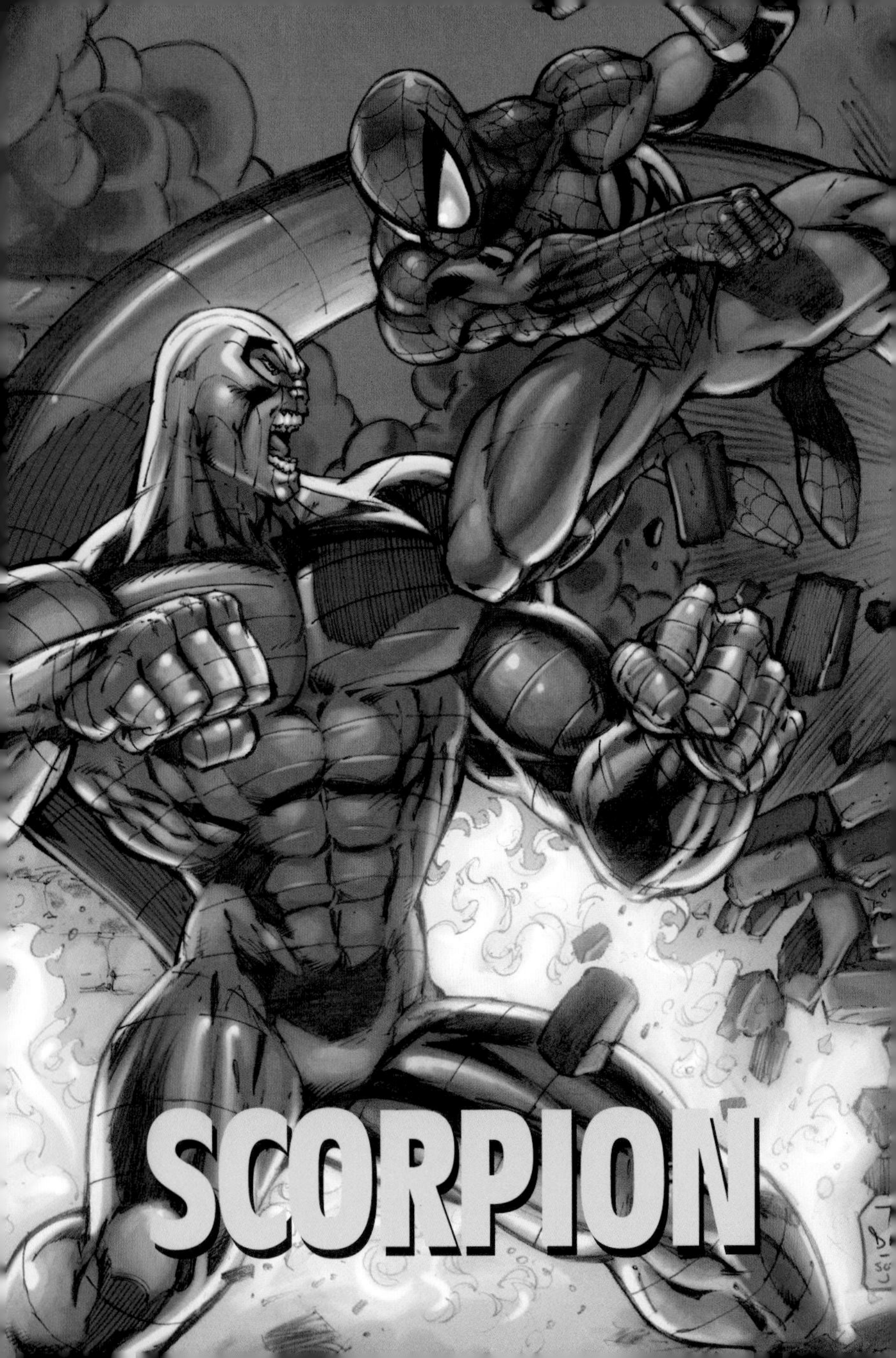
SCORPION

POWERS

As **Scorpion**:
enhanced strength and agility greater than Spider-Man's.

As **Venom:**
enhanced strength and agility, ability to cling to almost any surface, can block Spider-Man's Spider-Sense.

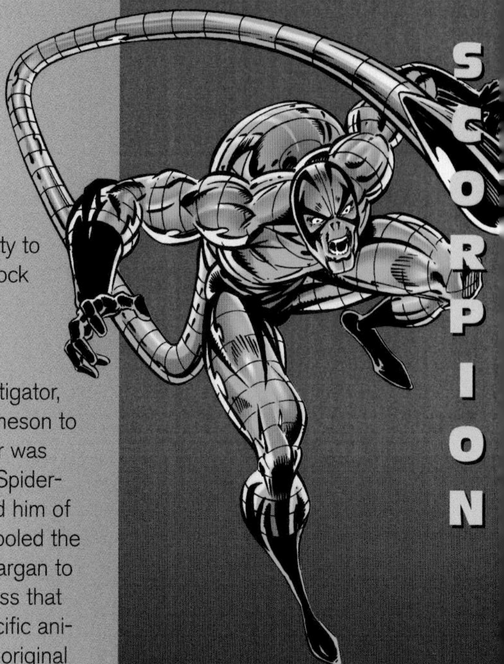
SCORPION

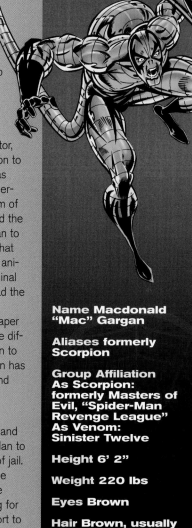

Mac Gargan, a private investigator, was hired by J. Jonah Jameson to discover how Peter Parker was able to get such good pictures of Spider-Man. Parker's spider-sense warned him of Gargan's schemes and he easily fooled the detective. Then Jameson asked Gargan to be the test subject of a new process that would give him the abilities of specific animals. A scorpion was used for the original process. The treatment worked, but had the side effect of driving Gargan insane. Gargan turned on JJJ, and the newspaper publisher suddenly found himself in the difficult position of rooting for Spider-Man to beat Scorpion. Over the years, Scorpion has battled Spider-Man numerous times and attacked Jameson as well.

Recently, while working for Norman Osborn, Gargan kidnapped Aunt May and used her as a pawn to force Spider-Man to break Osborn, the Green Goblin, out of jail. Shortly afterwards, Gargan became the new Venom, when he bonded with the Venom symbiote, which was searching for a super villain to merge with in an effort to destroy Spider-Man.

Name Macdonald "Mac" Gargan

Aliases formerly Scorpion

Group Affiliation
As Scorpion: formerly Masters of Evil, "Spider-Man Revenge League"
As Venom: Sinister Twelve

Height 6' 2"

Weight 220 lbs

Eyes Brown

Hair Brown, usually shaved

SECRETS

- Gargan was paid $10,000 by Jameson to be the first subject of the untested process that made him into Scorpion.
- As Scorpion, Gargan used his phony tail as a missile launcher.
- Norman Osborn revealed Spider-Man's true identity to Scorpion as part of his plot to escape from prison.

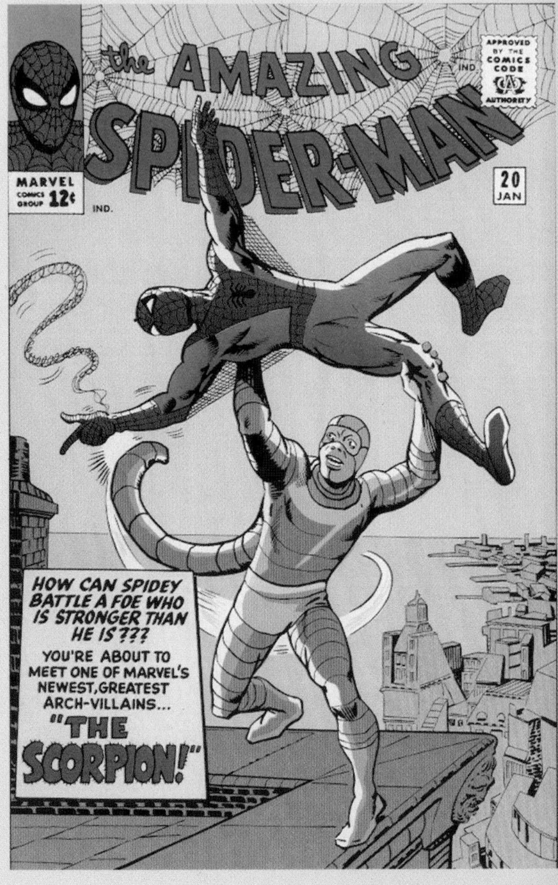

the AMAZING SPIDER-MAN
APPROVED BY THE COMICS CODE AUTHORITY
MARVEL COMICS GROUP 12¢
IND.
20 JAN
HOW CAN SPIDEY BATTLE A FOE WHO IS STRONGER THAN HE IS???
YOU'RE ABOUT TO MEET ONE OF MARVEL'S NEWEST, GREATEST ARCH-VILLAINS...
"THE SCORPION!"

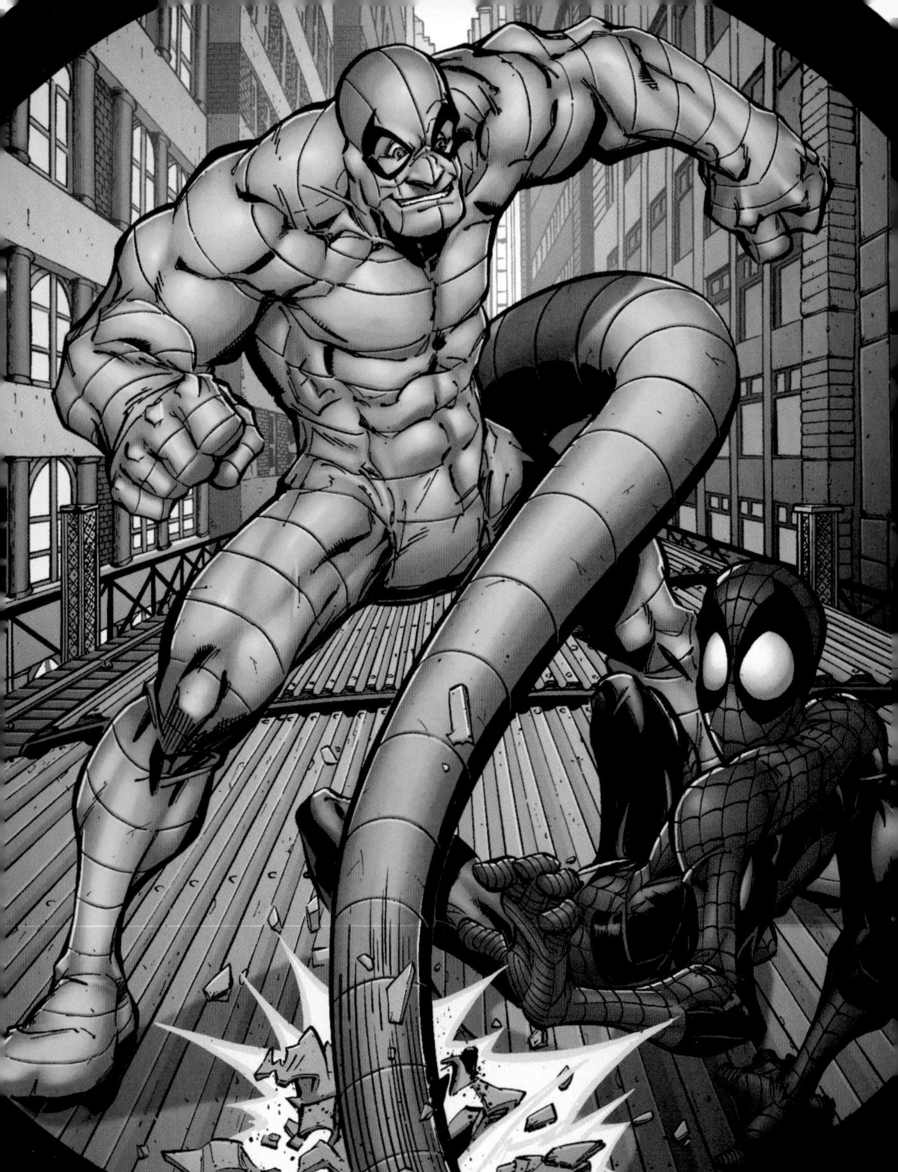

SCORPION

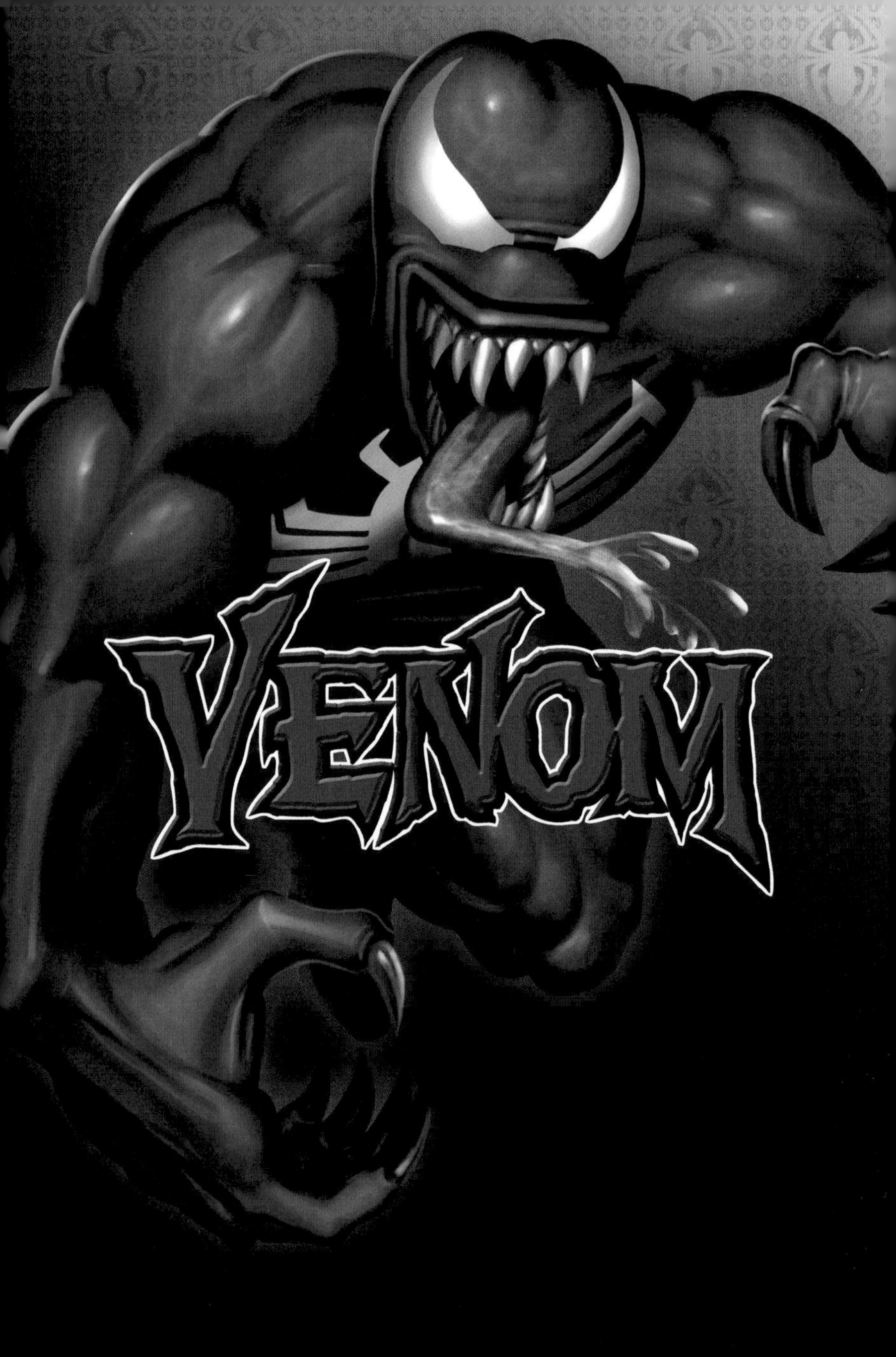
VENOM

POWERS

Venom (as Eddie Brock) has all of Spider-Man's powers and combines Spider-Man's strength with that of Brock's, making him stronger than the web-slinger. Wearing the alien costume also enables Brock to cling to walls and ceilings like Spider-Man. Venom can shoot webbing for a distance of 70 feet. This webbing is different than what Spider-Man uses, as it is actually part of the alien costume's substance and it dissolves after approximately 3 hours. The costume also endows Brock with a sixth-sense, much like Spider-Man's spider-sense. The alien can see danger approaching in any direction and warn Brock.

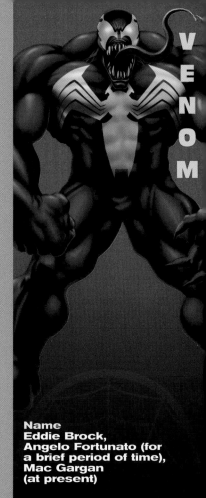

When Spider-Man returned from the Secret Wars on Battle World with a new and improved black costume, he had no idea he was actually clothed in an alien symbiote hoping to merge shapes with him. With the help of Reed Richards of the Fantastic Four, he learned that the symbiote was vulnerable to loud sound. Although enveloped by the black costume, Spider-Man was able to force it off his body by exposing it to the ringing church bells of Our Lady of Saints Church. The symbiote crawled off of Spider-Man's body and Peter Parker thought it was dead.

Not so. The creature slid down the walls of the church where it found Eddie Brock, a washed-up newspaperman, kneeling in prayer before the altar. Brock was dying of a rare form of cancer, which produced vast amounts of adrenaline, the symbiote's natural food. The alien was also attracted to

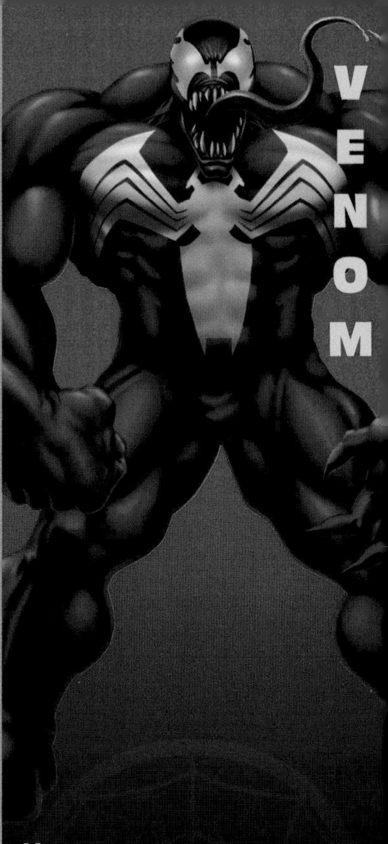

VENOM

Name
Eddie Brock, Angelo Fortunato (for a brief period of time), Mac Gargan (at present)

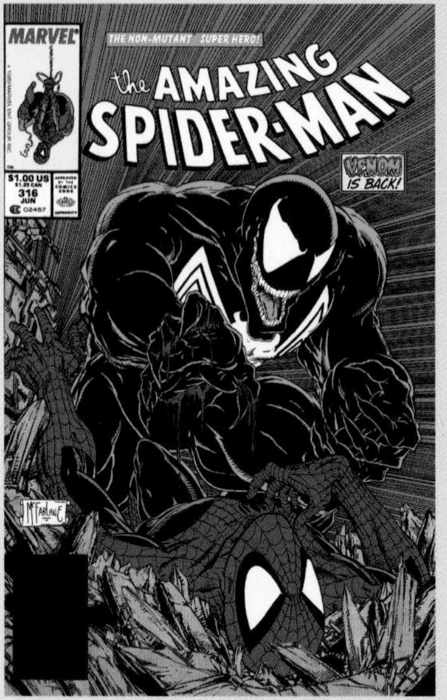
MARVEL
THE NON-MUTANT SUPER HERO!
the AMAZING SPIDER-MAN
VENOM IS BACK!
$1.00 US
316
JUN

Eddie because he was thinking about Spider-Man.

Months earlier, a killer called the Sin Eater had terrorized New York. Brock, a reporter for the *Daily Globe*, followed a shaky lead and wrote a series of columns identifying a man named Emil Gregg as the killer. When Spider-Man caught the real Sin Eater, Gregg was revealed to be a compulsive confessor to crimes and Eddie became the laughingstock of the newspaper world. Fired from the *Globe*, he was forced to make a living working for a scandal sheet, writing venomous stories about celebrities. Eddie was unable to admit that he had made a mistake by writing about Gregg, and he blamed Spider-Man for his problems. His discovery that he was dying of cancer only fueled his rage against Spider-Man.

When the alien symbiote bonded with Eddie Brock, it cured him of his cancer and turned him into a new and deadly being driven by an insane hatred of Spider-Man. Eddie named himself Venom, in reference to the tone of the articles he had written for the scandal sheets. Endowed with all of Spider-Man's powers, the symbiote was able to turned Eddie into a powerful duplicate of the web-slinger. The hybrid added a horrifying grin to its costume and began plotting revenge.

Because it retained many of Peter Parker's memories, Venom knew Spider-Man's secret identity. He was able to escape detection of Spider-Man's spider-sense and had the power to camouflage himself to blend in with a crowd. Venom delighted in tormenting Parker without revealing anything about himself. However, when the hybrid threatened Mary Jane at Peter's old apartment, Spider-Man quickly realized he was dealing with the alien costume on a new owner. Spider-Man tried to use a sonic blaster against Venom but because the alien costume had totally bonded with Eddie Brock, not even sound could separate them. Venom

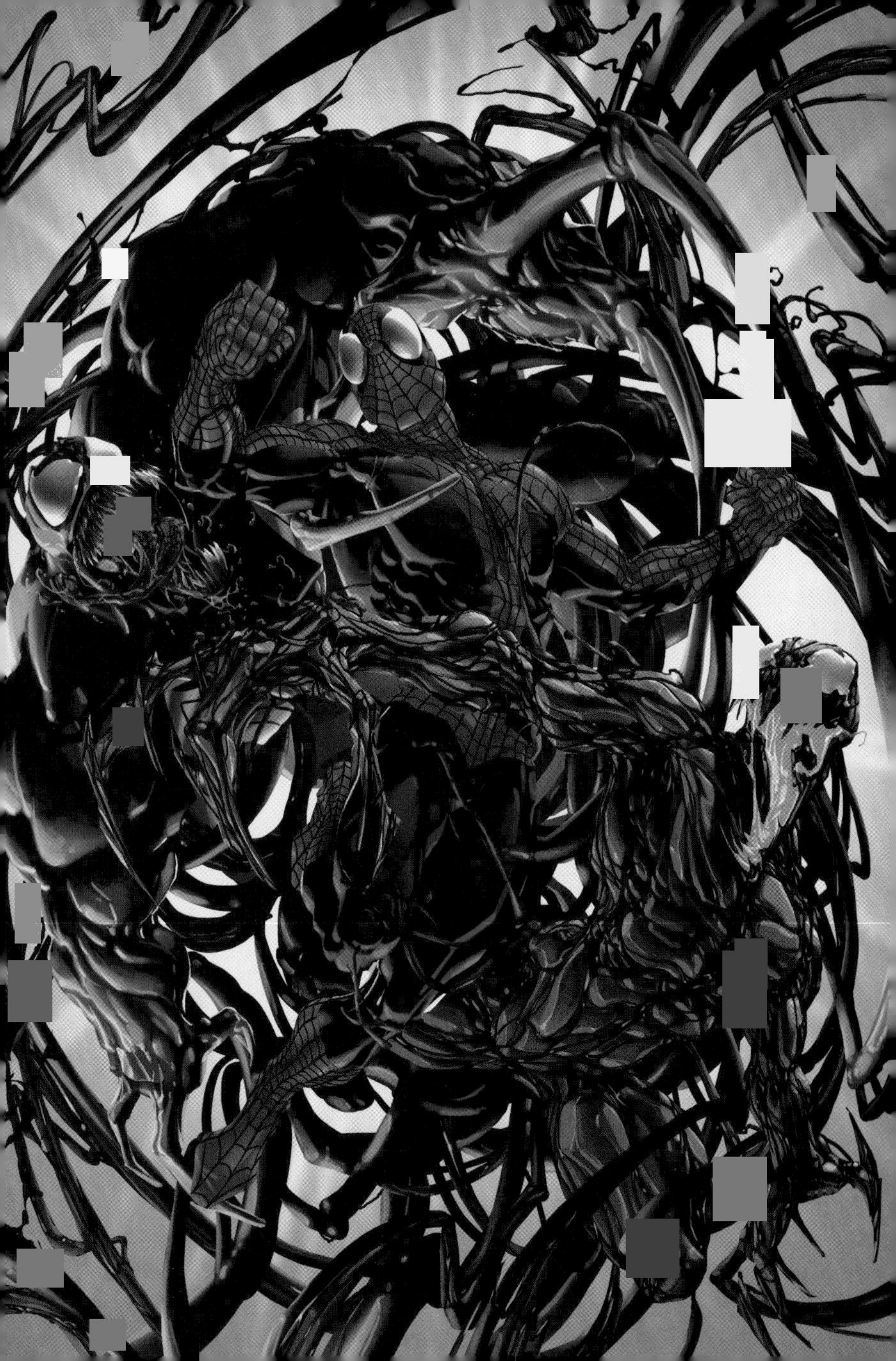

captured and almost killed Spider-Man. However, Peter knew that the hybrid used its own body as a source of webbing. By forcing Venom to use a huge volume of webbing in the being's efforts to capture Spider-Man, Parker exhausted Venom and took him prisoner. Venom was imprisoned in the government maximum-security prison in Colorado. The hybrid escaped once but was recaptured by Spider-Man, who again used his intellect to defeat Venom.

Eddie Brock was brought to trial with the alien symbiote in his body held in check by a chemical inhibitor. Then, Black Ops, a secret branch of the government, offered to let Venom go free if he worked as a counter-terrorist agent. Venom agreed, but because the government agents didn't trust him, they insisted that a remote-control bomb be put in his chest in case he had second thoughts.

After several missions, Venom tired of performing the government's dirty work. Operating on himself, he removed the bomb from his chest. Before Venom could expose the Black Ops operation, the agents dosed him with a massive amount of the chemical inhibitor, separating Brock and the symbiote and seemingly killing the alien.

The symbiote proved to be more difficult to kill than the Black Ops agents realized. It soon linked again with Eddie and Venom was reborn, although with much of his memory gone. Once again, Venom hated Spider-Man but it no longer knew the web-slinger's secret identity. For a short period of time, Venom joined a cabal of Spider-Man's enemies known as the Sinister Six but because he was not a team player he left the group.

When Brock's cancer flared up again, Eddie again turned to religion and broke the bond that existed between himself and the alien. Eddie offered up the alien symbiote to the highest bidder, with all proceeds to be donated to charity.

The winner of the auction was crime lord, Don Fortunato, who gave the costume to his son, Angelo. The Don hoped the symbiote would transform his son into a super criminal, but the alien proved unwilling to merge with a coward like Angelo.

Hunting for a new host that hated Spider-Man and who was not a coward, the symbiote chanced upon Mac Gargan, the villain known as the Scorpion. Gargan quickly agreed to bond with the symbiote and Venom was reborn, more powerful than ever before. The new hybrid soon joined the Sinister Twelve, a dozen of Spider-Man's worst enemies organized by the Green Goblin. They nearly succeed in killing Spider-Man, but the Fantastic Four and several members of the Avengers joined the fight and helped Spider-Man win the battle. The new Venom was sent to Ryker's Island, where he remains imprisoned, the alien part of his being controlled by chemicals. No one expects he will remain imprisoned for long.

SECRETS

- Venom always refers to himself as "we," making it clear he is the combination of two distinct personalities, the alien and whomever the symbiote has bonded with, in one merged body.

- Venom frightened Mary Jane so badly when she encountered him that she refused to let Peter ever wear a black costume again.

- Eddie Brock received ten million dollars for the alien symbiote.

- Eddie Brock is still alive and suffering from incurable cancer.

- When the symbiote determined the cowardly Angelo Fortunato was not a proper candidate to merge with, it freed itself from Angelo's body during a mid-air leap, leaving Angelo to fall to his death.

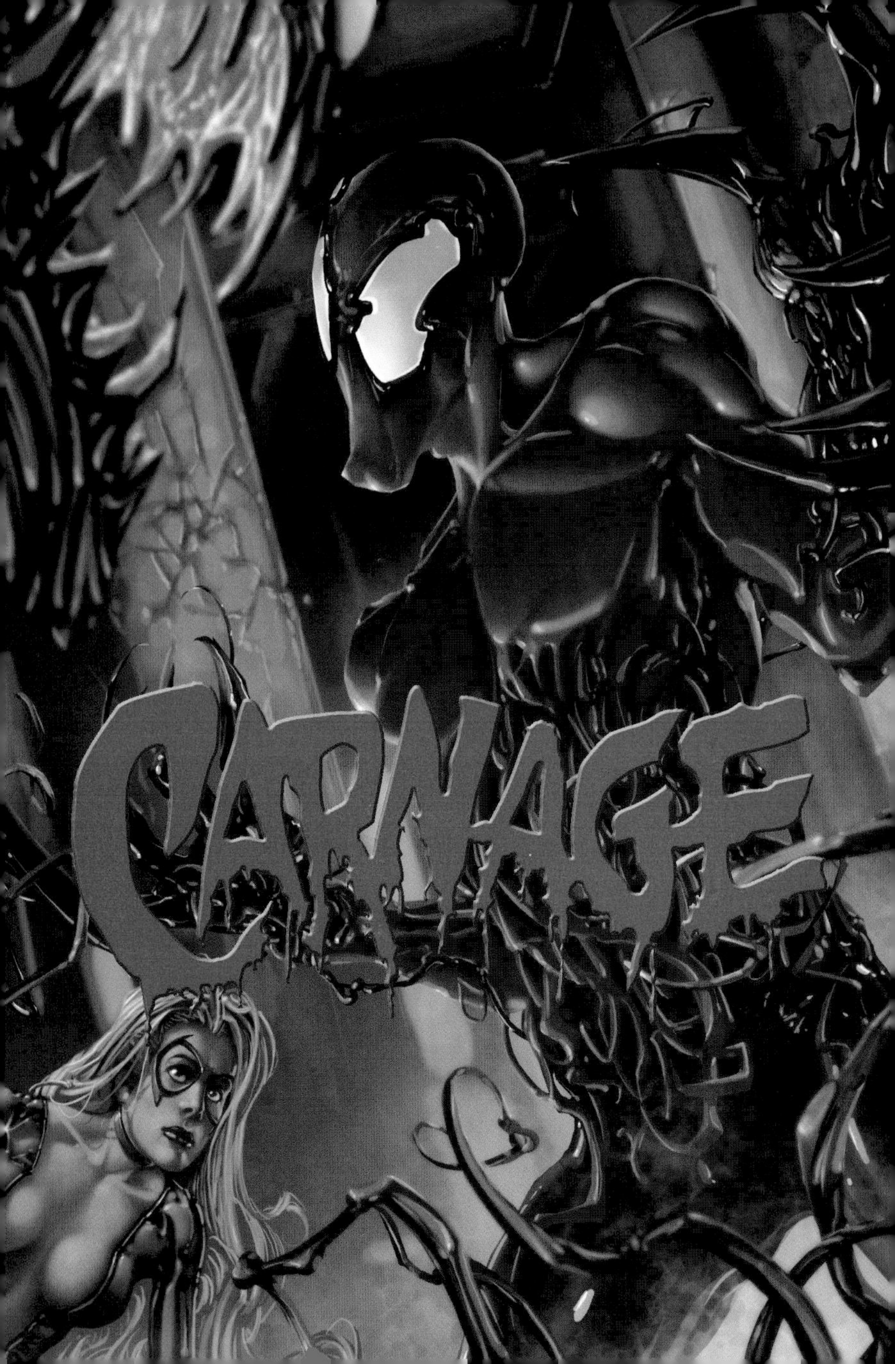
CARNAGE

POWERS

Carnage has powers similar to Venom's, and thus Spider-Man's: he can cling to walls, create tendrils to swing form place to place like webbing, and generate traps for his enemies. He is also capable of making detachable weapons from his skin, although they turn to dust in only a few seconds. The symbiote is impervious to normal gunfire. It is also able to mimic human clothing, but it does not possess Venom's camouflage ability. Carnage cannot be detected by Spider-Man's and Venom's spider sense. It is vulnerable to heat and sonic waves.

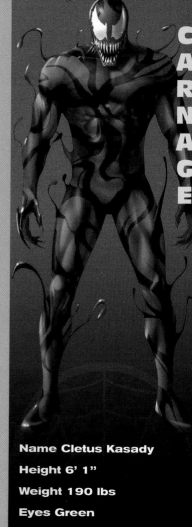

Cletus Kasady, a serial killer serving eleven life sentences, had Eddie Brock as a cellmate in prison at the time when Brock was separated from the Venom symbiote. One night, the symbiote returned and broke Eddie out of prison as Venom. But the symbiote didn't tell Eddie it was spawning, and that it left behind another symbiote that merged with Kasady. The serial killer and the symbiote became Carnage, a second-generation symbiote with much the same powers of Venom, but with the mind of an insane murderer in control.

The symbiote separated with Kasady several times, searching for a stronger host. It bounded for a short time with Ben Reilly, the Scarlet Spider, as well as with the Silver Surfer. But it always returned to Kasady. Even without the symbiote, Kasady continued to kill, covering himself with red paint to imitate Carnage.

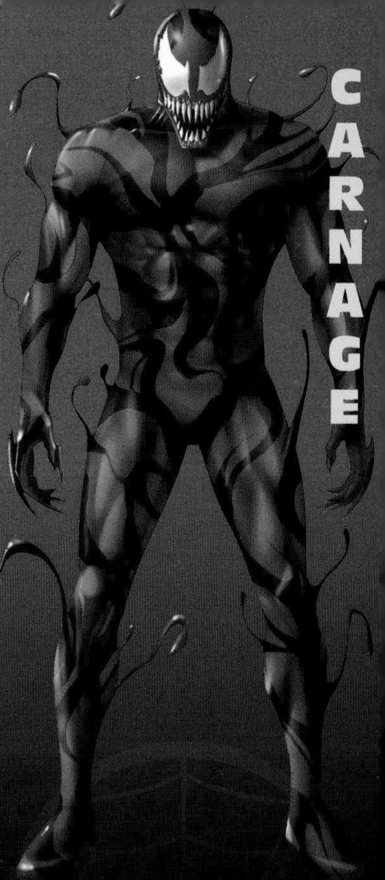
CARNAGE

Name Cletus Kasady

Height 6' 1"

Weight 190 lbs

Eyes Green

Hair Red

In the event called Maximum Carnage the being, along with a group of psychotic super villains, took control of Manhattan. They were defeated by Spider-Man, Venom, and a number of other super heroes.

Recently, when Electro freed a number of super villains from the prison known as the Raft, Carnage was one of the escapees. Caught by the being known as Sentry, he was dragged to outer space where the Sentry ripped him to pieces. Carnage has not been seen since.

SECRETS

- Cletus Kasady claimed to have killed his mother, his father, and even his grandmother, but no one knows the truth about his early life.

- Carnage is stronger than Spider-Man and Venom combined; he is able to lift objects weighing more than 50 tons.

- Kasady is a deadly hand-to-hand combat fighter and, when combined with the alien symbiote, is one of the most lethal of all of Spider-Man's enemies.

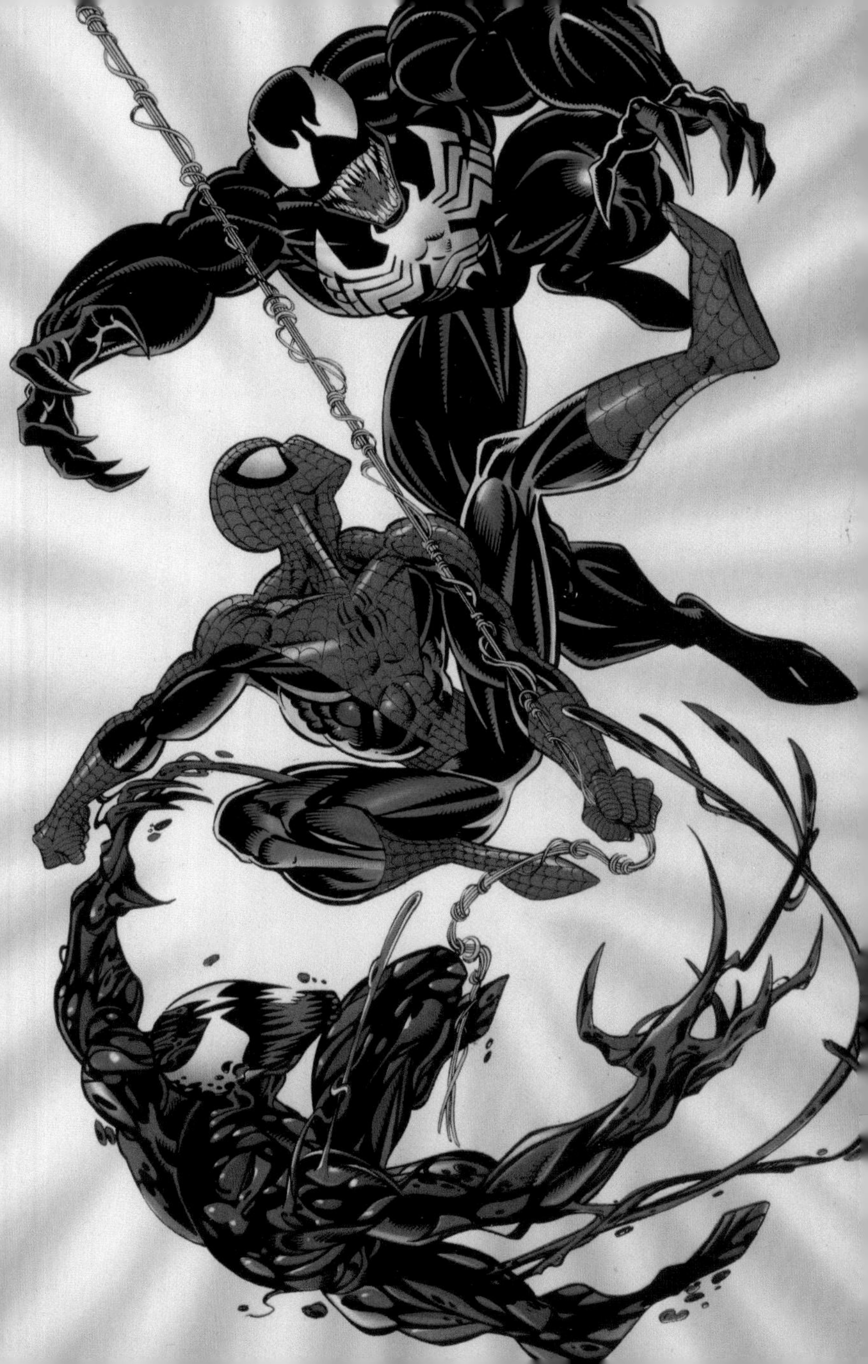

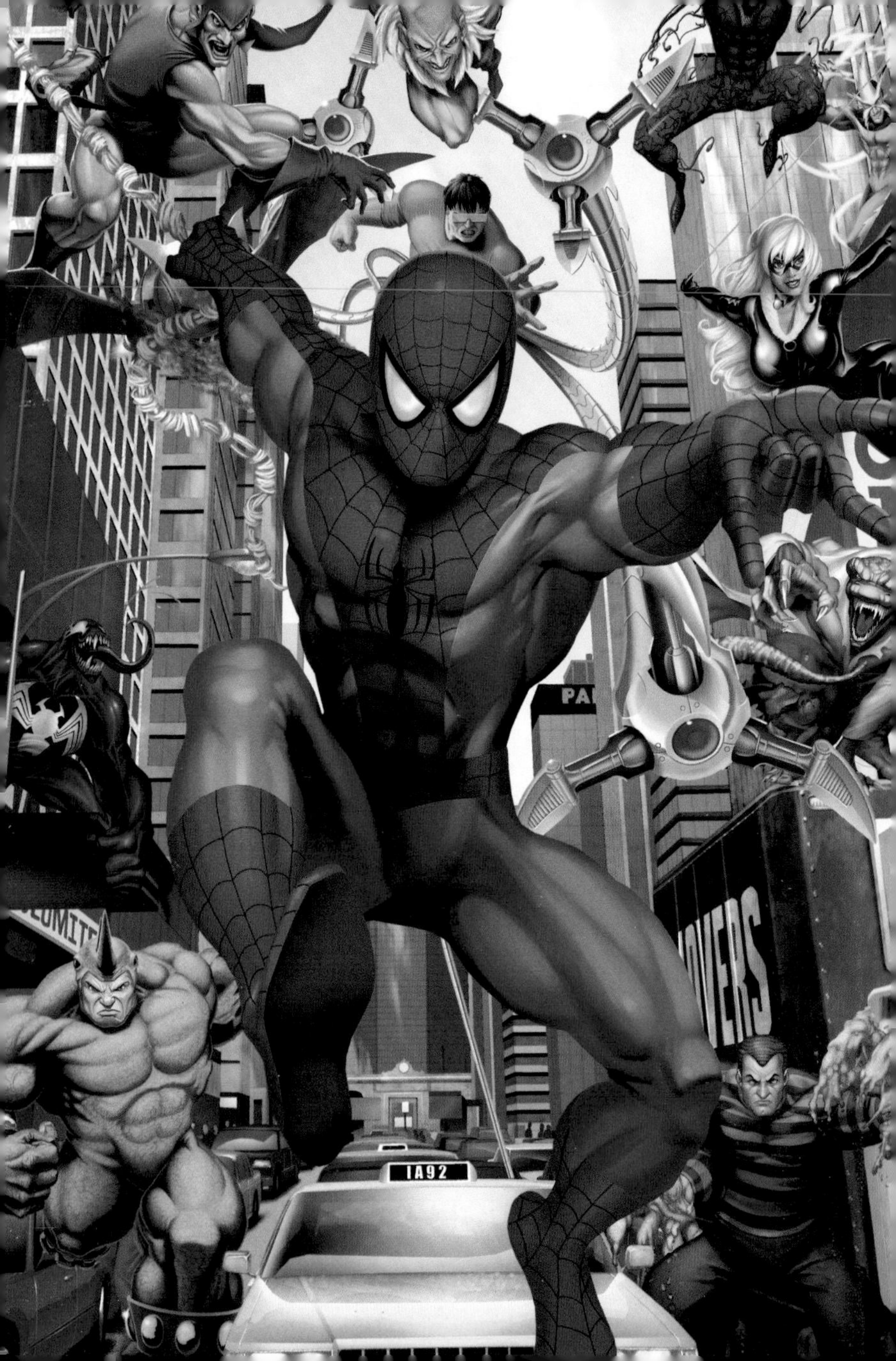
IA92